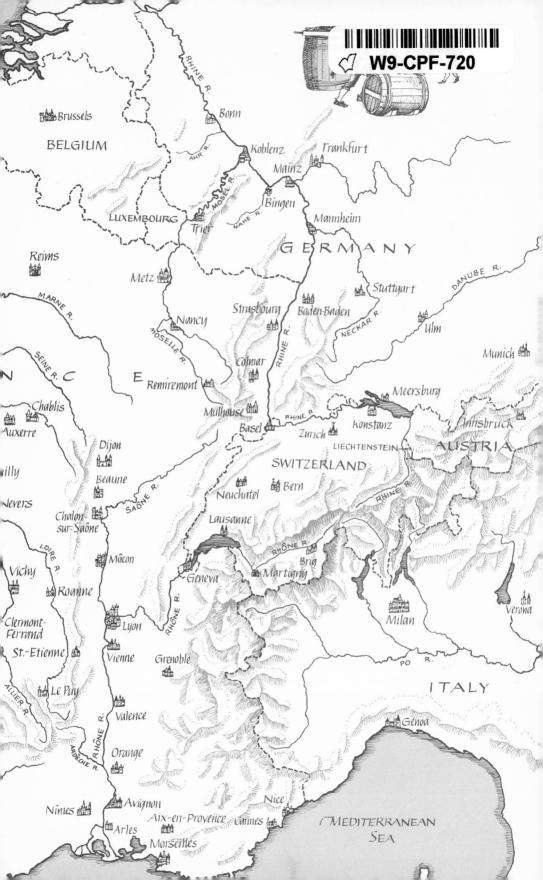

BELGIUM

Brussels

Bonn

Koblenz

Frankfurt

Mainz

Trier

Bingen

LUXEMBOURG

Mannheim

Reims

GERMANY

Metz

Strasbourg

Baden-Baden

Stuttgart

Nancy

Colmar

Ulm

Munich

Remiremont

Mulhouse

Meersburg

Chablis

Auxerre

Basel

Zurich

Konstanz

Innsbruck

AUSTRIA

Dijon

LIECHTENSTEIN

Beaune

SWITZERLAND

Nevers

Neuchatel

Bern

Chalon-sur-Saône

Lausanne

Vichy

Mâcon

Geneva

Brig

Roanne

Martigny

Clermont-Ferrand

Milan

Verona

St.-Etienne

Lyon

Vienne

Grenoble

Le Puy

Valence

Genoa

Orange

ITALY

Nîmes

Avignon

Nice

Arles

Aix-en-Provence

Cannes

Marseilles

MEDITERRANEAN SEA

RHINE R.
AHR R.
MOSEL R.
NAHE R.
MARNE R.
SEINE R.
MOSELLE R.
DANUBE R.
NECKAR R.
RHINE R.
RHINE R.
SAÔNE R.
RHÔNE R.
RHÔNE R.
RHÔNE R.
LOIRE R.
ALLIER R.
ARDÈCHE R.
PO R.

THE GREAT
WINE RIVERS

BY THE SAME AUTHOR:
A Notebook for the Wines of France
(New York, Alfred A. Knopf, 1961)

The World of Wines
(New York, Collier-Macmillan, 1964)

THE GREAT
WINE RIVERS

Creighton Churchill

The Macmillan Company, New York, New York

The Macmillan Company
866 Third Avenue, New York, N.Y. 10022
Collier-Macmillan Canada Ltd., Toronto, Ontario

Library of Congress Catalog Card Number: 79–158162

First Printing

Printed in the United States of America

To
my wife, Susan,
a collaborator whose patience
is rivaled only by her palate

Acknowledgments

For much valued assistance in the various researches necessary for this book, the author is especially beholden to:

Dr. Richard Müller of Reil-am-Mosel; Dr. Helmut Becker and Dr. Oberrat Walter Schenck of the State Viticultural School and Research Station, Geisenheim; Henri Louis Hess and Artur Meier of Mainz; Franz Karl Schmitt of Nierstein; Dr. Ludwig von Bassermann-Jordan of Deidesheim; Guy Dopff of Riquewihr; François Gilliard of Sion; J.-J. Ballif of Lausanne; Edouard Varichon and Louis Clerc of Seyssel; Paul Coulon of Châteauneuf-du-Pape; Edgard Baron of Thézée (Loir-et-Cher); Comte Georges de Vögué of Dijon; Guy Faiveley of Nuits-Saint-Georges; Robert Drouhin of Beaune; Pierre Maufoux of Santenay; Peter Allan Sichel, Comte Bertrand du Vivier and Baron Geoffroy deLuze of Bordeaux.

Contents

CONTENTS

Maps

Introduction

Wines are exciting—drinking them, collecting them, discussing them. You may drink or discuss or collect wines almost anywhere, yet the fact remains that to know their true colors, one must go to the place where they are born. Far too much has been written about which wines do or do not travel. The truth of the matter is that, to one degree or another, they do not. The sole exception is not strictly a wine. A few centuries ago it was discovered that Madeira, a wine fortified with brandy, markedly improved after a long sea voyage. Madeira tossed around the Horn was inexplicably better. But no other wine, however good or great, is quite itself after it has left home. A fragrant Burgundy or a venerable Médoc in London, New York, or San Francisco manifests *most* of its attributes—yet somehow, something is lacking. It is simply not the wine that was lovingly laid to sleep in a cellar in Beaune or Pauillac. No Moselle is ever its truly charming self unless consumed between Trier and Koblenz.

So-called little wines seem to come off worse yet. Muscadet

loses its bloom before reaching Paris; Château Grillet, the Rhône's most celebrated *vin du pays*, in Chicago is but a ghost of that orange-colored nectar served at the Pyramide in Vienne. No one has really ever put a finger on exactly why this is so.

In early Roman days some wines were calculated to last only a month; with others, one was lucky if they held over the winter, and it was expected that by spring they would have turned to vinegar. Winemasters of the ancient world were, of course, unaware of the existence or nature of bacteria, and of the fact that the alcohol in wine—generated by the action of bacterial yeasts on sugar—is itself a prey of yet another airborne yeast, the vinegar-making *acetobacter*. Eventually it was discovered that by sealing the amphorae wine could be preserved longer; often the *acetobacter* was kept at bay by adding spices or resin—in effect, pickling the wine.

The problem of wine's not traveling first became an important commercial challenge in Pasteur's day, and Pasteur himself was commissioned by the French government to solve it. His researches led indirectly to the science of pasteurization—in itself of no value to the problem at hand, since pasteurization kills the vital, residual bacteria that make wine "a living thing." But at least Pasteur opened the eyes of wine-makers to the existence of yeasts, both useful and otherwise, and to the value of proper stoppering of bottles. Today we drink far better wines than our forebears—wines that in general live longer, and are capable of a more perfect maturity, and travel better. Yet in the last analysis, wine is not made for travel. Wine is like a ravishing peasant girl whose country charms never quite make it when she moves to the city.

Nearly all wines of the world, great or small, are associated with rivers or bodies of water: the Rhône and the Loire, the Rhine and the Moselle, the Douro in Portugal and the Po in Italy, the Gironde, the Garonne, and the Dordogne—the lakes of Balaton in Hungary, Neuchâtel and Léman (Geneva) in Switzerland, Keuka in New York State.

The three vital factors affecting wine are the soil, the climate, and the nature or species of grape. The true wine grape is known botanically as the *vitis vinifera*—to be clearly distinguished from dozens of woodland or table grapes, such as the *vitis silvestris* and the *vitis labrusca*, which latter do not make wine as most men know or like it. No conclusive history of the wine-making *vitis vinifera* has ever been written: there are too many missing links in the chain of evidence. We know only that the *vinifera* grew in the Middle East before 4000 B.C., and that the Egyptians and Hebrews used it for wine. Greece acquired the art of wine-making from the Egyptians; the predecessors of the Romans drank Greek wine until the *vinifera* became developed on the Italian peninsula.

The Greeks took the *vinifera* to Marseilles in 600 B.C.—but here that particular story ends, and according to popular belief, it was the Romans who were its real colonizers in Europe. Yet this theory becomes increasingly nebulous as various discoveries are made. For although the Romans did indeed take some varieties of the *vinifera* with them to the corners of their empire, it turns out they also found the *vinifera* already growing in these places. How, then, did a plant supposedly indigenous to the Middle East make its way as far north as the Moselle or to Bordeaux and Portugal without the aid of man?

Lacking further evidence, one may only assume that the *vinifera* grew naturally throughout all of Europe—its qualities latent, until developed by man. In this sense, the Romans were ideal developers. Not only were they hearty wine-drinkers, but their homesick legions in distant lands needed wine, both for comfort and courage. The expansion of the empire to the west and north was important for two vital discoveries relating to the *vinifera*: first, the one that this particular vine was capable of producing its best in northern climes, as opposed to those of the temperate shores of the Mediterranean; second, that the true wine grape prefers poor soils to humus-filled earth upon which one might raise wheat or turnips.

The Romans were the first bona fide wine connoisseurs in history. It was they who first recognized, as all connoisseurs know today, that the wines of Gaul and Germany were superior to those made in their native Italy; they also learned that the *vinifera* produces its best under adverse conditions. The *vinifera* thrives in northern sunlight and in latitudes where it is forced into a hazardous race with killing frosts—a race it does not always win. It prefers slate and shale and gravel to lush meadows, and its roots have been known to penetrate scores of feet to gain the subsoil. In fact, the wine grape's predilection for eroded soil and subsoils is the geological factor that explains man's cultivation of it along rivers and on lakeshores. Probably the most graphic illustration of this is to be found on the Moselle, a river which over the millennia cut its way through hundreds of feet of slate deposited by the Devonian Sea. Wherever the river has left only a sparse covering of slate chips over subsoil or rock, the *vinifera* makes the best wine. As the often quoted phrase of the Moselle peasant has it: "Where no plow will go, the vine will grow." In Burgundy, likewise, whose greatest vineyards lie on hillsides once lapped by a prehistoric sea, the *vignerons* have a comparable saying: "Were it not for the grape, we would starve."

In the Old World, wines are an integral part of gastronomy— in fact, in most wine-producing nations, food without wine is almost unthinkable. Pragmatically speaking, then, to find good wines you should find good food. Good wines are usually not found at the corner bistro, or behind the green swinging doors of the local *weinstube*. A neophyte wanting to learn something about the wines of Spain's Rioja, for instance, would do better— before going to the Rioja—to dine at some of Madrid's best restaurants, inspecting and sampling the wine lists. When he eventually visits the Rioja, he will be in a position to know what wines to order and which vineyards to visit.

We do not rule out chance encounters, of course. They are part of the excitement of wines. We recall once being driven by a blizzard into a small village inn of Auvergne, where a refectory table by a blazing fire was set with a fresh *pâté de fois gras* the size of a plum pudding, surrounded by carafes of golden Monbazillac, all on the house—our first discovery of the potential of this little-known wine of the Dordogne. Or a corner *zinc* on the Rue Jacob, where the Anjou *en carafe* seemed more delicious than anything ever tasted before or since—except possibly a memorable Sylvaner made by an unsung cooperative in Alsace, drunk at a mountain inn in the Vosges. But such discoveries are exceptions. Hence our advice to the oenophile and wine-lover to seek out, wherever he goes, the good and even the best restaurants, those establishments where it runs in the blood of the proprietor to maintain a wine cellar that equals the excellence of his chef. If the pocketbook pinches, let it come off the night's lodging. A stimulating meal and a good bottle of wine may sometimes be more valid than a tiled bathroom. Perhaps we should allow the wine-wise Burgundians the last word: "Une bouteille de Nuits fait la votre. . . ."

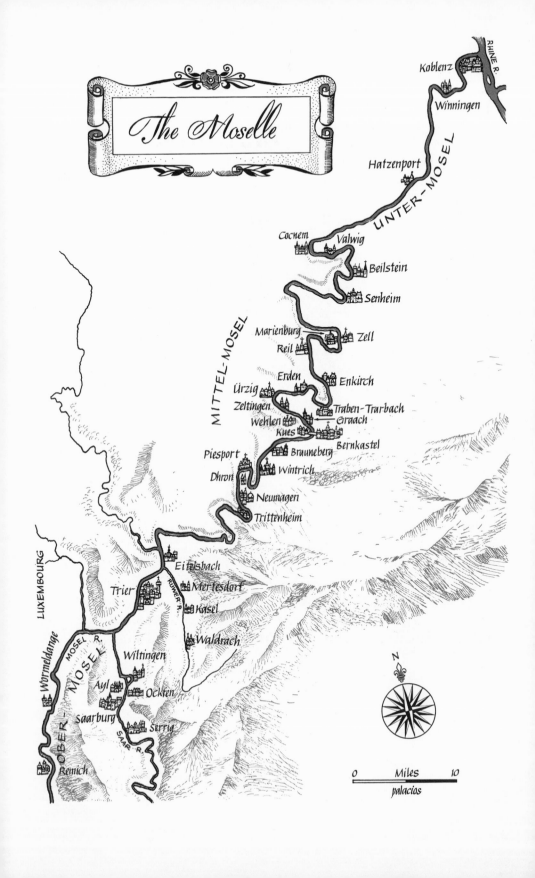

I

The Moselle

I : *From Its Headwaters to Luxembourg*

By curious coincidence, the headwaters of the Moselle, whose
wines were cherished by the Romans as early as the first century
of this era (*Vinum bonum, vinum generosum*), are almost at the
very epicenter of viticultural Western Europe. Six hundred miles
from the North Sea, the Moselle's source in the Vosges mountains
of France is nearly equidistant from Bordeaux, from the viticulturally prolific Po Valley of Italy, as well as the great vineyards of the Danube watershed—those of Austria, in turn but a
short step from the celebrated Hungarian hill of Somló and the
vine-covered shores of Lake Balaton. Not too many decades ago,
these Danube vineyards produced nearly a quarter of Europe's
wines.

Once fondly named by Schiller the "Virgin of Lorraine," the
little Moselle is born high in the Vosges, in a lush, two-pronged
meadow just above the tiny mountain village of Bussang. Bussang's only other claim to fame is that of being what the French

1

call a *station thermale*: one of the two freshets that join to form
the Moselle is fed by an icy spring endowed with iron and
arsenic. For centuries Bussang has been host to anemic pilgrims,
come to partake of its powerful waters.

Above Bussang, to the south, rises the Ballon d'Alsace, one of
the highest peaks of the Vosges. One may drive to within a half
hour's walk of the Ballon's bald summit, then climb upward
through dense pines and spruces until one suddenly comes out
on wild, rolling pastureland from which on a clear day one sees
the snowy peaks of far-distant alps. The nearby pass leading
along the Ballon, a creation of Louis XV and the first ever built
over the Vosges, is notably the most difficult and hazardous of
the entire range. Even the briefest wrestle with its intricate corkscrews makes one wonder why this particular route was ever
chosen, or even thought necessary. Only twenty miles to the
south, where the Vosges end, is the age-old water-level route to
Alsace and the Rhine, the Belfort Gap; and the next pass to the
north, the Col de Bussang above the Moselle's headwaters, is a
comparative thruway. Perhaps the answer is that Louis was noted
for doing things the hard way.

Racing down the valley from Bussang, the Moselle soon becomes a giddy little mountain stream, constantly interrupted in
its play to turn tiny farm mills, or forcibly canalized into little
ponds created for farmer's fish. At the valley's base, some twenty
miles downstream, it arrives, still out of breath, at the town of
Remiremont, where the "Virgin of Lorraine" appears to attain a
certain puberty. She still wanders capriciously from one side of
her valley to the other, but her waters have cleared to a lucid
green; her bed has turned to golden sand, and her rapids resound
with stiffled girlish giggles. Throughout her entire length, the
Moselle is as fascinating and feminine as any woman ever born.

Remiremont is not a wine town—the Moselle must follow her
course many miles yet before she begets vineyards. Yet the town
has its small share of history, however apocryphal; at least one
high attainment in gastronomy, plus a charming main street (la

Grande-Rue), in summer always bountifully decked with flowers. It is the palace of the ancient abbey that holds the bit of fascinating, if incredible, history. During the seventh century a noble Austrasian (Austrasia was the ancient name of Alsace-Lorraine) founded a monastery close by. For reasons never expounded, the monastery in some way became infiltrated by nuns, and as the account continues, "the whole valley commenced to be all smiles." Long before the last monk fled, the nuns had taken command, leading a life anything but nunlike. Only the abbess, who must have been something of a nonconformist in her own right, stuck to her vows. She is said to have conferred upon herself the title of princess, professing to answer only to Saint Peter and the king, and wherever she went she insisted that a bared sword be carried before her. Meanwhile the nuns led a life as free as the wind, blissfully heedless of God's commandments or the laws of the Church. Catherine of Lorraine, the daughter of Duke Charles III, once attempted to reform the Abbey of Remiremont, but soon took her high ideals elsewhere.

Just below Remiremont, on the road to Épinal, is one of those attractive and affluent country inns scattered throughout France, part of the loosely knit organization called "les Relais de Campagne." The watchword of this "chain" of tasteful and usually luxurious establishments, nearly always blessed by the presence of a truly talented chef, is attributed to, of all people, Saint Francis of Assisi: "Cherish your body, for your soul's sake." The great ascetic who shared his crumbs with lowly bird and beast may well be turning in his grave—but be that as it may. We have never yet stumbled on a "Relais" that wasn't a joy.

The Hôtel Claire Fontaine is by no means inexpensive, but well worth it. In accordance with our philosophy, it is far better to take advantage of such a windfall and, if one must, sleep the night in a comparative fleabag. Surprisingly, the cuisine is neither that of Alsace nor of Lorraine, nor even limited to France. You will go a long way before finding a better *borscht* or a more digestible *pirozhki*. A *volaille* or *cailles maison* (chicken or quails in Madeira sauce) will be superb; nor would it be wise to pass up the regional Münster cheese, particularly the version fortified with Kümmel. From the cellar one should draw on nearby Alsace's best: a Riesling called Les Murailles, or a fragrant Kaefferkopf made from the Traminer grape. These are wines we will meet again, but there is no need to overlook them now. Finally, provided one is willing to risk annihilation of the afterglow of a fine meal, try the *eau-de-vie* of the surrounding countryside, Gentiane, a clear liquor distilled from a yellow mountain flower. Gentiane, used to lend flavor to Schnapps, is conclusive proof that most *eaux-de-vie* and liqueurs were of curative or medicinal origin. Perhaps, like Greek Retsina, if one were to drink several bottles of it in sequence, one might thereafter start to crave it. Many Vosgians do, obviously.

The vast network of Europe's canals, connecting its great rivers and cities, constitute a never-ending source of color and fascination. Whereas they usually have little to do with vineyards or wines, except for transport of the latter, they are an indelible part and parcel of the civilizations through which they flow. Before the Moselle reaches its first city, Nancy, it is joined—specifically at the town of Épinal—by an extension of the Canal de l'Est, an important and comparatively recent short cut between the canal system of central France and, via the Moselle, the Middle Rhine at Koblenz. Not so long ago the only connection was through Alsace, from where barges had to be floated down the entire length of the navigable Rhine to Holland.

From Épinal to Nancy, one of the most intriguing stretches of the river, the Canal de l'Est is fed by (and parallels) the Moselle, on one occasion crossing the river by aqueduct. Unlike some French canals forgotten by today's commerce, such as the once busy Canal de Bourgogne, now so sadly bereft of traffic, stilled and filling with rushes, the Canal de l'Est is alive with activity. All day long, fat barges plow up and down it, but in the late afternoon one sees them tied up along the *quais* of the villages close to the canal-side bars or bistros. One is tempted to join the tanned and genial canal men relaxing over a beer or a glass of wine on a bistro's terrace. The wash is strung on the line; the barge's dog snoozes in his basket after the day's nerve-wracking watch; the womenfolk gossip across the water. For a home away from home, life on a French barge must be close to ideal.

Nancy is the capital of Lorraine, also its principal wine center and gastronomic lodestone. Actually, the city is not on the Moselle, but within a great bend of it containing the dense Forêt de Haye, though linked to the river by canals from both north and south. One should not be discouraged by Nancy's modern suburbs, but head straight for the minuscule *centre ville*, the Place Stanislas, one of the loveliest jewels of all France. Constructed during the reign of Louis XV, it and the adjoining palace were the work of a dethroned king of Poland who became Louis' father-in-law. Ex-king Stanislas was a remarkable, not to say talented and inventive, man. His career was one of many ups and downs, all of which he took gracefully in his stride. Deposed from his throne, he had fled to Alsace, where he lived modestly and in comparative poverty in the little wine village of Wissembourg, with his daughter, Marie-Thérèse. One day, quite unheralded, he was visited by representatives of the king of France, their mission to ask for the hand of Marie-Thérèse.

Stanislas of course accepted (there was no room for refusal), but he had to put himself in the hands of a Jewish moneylender in order to afford the dowry. When the marriage was finally consecrated at the cathedral at Strasbourg, with all the royal trappings, the king of France was fifteen; Marie-Thérèse was twenty-two.

Louis subsequently appointed his father-in-law governor of Alsace-Lorraine, one of the few appointments of its kind in history that ever bore fruit. Along with cherishing beautiful women and good food, Stanislas was gifted with an impeccable taste in many other things. Happily for Nancy, he loved above all else to build and invent. No man ever did more for Nancy, or

5

for Alsace-Lorraine. The square that bears his name contains some of the most exquisite ironwork in all Europe, and its pristine buildings are created in the noble tradition of French architecture at its best, reminiscent of the Place de la Concorde and the Rue de Rivoli, or the beautifully proportioned arcaded streets of Orléans.

Nancy is a rewarding place to spend the night, with good hotels at reasonable prices and superb restaurants. And although they are none of them great, or typical of Moselles as we shall know them later, this may be one's first and only chance to drink the indigenous wines of Lorraine, principally the *rosé* that goes by the name of *vin gris*. The term, naturally, does not mean gray wine—it is regional parlance for light pink. Lorraine's wines come from two officially accredited districts, the Côte de Toul and the Côtes de la Moselle. Both produce token amounts of red and white wine, but *vin gris*—strangely fragrant and refreshing though a bit on the harsh side—is the best known. In effect they are all simply *vins du pays*, or country wines, that have earned sufficient recognition to merit the official vinous classification of *Vins Délimités de Qualité Supérieure* (abbreviated to *V.D.Q.S.*), the classification next below France's highest title of *Appellations Contrôlées*.

Fortunately Nancy's gastronomy is on a far higher level than Lorraine's wines, even though the cuisine of Lorraine, as such, is rarely ever posited as outstanding as compared with that of most other French provinces. Lorraine has never been rich. Forestry and mining have been its chief industries, with agriculture playing a relatively minor role in the economy. And great traditional cooking is nearly always rooted in a bountiful agriculture. Hence Lorraine's fame rests on such dishes as *pâtés* made from game or pork, roast suckling pig (from a countryside where it was not always economically feasible to raise every pig to full growth), sausages with pickled cabbage (*choucroute garnie*, a staple in Alsace-Lorraine), or the familiar *quiche Lorraine*, basically a farmer's custard pie with added bits of leftover meat and onions. Some of these dishes, embellished by sophisticated chefs trained in the kitchens of Paris, will be glorified *in excelsis* at some of Nancy's hostelries. Wash them down with *vin gris*, even though you may consider it a crime to drink so humble a wine with expertly prepared food. The sooner one discovers the irrefutable affinity of native wines to native dishes, the better. A white Graves or a rich Burgundy with suckling pig *en gelée* will be an unhappy experience; yet the simple, slightly acidulous *vin gris* turns out to be mutually enhancing.

Anyone staying in Nancy will want to be as close to the Place Stanislas as possible—thus the logical first candidate becomes the Grand Hôtel on the decorative Place itself, housed in one of the ex-king's original buildings and facing the statue of Louis. But there are several others within easy range, to fit a flattened or diminishing pocketbook. One is the Hôtel de l'Europe et Univers; another, simpler but nonetheless recommendable, the Portes d'Or on the Rue Stanislas. Besides the restaurant at the Grand Hôtel, visiting gourmets tend to flock to the Rôtisserie des Cordeliers or the more intimate Capucin Gourmand. Notwithstanding, our own favorite, rarely mentioned in any guide, is the Rôtisserie Gourmet Lorrain, next door to the Portes d'Or. Small and charming, the Gourmet Lorrain is owned and managed by an exceptionally talented restaurateur. We can testify that almost anything one orders will be more than just an example of honest French cooking: snails that are not overly seasoned, fresh *pâté de fois* (October to March), succulent game, and a *soufflé maison* light and fluffy to the very bottom of the dish, its sugared crust burned at the table with Grand Marnier. While awaiting your dessert, you hear your *soufflé* being whisked by a rosy-cheeked young apprentice operating in the tiny kitchen behind a screen at the restaurant's rear. Ascertain, too, whether that most unusual of wines, Champagne *pétillant natur*, is available in carafe. Only to be had in certain seasons, this will be Champagne as made in the eighteenth century, when it became popular in England years before the French themselves ever drank or appreciated it.

7

Made without the extra dosages of sugar and yeast that go into the modern-day version, Champagne *pétillant natur* is deliciously light and almost imperceptibly bubbly, often more reminiscent of hard cider than wine. Beware of Champagne *natur* in a bottle: it can often be an unpleasantly acid wine, gone flat.

To find the first vineyards of the Moselle one must drive westward from Nancy through the Forêt toward Paris, to the town of Toul; thence across the Moselle and a short distance northward into the hills. This is the Côte de Toul, where the vineyards climb the hillsides behind the little hamlets of Pagney, Lucey, and Bruley, the three best known. The Côte de Toul is reputedly the home of the best *vin gris*, made here by an almost unique method. *Rosés* are born in a number of ways. The least desirable method is to add coloring, however harmless, to white wine. Another, to mix red and white wines that have been independently fermented. The third (and traditionally the best) uses red-skinned grapes only, which are withdrawn from the fermentation vat as soon as the desired color and flavor have been obtained. Yet another way—that employed for the *vin gris* of Lorraine—is to ferment both red and white grapes together, again lifting the skins when the liquid becomes pink. The authorized grapes for this region constitute a somewhat motley assortment, no doubt accounting in part for the wines' special tastes: two varieties of the red Gamay, as well as the Pinot noir (both Burgundian); for white grapes, two indigenous ones, the Aubin and the Envezin, together with an inferior native of Burgundy, the Aligoté, never used for the best Burgundies. Lorraine's other Côte, the Côtes de la Moselle, centered downstream around the town of Sierck, draws on an even wider spectrum. Here two more white grapes once used around Chablis are added, along with Alsatian Gewürztraminer and three German grapes, the Sylvaner, Riesling, and Elbling. Needless to say, the character of the wines of the Côtes (the official appellation on a label will be Vin-de-la-Moselle) is more pronounced and peculiar yet.

One should not linger too long at Toul, since far more spectacular vineyards (and wines) are to come, and just around the corner is yet another intriguing stretch of the Moselle, its end marked by a distinguished inn. Shortly below Toul the river flows through a deep gorge of brick-colored limestone, neck and neck with the canal. One should not make the mistake of taking the main road here, but instead seek out the country road on the west bank of the river, and follow the lonely gorge to the walled town of Liverdun, overhanging the topaz river.

Liverdun is no Carcassonne or Saint-Malo: in fact, if one were not forewarned of its charms and of the presence of the Hôtel des Vannes, one might well pass it by as just another of a thousand or so fortified towns on a hill. Liverdun's only entrance leads through a towered medieval gate, giving immediately on to a tiny square, shaded by a single great spreading tree, and only large enough to accommodate a half-dozen cars. Beneath the tree is the doorway of a little Romanesque church that appears to have undergone several architectural migrations, and opposite, an ancient gate through which one sees the gardens of a legendary governor's palace—now fallen into disrepair and used as a parsonage. No citizen of Liverdun could possibly tell you why, or when, this doll house of a *château fort* merited a governor. But such is the legend.

Just off the square is the Hôtel des Vannes, as unusual and delightful a hostelry as may be found in all Lorraine. Its cuisine— *haute cuisine* in the very best sense—is equaled only by the breathtaking view of the clear-running Moselle several hundred feet directly below the inn's windows. In the Vannes' kitchen, no corners are cut, no imagination spared, and the cellar is a credit to all France. Even though they may be the best of their kind, this is no place to settle for *vins gris*. In the happy afterglow of your repast the chances are that you will have risen above such mundane matters as the large check. But the thoughtful management has taken pains to provide for a relief of your conscience: upstairs there is a limited number of comfortable rooms, priced at approximately a quarter the cost of the princely

9

meal you have been served below in the unforgettable gallery cantilevered over the Moselle. Be sure you get one on the river side, to prolong the dream.

For the next seventy-five miles or so to Apach, where the Moselle leaves France to intersect Luxembourg and Germany, the river passes through her one and only unattractive stage— we might call it her unadorned adolescence. The valley widens and becomes distinctly impersonal, and especially after the city of Metz the river is beset by every conceivable deviltry of man and industry. Towering chimneys belch fire and putrid fumes; mile-long conveyor belts and giant pipelines cross and crisscross the landscape, the river, and the road. Happily a fast *autoroute* eases the pain of the last part of the trip.

If your schedule is ripe for a meal, you would do well to stop off at the hamlet of Corny-sur-Moselle and sample a Vin-de-la-Moselle at a creditable roadside inn, also called Gourmet Lorrain. Industrial Metz, the city to come, is by no means the most fetching city of France and, with one exception, contains no restaurant or eating place worthy of mention. In fact, until the Hostellerie Marne (near the principal square and virtually the only parking place) came into being a few years ago, Metz was a gourmet's Sahara. Nowadays at the Marne, between walls serving as a gallery for local artists, one may lunch or dine with luxury and confidence—though one should be equally confident that the check will be as high as the food will be exemplary. Metz will be the last place to indulge in a suckling pig *en gelée* or a *quiche Lorraine* washed down with *vin gris*. But here a word of advice: we are about to enter and dwell in the white-wine country of Germany. It would be prudent to fill up on a hearty French red.

I I : *The Ober-Mosel: From Apach to Trier*

"Only a Frenchwoman," in the words of an anonymous German writer of the last century, "could show such caprice or indecision with a new suitor." No words better describe the flirtatious contortions of our "Virgin," once she meets with foreign soil. On one celebrated stretch below Trier, her philanderings—covering only forty miles as the crow flies—nearly treble the length of her travels.

Below Apach we find the valley narrowing once more, and the first of those uncountable romantic little castles that we shall encounter appears on a steep, vine-covered hillside. On the river's left bank are the vineyards of Luxembourg; on the right, those of Germany—the district officially called the Ober-Mosel (Upper Moselle). Although neither the wines of Luxembourg nor those of the Ober-Mosel may honestly be compared to the fragrant nectars made further downstream (to travel *up* the river to taste the wines would be a bitter anticlimax), the fact remains that Luxembourg's wines deserve passing attention, if only to round out one's experience. With impunity you may skip the vineyards on the German side. They are planted predominantly with inferior grapes on inferior soils, and their situation deprives them of a full day's exposure to the sun—whereas those of Luxembourg, with a southwest exposure, are at an advantage.

Notwithstanding, in all but the very best years (about two in ten) Luxembourg's wines tend to be high in acid and relatively low in alcohol (8 percent is a good average). They will probably improve when the Grand Duchy gets around to prescribing fewer and more suitable grapes. As the *Appellations Complètes*— Luxembourg's equivalent to the French *Appellations Contrôlées*— now stand, nine or ten different grape varieties may be used, individually or all together. Unfortunately, the most popular vine is still the Elbling, a high producer yielding a notably poor wine—in effect, a curse on the entire Upper Moselle. Even so, a quarter of Luxembourg's annual production (approximately three million gallons) is currently exported to Belgium and Holland.

The road that follows the Luxembourg bank is both better and more scenic than the one that cuts through the Ober-Mosel, another inducement for the inquiring oenophile to cross immediately to the town of Remich, where he may pause at one of the many simple Luxembourg inns or *weinstuben* on the river's bank. Among many providing honest meals and comfortable beds is the Hôtel de la Moselle at Ehnen, just above the wine town of Wormeldange. In ordering a Luxembourg wine one should know that the highest official qualitative classification involves mention on the label not only of the name of the town, but of the vineyard and grape as well. Pick one labeled Riesling or Traminer if possible, and especially look for a little round sticker on the bottle's neck with the words *Marque Nationale*, indicating the wine has merited the blessing of a governmental tasting committee.

Although classifications and labels of the relatively minor vineyard districts visited so far present few problems, any oenophilic visitor to Germany will be at a distinct disadvantage without a bit of preliminary study of German systems of labels, including a knowledge of the principal grapes used for the wines. Once one has caught on to the principles of German classification, one will see that it is by far the most logical of any nation on earth. To begin with, for the convenience of the consumer, the Germans bottle Moselles in green bottles (*flaschen*), as opposed to brown bottles for the Rhine. Additionally, labels always bear the name of the district from which the wines come: Moselle labels, for example, will always have the term Mosel-Saar-Ruwer. Similarly: Rheingau, Rheinhessen, and so on.

German wines divide into two general classes: those labeled with generic names, usually inexpensive blends, and those labeled with specific geographical names indicating the town, the vineyard, and often the name of the grape—though, as we shall see, the two latter may be omitted. The most widely known generic name on the German Moselle is Moselblümchen, a vinous vagary useful principally for export. Legally Moselblümchen ("Little Flower of the Moselle") may be a blend of anything from the German watershed of the river. Its Rhineland opposite number is

Liebfraumilch. Happily they are rarely, if ever, found on German winelists.

The finer German wines are required to carry the year the wine (or most of it) was made, the name of the town, and (in the case of the best) that of the vineyard, along with the name and address of the producer or vintner. Thus, a wine labeled only with a town name accompanied by a grape name means, in essence, a blend of wines from anywhere within the town's viticultural limits. An example would be Bernkasteler Riesling 1964er: a blend from anywhere in the town of Bernkastel on the Moselle. Two-thirds of it must by law be the vintage of 1964, and its producer certifies it is made from Riesling grapes, the best. Parenthetically, on the Moselle, mention of the grape name is largely a matter of superfluous window dressing. All the good wines of the Moselle are made from the Riesling.

One may be sure that if our Bernkasteler came from a well-known vineyard, the producer would so indicate, in order to get a better price. A label reading Bernkasteler Doktor 1964er, then, means a wine from the celebrated Doktor vineyard in the town of Bernkastel. Its distinguished and sophisticated producer does not insult his public's intelligence by using the word Riesling; and in the case of so great a vineyard as this, his public incidentally may be sure the wine will be made entirely from the 1964 vintage, though by law the producer must mention it. You may be confused by the suffix "er" tacked on the word Bernkastel, as well as on the date. This "er" is adjectival, as in New Yorker or Vermonter. It signifies Bernkastel's, and 1964's product of the Doktor vineyard.

German wines are also all conveniently graded by their comparative degree of sweetness, and usually priced accordingly, since the sweeter wines cost more to make. A label without one of the following terms will usually indicate a dry wine made from grapes picked when they are considered ripe. However, the term *Spätlese* on a label signifies a sweeter wine, from "late-picked" grapes left to ripen longer on the vine; *Auslese*, sweeter yet, is from very ripe grapes, hence ones with even more sugar, picked bunch by bunch. Two further categories exist: *Beerenauslese* (from overripe grapes literally picked one by one) and *Trocken-beerenauslese*, a veritable liqueur made from grapes left so long that they have almost become raisins. The Germans prize (and price) them highly: it is nothing for a *Trockenbeerenauslese* from a good vineyard to cost eighty or ninety Marks ($20–$25). These excessively sweet, luscious, and delectable wines are never consumed with meals, but with the coffee, or as a liqueur—when they may be sipped and savored. Sometimes the medium-sweet ones are drunk alone, very much as we would drink coffee at a coffee break, or afternoon tea.

Other pertinent terms on German labels are *Natur, Naturwein,* or *Naturrein,* meaning wine from grapes that were sufficiently sweet at harvesttime to render added sugar unnecessary. In poor years the addition of sugar to the ferment is both necessary and legal. But since it does not improve the overall quality of the wine, all vintners are eager to disclaim the practice, when possible. *Feine, Feinste,* or *Hochfeinste* ("fine," "finest," or "the very finest") are terms indicating a producer's high opinion of his product; likewise, *Kabinett* or *Cabinet,* a term in effect meaning "Special Reserve." *Original-Abfüllung* (often abbreviated to read *Orig-Abfg.*), *Kellerabfüllung, Kellerabzug* or *Schlossabzug* all testify to bottling on the producer's own property, rather than in the far-distant cellars of some merchant who might be a surreptitious blender. *Wachstum* supposedly guarantees a wine that is both unblended and unsugared; *Weingut* means property or domain, but does not necessarily assure estate-bottling. Finally we come to the use of the words *Fuder (Fud.),* indigenous to the Moselle, or *Fass,* with a number. The average vineyard holding in Germany is around three acres, and especially with the very sweet wines, it can happen that only a few casks are made by a producer. Since one of them may contain a better wine, or a wine of different character, numbering the casks affords the consumer an opportunity for identifying (and reordering) something that particularly takes his fancy.

In descending the Ober-Mosel one increasingly notices the meandering curves of the "Virgin of Lorraine," seemingly aimless twistings and turnings, as well as the growing preponderance of slate on her hillside vineyards, chips of stone that here tend to be hard and reddish, but are soon to change to a softer texture and a warm gray. Not too far downstream the meanderings are to turn into contortions. Below Trier they become so peristaltically severe that on one stretch, where the river's predominant direction is northeasterly, she flows due north eight times, due south seven times, and on one occasion reverses herself completely and flows due west. Both these geological factors—the slate and the contortions—are of the utmost significance in the making of great wines, especially the unique wines of the Moselle.

In prehistoric days this particular part of the world lay beneath the Devonian Sea, whose fossilized vegetation, after the sea receded, left a deep layer of a shaly slate that the Germans call *scheifer*. Over the millennia the river, in carving its way through the slate, was again and again forced back on itself at those spots where the slate was hardest and most resistant. On the inner side of each sharp bend, it deposited alluvial soil—soil too fertile for the making of great wines. But on the outside of these bends it left precipitously steep hillsides, covered with large slate chips mixed sparsely with soil. These slate-covered slopes sometimes attain a height of six or eight hundred feet above the water. The best for wine-growing face south or southwest, and are painstakingly terraced against erosion. The hills above shield them from cold, damaging winds, while the slate, reflecting the sun's heat by day and holding it by night, protects them from early frosts.

Even so, the grapes of the Moselle require a minimum of a hundred days of warm sunshine to reach maturity, and many more yet to produce the sweeter wines held in such high esteem.

This is why the Moselle, with a latitude approximately that of Newfoundland, produces only great or good vintages three or four years in each decade. In other years most wines are too acid for anything but generics, such as Moselblümchen or Sekt (German "Champagne"), both receiving added sugar.

The variation of slate types, combined with soils, is also significant. On the Ober-Mosel the red slate is hard and mixed with a soil that is mainly chalk, comparable to the chalk of Champagne, another northern district where nearly all wines are perforce sugared. Even with the best exposures, the wines of the Ober-Mosel are weak in flavor and too acid, and no vineyard is really famous. On the Mittel-Mosel below Trier, on the other hand, the soil is not chalky, and there is far less of it in proportion to the soft gray slate. With every rain, the slate—once upon a time sea-bottom humus, fossilized vegetation—erodes a little, adding just enough fertilization to the vineyards. By the same token, on the Unter-Mosel (Lower Moselle) below Zell, the slate is too hard to erode, with the result that the wines here are not as good.

The resistance to the river as it carved its path downstream is most apparent below the town of Zell, where the stream undergoes the most severe peristalsis of all. One impressive example may be seen from the heights of Marienberg, at the neck of the Zell bend, where the river has bent back on itself to such a degree that, had it cut into its banks another few hundred yards, the result would have been an oxbow.

Trier, the largest city of the Moselle, is reputedly the oldest in Germany. Legend would have one believe it was founded in 2000 B.C. by the son-in-law of Semiramis, Queen of Assyria. What is more likely is that Trier, undoubtedly very old, was originally a trading post and meeting place for Celtic tribes, and that its name derives from Treveri, a tribe from eastern Gaul. Later Trier became a meeting place between these northern tribes and the Romans, and subsequently—under Augustus in the first century B.C.—a strategic bastion of the empire. As is the case today, the river afforded the easiest route for trade and transportation to the Rhine, thence northward to the sea.

The Romans arrived at Trier by way of the Rhône and what is now Paris, probably several centuries before they ever visited the Rhineland. They built an amphitheater, elaborate baths (parts of which still exist), and a remarkable four-story gate to the city, the Porta Nigra, which still stands. Built without mortar, the Porta Nigra (its name supposedly derives from a smoky patina that the weather imparts to its limestone) was as ingenious a concept for defense as the Trojan Horse was for the opposite. The arcades of its top stories being deceptively "blind," an enemy was thus tempted to enter the courtyard of this innocent-looking building, exposing himself to attack on all sides. The Romans also built an important arterial highway from Trier to Koblenz. Just east of Trier, where the highway followed the valley, are the two towns of Quint and Detzem, respectively five and ten Roman miles on the way to the Rhine.

Rome's legions were driven from Trier by the Franks in the third century, but one should not end their story without some mention of them as husbandmen of the wine grape—especially of the shy-bearing Riesling, which so excels on the hot slate terraces of the Moselle and the Rheingau. The Riesling is the "noble" grape of the north—only one other white-wine grape in the world, the Chardonnay of Burgundy, produces wine of equal finesse and character, and then only in its native clime. So many nonsensical and nebulous theories have been advanced, picturing the Romans as the great colonizers of the Riesling, that the record must be set straight. The impression is conveyed that the Riesling was brought to Germany by the Romans; hence a common ancestor, originally rooted somewhere in Italy, is responsible for all the wines called Riesling—from the Moselle to Chile and California, Portugal to Yugoslavia. The best German oenologists insist that such was just not the case. When the Romans arrived at the Moselle, they found a wild grape that we now know as the true German or Rhine Riesling. But there is no evidence that

wine was even made there at the time. This latter is confirmed
by Caesar himself, who visited the Moselle twice in the sixth
decade B.C., and who in his accounts of both visits never once
mentions viticulture. Without doubt, had there been, this meticu-
lously observant historian of his day would have recorded it. One
assumption that the Romans were the colonizers of the grape in
the north, bringing the Riesling with them from Italy, is based
on the fact that amphorae have been found on the Moselle,
principally at Trier and Neumagen. Here again, historians have
put two and two together to make five. These amphorae had
nothing to do with wine-making. The Romans habitually brought
wine for their legions, wherever they went; they also used it for
trading. Records found on the Moselle indicate that an amphora
of wine in the north country was worth one slave.

Even so, wine was an important staple for Roman civilization,
and it was always more economical to raise it on the spot. Unquestionably wine was made from the difficult Riesling, but not
for the masses or the legions. In fact it was not until many centuries later, when the Cistercians and Benedictines, history's
true colonizers of the wine grape, took over German viticulture
that the Riesling came into its own. For purposes of mass production the Romans did indeed bring a grape from Italy, in this
case an inferior plant, the Elbling. It is the lowly Elbling, traces
of which exist in Italy in archaeological findings, that is the
principal grape of the Ober-Mosel. Only since the edict of 1787
of the Prince-Bishop of Trier has the Riesling become the official
grape for the balance of the Moselle.

This flimsy theory about the origin of the German Riesling
should be briefly demolished. The Rhine Riesling of the north is
not the Riesling of Italy, Portugal, or many other parts of the
world, yet how did this totally unrelated grape come to be so
named? It requires no oenologist to spot the difference: the leaf
of the German grape has five marked contours or lobes, whereas
that of the so-called Riesling of the south has only three. The
veins of the former tend to be reddish, and one of the leaf's

surfaces is rough; with the latter, the veins are snow white, and both surfaces are smooth. There are other differences, such as the marked dissimilarity in taste between the two wines—non-German Riesling lacks bouquet and "bite." We can only assume that the Romans, or rather their descendants, having once tasted the glorious Moselles, must have given the name Riesling to a grape that produced the closest approximation. The practice of borrowing famous names in the world of wines is not unique to our era alone.

III : *The Mittel-Mosel*

Although Trier is the traditional wine center for the Ober-Mosel and the Mittel-Mosel, one will have difficulty finding representative vintages of the region in most of Trier's restaurants or *weinstuben.* Until the celebrated Ratskeller Steipe on the Hauptmarkt (Market Square) was torn down a few years ago, the situation was different. The Steipe's cellar was a veritable library of the best Moselles; without it, Trier seems to have few merits. The two large hotels, the Römischer and the Europäischer are moderately expensive, comfortable, cold, and modern. As an alternative, try the popular Hotel Central—smaller and with its own shady parking lot. About the only passable restaurant within the city limits, with only a passable wine list, too, is the Zum Domstein, also on the Hauptmarkt. On a hot summer's evening one will enjoy the Moselterrasse Zurmaien, where one may sit over a bottle, watching the barges chug by and the river life in general. The Zurmaien is headquarters for the local rowing club. Along with sailing small catboats, rowing is taken very seriously on the Mittel-Mosel. Nearly every town between Trier and Zell has its fiercely competitive club, and rain or shine, the early evening brings out the four- and eight-oared shells manned by grim-faced amateurs of all ages and both sexes, straining for the great day.

If one is not forced by circumstances to have a meal or stay overnight in Trier, a recommendable inn may be found across the river in a lovely park overlooking the city: the Hotel Weisshaus. The Weisshaus is not mentioned in every guidebook, nor is it easy to find the entrance at a sharp curve of the winding Route 51 (the road to Cologne), about a mile after crossing the river. The quiet terrace of this simple inn has a compelling view of the city and the river; the food is far better than average; the wine list includes some of the best. Two specialties are poached trout (*forelle blau*) and *zigeunerschnitzel* (a hot, exotic veal dish with a sauce containing paprika, red peppers, onions, and pickles). One will be perhaps amazed to find that even this spicy concoction does not impair the delicacy of one of the establishment's greatest wines, Scharzhofberger. This is a unique quality of all Moselles: they live with almost any food.

Scharzhofberger stems from the Saar valley, one of the Moselle's two important wine tributaries. These exceptionally delicate, light-colored and fragrant wines, made in the narrow Saar valley upstream from Trier, are from the Riesling, and not the Elbling; but one should be warned that good or great Saar vintage years are even less frequent than those of the Mittel-Mosel. So narrow is the valley and so swift its tiny river that despite the slate hillsides, next to no heat is retained. Saar vineyards are subjected to merciless temperature changes between day and night, leaving even in the best years more acid and less sugar in the grapes. Yet these very best years, when the sugar-acid balance approaches perfection, may often be responsible for the finest wines of the entire Moselle.

The principal wine towns of the Saar are Oberemmel, its famous vineyard being Scharzberg; Ockfen, with its Bockstein, and Wiltingen, whose Scharzhofberg is largely owned by one of Germany's most distinguished growers, Egon Müller, a name to note well. Another section of the Scharzhofberg is the property of the Cathedral of Trier. Its labels bear the name Dom Scharzhofberg. Perhaps the other most notable vineyards are Gottesfüss and Braune Kupp in Wiltingen, Kupp and Herrenberg at Ayl.

At Ayl, too, is the only creditable inn of the Saar, the Hotel Peter Lauer; its wine list will be endowed with local pearls. The valley's last wine town, whose symmetrically laid-out vineyards look for all the world like green linen set out to dry, is Serrig. A cleft in the western hills exposes Serrig's vineyards to fierce winter winds; yet in propitious years Serrigers can be little short of remarkable. Its two traditional vineyards are Heiligenborn and Schloss Saarfels—but there is another yet, Schloss Saarstein, in recent times so improved by good management that its wines rival the great Scharzhofberg and Scharzberg. Serriger Schloss Saarstein is definitely a name to remember.

The other tributary of the Moselle is the Ruwer, a bubbling trout stream that joins the Moselle just below Trier. Among the most highly prized of the entire Moselle, Ruwer wines are capable of remarkable, subtle bouquets and hauntingly spicy tastes. Some think they taste faintly like cinnamon. And like Saar wines, they are often charmingly *spritzig* (the German equivalent of the French *pétillant*), imperceptibly bubbly. The Ruwer can boast only five significant wine towns, and but a handful of important vineyards, all with world-famous names. The best known is perhaps Maximin Grünhauser Herrenberg. In the village of Mertesdorf are Brutusberg, Lorenzberg, and Treppchen. Kasel is celebrated for its Neisgen; Eitelsbach for Karthäuserhofberger Sang, and Waldrach for Schloss Marienlay.

After leaving the Ruwer we descend that part of the Moselle whose vineyard names are, as a rule, more familiar to the average wine-lover. Here is the most famous part of the river, where no curve or stretch is ever quite the same as the last, each with a backdrop of precipitous green hills, ruined castles, and unfrequented chapels and shrines. The spell is other-worldly: one never pauses to reflect on the cruel upheavals of nature that created it, or of the millions of years that passed during its making.

At the risk of emulating the format of a guidebook, we give here a list of the principal wine villages of the Mittel-Mosel, with their best vineyards. The seven principal villages are marked with asterisks. Yet another five are only of slightly lesser importance, and once or twice we come across an occasional joker. Downstream from Trier, they are:

Trittenheim. About ten miles below the towns of Schweich and Mehring, where vines again appear on the hillsides, we come to Trittenheim, set in a sharp bend in the river, its vineyards crowned by the chapel of Laurentiusberg. Trittenheim's wines are known for their freshness and lightness. They are rarely exported, though entirely typical of the Mittel-Mosel. Besides Laurentiusberg, two other Trittenheim vineyards are worthy of mention: Altärchen and Apotheke.

Neumagen. The name is probably derived from the nineteenth milestone on the Roman road to Koblenz. Neumagen is one of the oldest wine settlements on the Moselle—a Roman village mentioned by Antonius in his *Mosella,* especially important because of its hazardous rapids (nowadays under water). A respite was always taken at Neumagen for craft bound downstream, as well as for traders mounting the rapids. The village's best vineyard is Laudamusberg, whose wines are often described as tasting, somewhat paradoxically, like "bitter almonds" and "ripe currants."

Dhron. At Neumagen the road leaves the river and crosses the peninsula to Dhron, a charming village on a small river of the same name. Its best vinyard, whose wines can be of the greatest in fine years, is Dhronhofberger, owned by the Bischöfliches Priesterseminar in Trier, a Catholic institution with other important holdings throughout the Saar, Ruwer, and Moselle.

*Piesport. As you mount the top of the hill after Dhron, you get your first view of these celebrated terraced vineyards, mounting precipitously above one of the Moselle's more generous bends, exposed to every ray of the southern sun. On approaching, you will also observe that many of them extend out on bastions, some man-made, some natural, like boxes in an opera house. Every precious square foot of slate and soil must be used. Like many others on the river, the Piesport vineyards must be worked

entirely on foot. One of the best is named Treppchen—after the stone steps that the workers climb to tend the vines in summer and, in winter, to carry the slate chips up the cliff to replenish those that have slid off the terraces.

If one crosses the river to the village and drives along its quay, so low that the river laps its edges, one will see at first hand the vineyards wholly covered by the gray slate considered so important in making the best wines. High above you will see Piesport's finest traditional vineyard, that of Goldtröpfchen or the "little golden drops"—romantically depicting the Riesling at its full stage of juicy ripeness. After Goldtröpfchen and Treppchen, Piesport's finest are Güntherslay, Taubengarten, Schubertslay, and Lay, a word which, incidentally, means slate. But one single word of caution about the wines of Piesport: be wary of a wine labeled Piesporter Michelsberg. The term no longer applies to a specific vineyard, but to a blend of any wines from thereabouts.

Wintrich. Around yet another curve we come upon the town of Wintrich, its three best vineyards being Grosser Herrgott, Ohligsberg, and Geyerslay. Superb wines from the Grosser Herrgott (as well as from Piesporter Güntherslay) are made by the Erbhof St. Michel at Wintrich, a winery that also owns a delightful inn at the upper end of the village. The Stube St. Michel is family-operated. On this part of the Moselle, anyway, one will not find comparable cooking or, specifically, a more tempting version of the ubiquitous *schnitzel.* Nor should you depart the St. Michel without having sampled the house-distilled fruit *eaux-de-vie* (*geists*)—especially the apple "Calvados," of which the genial proprietors are justifiably proud.

Kesten. A tiny village, across and away from the river. Its wines are of rare value, though rarely seen. Those from the vineyard of Paulinshofberg are both "big" and delicate, much sought after by the Germans themselves.

Brauneberg. Kestener Paulinshofberg's wines are more unusual and rare than those of the next town, Brauneberg, though vintages from the two best vineyards here, Juffer and Falkenberg, are also much in demand by knowledgeable Germans. Hearty, sound, rich—and a little earthy—they were evidently liked by the Romans, too. The town's original name was Dusemond, derived and Germanicized from the Latin *mons dulcis* ("sweet mountain").

Bernkastel. Bernkastel is no village, but an exciting medieval town, a wine center of the Mittel-Mosel dating back to the beginning of the valley's viticulture. Bernkastel is a fascinating hodgepodge of timbered houses and narrow streets, with a colorful marketplace and an ancient Rathaus, or town hall. A half-hour's climb takes you to the ruins of Landshut Castle above, once a favorite retreat for the bishops of Trier—men who knew their wines.

Bernkastel's most renowned vineyard is known as the Doktor, nowadays divided three ways between the family of a certain late Dr. Thanisch (no connection with the name), the large German wine-shipping firm of Deinhard, and a progressive vintner named Lauerburg, who owns the smallest section. The Doktor (the hill is called Doktorsberg), is and has for decades been considered by many to be the best vineyard on the Mittel-Mosel, its fame having spread so far and wide that the supply has long since failed the demand. Consequently, the Thanisch heirs combine its wines with those of another excellent vineyard, Graben; the Deinhards use Badstube, and Lauerburg, Bratenhöfchen.

Competitors of the Doktor, without much backing from experts, claim the wine's universal fame has resulted from its catchy name. Our own viewpoint would be the reverse. Only a truly great wine could possibly have survived all the nonsensical legends that have been spread about it. Nearly everyone has his own version; but the basic theme is that some dignitary—a king of England, a noble Metternich, or a bishop of Trier—lay one day at death's door. As a last resort, he was given a drink of wine from the greatest vineyard of the Moselle—but need we finish? Without question the wines of the Doktor deserve their fame. Fragrant, with more body than most Moselles, they also defy age, an attribute of any great wine, and most particularly a Moselle. Their producers age them in icy cellars beneath the berg, usually releasing them for sale only after two or three years. A unique characteristic of the Doktor is a subtle smokiness, best detected when the wine is very young.

Other great vineyards of Bernkastel—and there are many— include Lay, Rosenberg, and Schwanen. Parenthetically, since wines of the Doktor have become too expensive for most people, one should seek out wines of these others, almost as good and in some years even better, which command more realistic prices. Be wary of a label with the town name of Bernkastel-Kues. These are wines from vineyards on the opposite, alluvial bank of the river. They are not bona fide Bernkastelers.

*Graach. Like some of the Grands Crus of France, a handful of famous vineyards in Germany, with official consent, omit the name of the town from their labels, their owners assuming that the wines are so famous everyone knows where they are. In this latter category are Marcobrunn, Steinberg, Schloss Vollrads, and Schloss Johannisberg on the Rhine; Scharzhofberg on the Saar, and Josephshof on the Moselle. Josephshof, at Graach, is owned by a famous wine-making family, the Kesselstatts, who have other holdings in excellent vineyards in Piesport, as well as on the Ruwer. The wine of the Josephshof is unbelievably redolent, always well made and well balanced. Visitors to Graach will find the vineyard just behind and above a bulbous-spired chapel of its one-time owner, at the downstream end of the village. Graach's other notable vineyards, all surveying the river from risky heights, are Himmelreich, Domprobst, and Abtsberg. The town's joker is Graacher Munslay, the name for a regional wine shared with adjacent Wehlen.

*Wehlen. Except for those ruined castles and chapels perched high on nearly every hilltop, perhaps the most frequent sight on the Moselle are the white sundials, affixed to rocky crags among the vineyards. Whether coincidental or not, the presence of one of these sundials on a hillside is usually indicative that a good vineyard hangs somewhere on the nearby hill; more often than not, it will be named Sonnenuhr or Sonnuhr. Some Germans, spurning the Doktor, think that the vineyard of Wehlener Sonnenuhr is the greatest on the Moselle. Its reputation for quality and consistently good vintages is certainly high—but no more so than that of its principal owners, the famous clan of Prüm. Their affluent houses, side by side and lining the quay of the town, are an impressive sight from the opposite bank. A local saying goes: "What the Duponts are to Delaware, the Prüms are to the Moselle." The family holds vineyards in Zeltingen, Wehlen, Graach, and Bernkastel, and almost without exception, any or all wines with the name of Prüm on the label will be nothing but the highest quality. Notwithstanding, made by the Prüms or not, Wehlener wines—combining delicacy, richness, and fruitiness—have for years won a clear majority of prizes at expositions throughout Germany. After Sonnenuhr, the best-known vineyards are Lay, Klosterlay, and Nonnenberg. As mentioned, Wehlener (or Graacher) Munslay is a regional wine. It can be nearly anything.

Zeltingen. Sharing the same stretch of the river with Graach and Wehlen, Zeltingen is the largest producing village (well over two million bottles annually) of the Moselle. The finest of Zeltingen are equals of Wehlen, but mediocre Zeltingens so flood the market that it is especially important to know the names of the best. Once again the magic name of Prüm will bring forth outstanding bottles; the best-known vineyards are Sonn(en)uhr, Schlossberg, Rotlay, Himmelreich, and Stephanslay.

Ürzig. At the next bend we encounter the steepest vineyards so far, along with an appreciable change in the color of the slate. Here the river has run into a volcanic strata rich in iron. The result is that the wines of Ürzig are spicier, and often *spritzig.* Once more the most important owner in the town is Bischöfliches Priesterseminar of Trier, and the great vineyards nestled among the crags and bastions are Würzgarten, Lay, and Kranklay. There

26

is also an inferior regional wine, Ürziger Schwarzlay, an author-ized blend from vineyards even as far distant as Zeltingen and Kinheim. Kinheim wines are not well considered, though two vineyards, Rosenberg and Hubertuslay, are certainly worthy of mention.

Kröv. What's in a label? One need only drive through the village of Kröv on a summer's weekend to see. History does not record the identity of the marketing genius who first thought up the idea of affixing—to bottles from this hitherto unspoiled village—a label depicting a child being spanked with its pants down. One only hopes that wherever the genius is now, he is enjoying his just deserts. Krövner Narktarsch ("bare bottom") is as pleasant and inoffensive a little wine as its label is the converse. Yet it has earned an international notoriety—as invariably evi-denced by the disproportionate number of buses pulled up in front of the *weinstuben* crowding the main street. Kröv is a tourist trap, so drive on. There are some good vineyards at Kröv (Nieder-berg, Heislay, and Petersberg), but they are best found on a wine list at a respectable distance.

Zell. Zell's vineyard of Schwarze Katz ("the black cat"), when its pure product can be found, produces a delightful, soft wine. But somehow over the years this catchy name has led to a world-wide popularity, a demand far exceeding the tiny vineyard's conceivable output. Today, Zeller Schwarze Katz is an exploited blend that should never be thought of as anything but a localized Moselblümchen. Good wines from this picturesque and historic little town come from the vineyards of Burglay, Dommhen, and Nussberg—nor should one pass up a bottle of the true, pure Schwarze Katz, which may be found only at the Hotel Schloss Zell. The hotel's owners, the Bohn family, have been proprietors of a part of Schwarze Katz for generations.

The village of Zell has much to recommend it, one of its pleasantest assets being a lazy, tree-lined quay with more than its share of little *weinstuben.* Because the main road to Koblenz bypasses the town, Zell gets less than the normal numbers of trippers. Across the river are the heights of Marienberg where, as we have mentioned, the Moselle barely missed uniting with itself. Marienberg should not be missed. It commands three glorious stretches of the river, all from the same vantage point. You may spend the night at the somewhat sketchy hotel: it will be a quiet night, high above the twinkling lights of the valley, though on a weekend one's sleep may be terminated at any early hour by hundreds of pilgrims come to visit the little church, profitably designated as a shrine. Under these circumstances it is wise to be either very early or very late for breakfast, since the male members of these pilgrimages have a way of gravitating to the dining room (also the *weinstube*), while their wives attend mass. Usually by midmorning the respective adherents of God and the grape have been herded back into their buses and bounced down the mountainside, and peace restored.

From Trier to Zell, as the crow flies, is a mere thirty miles; but by road the distance is nearly tripled. Hence it is best to put up at some central point. Two obvious ones—those that also have the best hotels—are Bernkastel and Traben-Trarbach. For modern comfort accompanied by good taste and a view of the river traffic, the best is the Park Hotel at Traben-Trarbach. It is also the most expensive.

Before the Park existed, the traditional hostelry in Traben-Trarbach was the Clauss-Feist, small, ornate, and old-fashioned. The Clauss-Feist, also overlooking the river, provides above-average food, and wines drawn from some of the best vineyards of the region. Germans of the old school tend to frequent it: dowagers in high, boned collars, white-thatched gentlemen in waistcoats with prodigious watch chains, many of them come to take the baths, for Traben-Trarbach, besides a wine town, is also a well-known spa. A leisurely walk up the narrow gorge leading to the lovely Hunstück plateau takes you to the Kürhaus—and having come this far, you might climb a bit farther to the village of Kautenbach. On one side of the street the citizens of Kautenbach are Catholics; on the other, Protestants. Kautenbach's citizens are good neighbors, but until the last war there had never been an intermarriage.

Bernkastel's best hotel, also reflecting a past era, is the Drei Könige. Its rooms are moderately priced, and one will be graciously served on a large terrace by the river, with a view of the Landshut Castle above the town. Bernkastel has many other good hotels, all mentioned in guidebooks, but none more pleasantly situated, nor with a more excellent cellar.

Traveling on toward Koblenz, there are few more comfortable places to stay on the entire length of the Moselle than the Hotel Schloss Zell at Zell, in the thirteenth century a fortified palace of the archbishops of Trier. The Schloss has been so skillfully modernized that hardly a stone appears to have been dislodged since the day it was built. The kitchen distinguishes itself with Moselle specialties: trout (*forelle*), subtle variations of the local favorite, Moselle eel (*Moselaal*), and game of all kinds, furred or feathered. As we have already mentioned, this is one's chance to taste a bona fide Schwarze Katz, made by the Schloss management.

For those whose compelling interest is simply local wines combined with an honest meal and an unpretentious room, there are dozens of inns in many of the river villages. We have already praised the Stube St. Michel at Wintrich. Another is the Hotel Nicolay at Zeltingen, where one may sit by the river's edge and enjoy a Zeltinger Schlossberg or a Wehlener Sonnenuhr at realistic prices. The villages of Ürzig and Wehlen also each have acceptable establishments in comparable settings, where lazy hours may be well spent. The virtue of these places may evaporate, however, if one expects snappy service or *haute cuisine*. German cooking, even at best, is not *haute cuisine*. Instead, it is rugged, hearty, and nourishing, and always served in overgenerous portions. Contrary to popular notion, it is not greasy, only rich—especially along the Moselle. Rare is the sauce, either for meat or fish, that is not embellished with heavy cream. Typical

German soups are thick, but infallibly satisfying: in fact, in most restaurants one could keep body and soul together by simply ordering the *tagesuppe* (soup of the day). Freshwater fish, especially trout and pike, are always good, but with the meats there is a cloying lack of variation. One soon tires of the perennial veal or pork *schnitzel*, or beef prepared with wild mushrooms (*pfifferlinge*) and the invariable cream sauce. In desperation one searches for that section of a German menu headed *Geflügel und Wild* (fowl and game). The Germans know how to cook game, and they excel with partridge and pheasant, venison and wild boar. When it comes to wines, break convention and let them all be white. No German red wine has ever been more than mediocre; German whites, especially Moselles, harmonize with anything. In Rome, do as the Romans.

I V : *The Unter-Mosel*

If you ask any Mittel-Mosel vintner about the wines of the Unter-Mosel, he will usually tell you that no wine made between Zell and Koblenz is worth drinking. For the enthusiastic oenophile this is not quite the answer. When made from the Riesling (and most are), many wines from the Unter-Mosel stand up well, even though they lack the perfume and character of those upstream.

Below Zell, on the sharpest of curves, are the vineyards of Bremm. Here are the steepest slopes we have met so far—so precipitous that only parts of the hill can be cultivated, even for vines. With a growing shortage of manpower in the last few decades, vineyards such as these have fallen into neglect. A few miles further downstream and across the river, we pass the medieval town of Beilstein, shadowed by the ruins of a castle once the seat of the Metternichs. Beilstein, like Bernkastel, is a maze of narrow streets and timbered houses, and its most venerable *weinstube* and restaurant, the Ratskeller Haus Lipmann, was once the wine cellar for its noble rulers. Here one should try a bottle of Beilsteiner Schlossberg or Klosterberg, two exquisite wines, though they may not compare with a delicate Saar or a Piesporter. Better yet, you may discover a bottle from nearby Valwig, a village whose wines in good years are considered as fine as almost any from the Mittel-Mosel.

Passing down the river, one comes to many another wine town of fame: Senheim, with its vineyards of Blenengarten and Kircheberg; Kobern, with Pfennenberg and Weissenberg, and Winnegin, whose best bottle will be a Rosenberg Hann. Probably the best place to find these wines is Cochem, the principal town of the Unter-Mosel. More frequented by tourists than is good for its soul, Cochem nonetheless provides a convenient and colorful stopping place. At the Hotel-Restaurant-Ratskeller Brixiade on the right bank you may lunch or dine well, with access to a list of excellent local vintages and a view of the ancient town and its two castles—the first a very live castle indeed, atop a vineyard-covered mound; the other an ancient ruin crowning a lofty pinnacle downstream. If one objects to the comparative modernity of the Brixiade, a contrasting atmosphere may be found in the town itself at the Alte Thorschenke, a fourteenth-century building that is as much museum as restaurant. Cochem is a busy place, filled with hotels, souvenir shops, and trippers. But if you can bring yourself to overlook it all, linger a while in this, the last and among the most luminous of so many jewels that have studded the banks of the little river born in the Vosges.

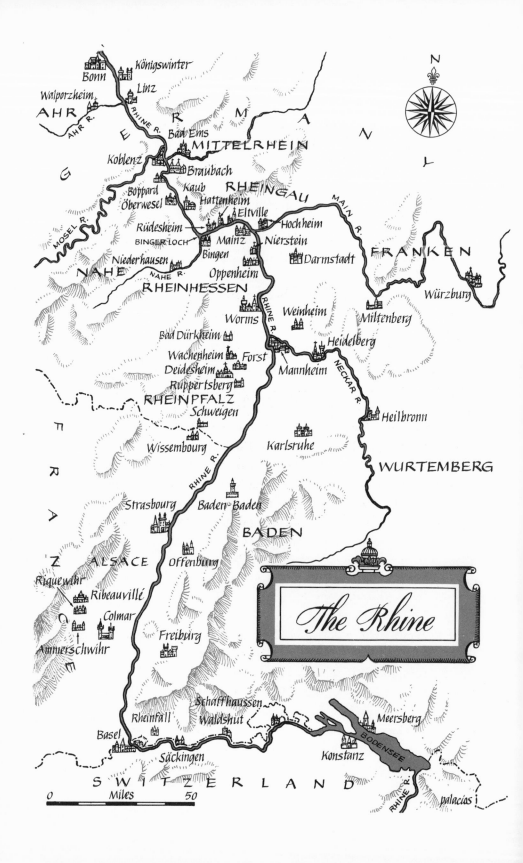

The Rhine

I I

The Rhine

I : *The Rheingau*

The Rhine—"Father Rhine" to every German schoolchild—
rises in the Swiss Alps and flows to the Hook of Holland. In the
course of nearly nine hundred miles of its journey, this "Nile of
the Occident," as Lamartine once called it, is the backbone of a
great network of waterways that serves six countries and forty
cities. From Basel (its highest navigable city) to the sea, it carries more than seven million tons of cargo annually and generates
about five billion kilowatts of power. Passing through some of the
most beautiful and variable country in Europe, the Rhine (including the Moselle) drains four of Europe's greatest wine
districts, along with several lesser ones.

At Koblenz, where it is joined by the Moselle, we find a river
that is bold and swift, its rough waters churned from the bottom
by boulders and ledges, its surface incessantly roiled by craft of
every kind and description. The Rhine—and everything that
rides it—is always in a hurry. It is a river that never seems to
pause to rest.

33

The name Koblenz derives from the Latin *castrum ad confluentes*, the name the Romans gave to their fortified trading post at the confluence of two important arteries. Viewing Koblenz today from the heights across the busy river, with its massive neoclassic schloss and church spires rising dimly amid smoke and haze, it is difficult to imagine what it must have been in Roman days: a quiet little port where oared Moselle boats tied up at the quays above the Deutsches Eck ("the German corner") with casks of wine for trade and transshipment. Equally hard to imagine, too, is how this busy, modern city, proudly presiding over the great river and its commerce, must have looked twenty-five years ago. Three-quarters of it were destroyed in World War II.

One leaves Koblenz on the right or eastern bank, to drive about thirty miles up the Rhine through a twisting gorge, its hills at times darkly wooded, at other times covered with terraced vineyards—and a castle at every turn. Viticulturally this section of the river is called the Mittel-Rhein: but we need not linger, for none of its vineyards is of any importance, most of the wine going into blends or Sekt. Across the river we see Stolzenfels, described in some guidebooks as "the most romantic fortress of the Rhine." The guidebooks are wrong; nor is Stolzenfels by any means typical of what is to come. A garish yellow horror, it was rebuilt by Frederick Wilhelm IV in the early nineteenth century, its walls embellished with ersatz crenellations and its style revamped to reflect the emperor's schizophrenic love for Spanish architecture and English country houses. Far more rewarding are two other castles soon to appear, intriguingly named Burg Katz and Burg Maus (Cat and Mouse Castles). Beyond Burg Maus the road passes under a high jutting cliff, the Lorelei, beneath which legendarily lived the man-eating siren whose story has been glorified by Heine, Liszt, and many another. Few other stretches of the Rhine are more adorned with legend or natural beauty.

The only significant wine town one meets in ascending the

Mittel-Rhein is Assmannshausen—as it happens, Germany's best-known red-wine town. Red wines are also made on the Ahr River, which joins the Rhine below Koblenz, as well as in two other predominantly white-wine regions, the Rheinhessen and the Rheinpfalz; but those of Assmannshausen are the most sought after when a German decides he *must* have a German red. The best vineyards of Assmannshausen are not to be seen from the main road, but lie in a pocket of the valley that rises behind the town. Here you will find immaculately kept vines, nowadays largely the property of the German state, which latter logically has a high stake in the development of red wine in a nation that must import most of the red wine it drinks. The grape most used by the *Staatsweingut* at Assmannshausen, as well as in the Ahr region to the north, is the Spätburgunder, a strain of the Burgundian Pinot noir developed specifically for the abbreviated growing season and arduous winters of this part of the Rhine. At best its wines have the familiar bouquet of a red Burgundy, but the tastes that follow are unfamiliar and not always even attractive. The Germans, like the Swiss, are in the habit of drinking their red wines at a youthful age and seem to prefer them slightly on the sweet side. Yet even wines from the most famous vineyards of Assmannshausen—Höllenberg, Hinterkirsch, and Frankenthal—are ones that profit little by laying down.

Since you undoubtedly will want to taste a red Assmannshauser, there could be no better place for it than on the terrace of the ancient Hotel Kröne, situated on the main road and overlooking some of the river's busiest activities. The Kröne, nowadays considered one of the superior restaurants in Germany, has been an important hostelry for more than seven centuries, by virtue of holding—with Assmannshausen itself—a commercially important vantage on the river's life. Just upstream from Assmannshausen lies that notoriously hazardous bend of the Rhine, the Binger Loch, about which we shall have more to say later. Until modern times, every passage through the raging waters of the loch was fraught with danger; hence it was common practice to unload valuable cargoes and transport them by land between Assmannshausen and Rüdesheim, the next town around the bend. Today parts of the worst reef of the loch have been cut away, and Assmannshausen is no longer a port.

During the war, the R.A.F. used the Binger Loch above the Kröne to good advantage. By flying close to the water to escape the hail of antiaircraft guns set on the hills, it managed to plug the river many times over with sunken tugs and barges, effectively crippling the vitally important traffic of the Rhine.

At the Binger Loch there is an abrupt right-angle turn, and for the next fifteen miles upstream the Rhine's valley points from east to west. It is this stretch of the Rhine, specifically along the low hills of the northern bank facing the sun, that is the most illustrious wine land of Germany: the Rheingau. According to legend, it was Charlemagne who first recognized the viticultural virtues of the Rheingau. From his castle across the river at Ingelheim, he observed that the snows melted faster on these hillsides than in any other part of the surrounding countryside, and he commanded that grapes be planted there.

The Rheingau is the smallest wine region of Germany, producing about one-third of what is produced on the Moselle. Its vineyards are by no means as scenic or spectacular, for with the exception of those of Rüdesheim, which rise to dizzy heights above the river, most grape-growing land of the Rheingau is only gently sloping. The best vineyards are usually found back from the river, where they are protected from the north winds by the high Taunus mountains that rise behind—though still close enough to the Rhine to benefit from the valley's warmth and the reflection of the sun on the water. The soil is quartz and slate, mixed with considerable fertile earth. Even so, it is eminently suited for the noble Riesling, grown on nearly three-quarters of the Rheingau's total acreage.

Two other grapes share the balance of the Rheingau: the Sylvaner, and the Müller-Thurgau. The Sylvaner, far more prevalent in the Rheinhessen and Rheinpfalz to the south, is known as the second grape of Germany. Contrasted with the Riesling, it is a bountiful producer and easy to raise, but its wines never approach the style or delicacy of the former. The Müller-Thurgau is a cross of the two, its wine less distinguished yet. Principally the Müller-Thurgau is useful in blending.

Between Mainz and Rüdesheim the river, dammed by the reefs of the Binger Loch, becomes extremely wide, an important factor to the viticulture of the Rheingau. In very hot summers evaporation from this large expanse of water is beneficial to the vines, and in the spring and autumn its mists and fogs guarantee their protection from the settling frosts and prolong the growing season. In the Rheingau it is not unusual for the harvest to last well through November, on occasion even into December. This is particularly applicable to the overripe, sweet grapes, those which have been attacked by the so-called *edelfäule*. The natural phenomenon of the *edelfäule*, known in France as the *pourriture noble* and botanically as the *Botrytis cinerea*, is responsible for all the great sweet wines of the world, not only including those of the Moselle and the Rhine, but also the classic Sauternes, Anjous, and Hungarian Tokay. Briefly, the *edelfäule* is a minute organism or mold that, under conditions of sufficient humidity, settles on ripened grapes and, by virtue of its tiny roots that penetrate the skins, saps the water from the juice—leaving a concentration of sugar and other elements within. Grapes so affected are not exactly an appetizing sight. But without the aid of this predatory organism, man would never have known the delights of some of the world's greatest wines.

As compared to the colorful and intriguing wine villages we have met on the Moselle, few of the Rheingau offer much temptation to linger. Especially those near the river have a commercial tinge; most others are simply devoid of charm, even though one occasionally comes across a pretty church or square. Tourist trap that it is, the outstanding exception is Rüdesheim. Rüdesheim's teeming river life alone is enough to recommend it. This is where the tugs, having struggled with the swift and dangerous waters of the Binger Loch, take leave of their barge trains, to dart once more down the river to pick up another. The loch is considered so hazardous that pilots are trained and licensed to navigate it only in one direction. Hours of rapt fascination may be spent watching the river or studying the complex system of flags and signals of the control towers that guide the traffic around the bend. One slip or oversight on the part of the controller would bring disaster. If Rüdesheim's main street, where every establishment is either a hotel, a *weinstube*, or a souvenir shop, is not enough to convince you that this is where the world congregates to drink wine, we suggest a visit to the Drosselgasse, a celebrated back alley wholly taken up with *weinstuben* from one end to the other. And one of Germany's best wine museums is to be found in the Brömserburg Castle at the lower end of the town.

In good years Rüdesheim's wines are considered to be among the Rheingau's finest, exceptionally endowed with body and an individualistic flinty flavor. The best are known as the Berg wines, meaning ones that are grown on the *berg* or mountainside above the town. For an exhilarating view of the Rhine one should climb through these precipitous vineyards to the ruins of the Ehrenfels Castle commanding the scope of the Rheingau and the Binger Loch. The soil in these slate-covered vineyards, reminiscent of the Moselle, is so shallow that in seasons of scant rainfall the vines dry out, leading to wines that are harsh and coarse; yet in rainy years the wines excel. Labels of Berg wines always carry the term before the vineyard name, such as Berg Burgweg, Berg Bronnen, and Berg Schlossberg—to name the best. Two other good non-Berg vineyards are Bischofsberg and Hinterhaus.

Again, in the following pages asterisks indicate the best wine towns:

Geisenheim. Next to Rüdesheim on the river, Geisenheim is well known for its wines, but perhaps best known for its famous school of viticulture, in whose experimental vineyards nearly every grape variety of the world is grown. Geisenheim's best vineyards are Rothenberg, Kosackenberg, Decker, and Lickerstein.

Johannisberg. Even those who know nothing about wines have heard of Schloss Johannisberg, the massive, institutional-looking building that sits proudly on its hill, overlooking the Rhine. The schloss and its vineyards have a long and lofty history. Founded by the Benedictines in the eleventh century, it was the property of various religious hierarchies until the beginning of the nineteenth century, when German church lands were secularized. Thereafter successively owned by the House of Orange and the Habsburgs, it was finally presented by the latter to the distinguished family of Austrian statesmen, the Metternichs, whose descendant is the present owner. The Habsburgs reserved a tithe—one-tenth—of the production for themselves—an obligation that must still be paid today.

Traditionally, the wines of the schloss are among the very finest of the Rheingau, and there is no doubt that under the Metternichs they were developed to a point of near perfection. However, within the last decade, some experts are beginning to wonder. The wines do not seem to be as carefully made as in days of old, and the management of the schloss appears to be relying on its past reputation. Additionally, the labeling and classification of the wines seems calculated to confuse rather than clarify the mind of the consumer, who must sort out seven categories or label types from the same vineyard. Given in their approximate order of quality, price, and degree of sweetness, they are labeled and marked as follows: *Rotlack* (red label), *Grünlack* (green), *Rosalack* (rose), *Orangelack* (orange), *Weisslack* (white), *Himmelblau* (blue), and *Goldlack* (gold). With all this in mind, one should seize the opportunity to visit the schloss and its impressive cellars. Visitors are welcome, and a lackey exuberantly explains the wines, expounds the history, shows you the cellar, with its neatly raked gravel floor and its one thousand candles that are lit when the incumbent Prince von Metternich entertains dignitaries. You will be given a glass of wine, generally at the *Rotlack* level; and along with considerable scuttlebutt about the prince and princess, who occasionally occupy the castle, your heartstrings will be pulled by learning that the prince has no heir, and thus the schloss stands in danger of reverting to the Habsburgs.

Even though one may gain the impression that they are traitors to their past, some of the higher-priced wines of the schloss in good years will be superb, and worth every penny. It is valuable to know, too, that the schloss's wines are by no means all that Johannisberg has to offer. Happily there are other excellent vineyards of the town, such as Hölle, Mittelhölle, Klaus, and Erntebringer, whose wines may nowadays be as good or better. Some of these may be had at the nearby hostelry, the Berg Schwarzenstein, perched on a hill overlooking the schloss itself. Good restaurants in the Rheingau are few and far between. The Schwarzenstein offers German home cooking. With your dessert, invest in a bottle of Rüdesheimer Eiswein ("ice wine") made from the Rülander grape, a comparative stranger on the Rheingau. Eiswein itself is an expensive and much prized rarity: an exceptionally delicate, luscious wine made from overripe grapes that have been partially frozen before picking.

Winkel. Winkel's great vineyard is Schloss Vollrads. The impressive schloss, with moss-covered slate roofs and a surrounding moat, is the residence of one of the Rheingau's leading vintners, Graf Matuschka-Greiffenclau—as it has been for his ancestors since the fourteenth century. The wines are distinguished by what, for want of another word, may be called their elegance. Moreover, a bottle of Vollrads will always be a good bet—else it would not have been sold by the vineyard's eminent owner. The only detraction lies, once again, in the system of labeling, even more complicated than that of Schloss Johannisberg. Summarized very briefly, they divide into four groups: those marked *Original-Abfüllung* are the least expensive and most ordinary, however desirable; the addition of the word *Schlossabzug* means a better wine, probably a Spätlese; *Kabinett,* the next higher; after which come the *Auslese, Beerenauslese,* and *Trockenbeerenauslese.* In addition to Vollrads, the other good vineyards of Winkel include Hasensprung, Jesuitengarten, Honigberg, and Dachsberg—all producing wines of distinction.

Hallgarten. Hallgarten's vineyards climb the Taunus range to almost one thousand feet, making them the highest of this part of the Rheingau. The wines can be very good or very bad, for Hallgarten's soils are heavier than most, containing more than their share of clay. This results in full-bodied and fruity wines in good years and very ordinary products in poor years. Hallgarten's best-known vineyards are Schönhell, Deutelsberg, and Jungfer.

Östrich. Experts disagree about the quality of wines from this largest-producing town of the Rheingau. In general they tend to be less delicate than those of adjacent towns, yet there are classic exceptions, as will be noted. Bouquets of many Rheingau wines may frequently be likened to specific fruits; to many of us, Östrich's wines smell and even taste like fresh apricots. The famous vineyards are Doosberg, Eiserberg, and Lenchen, and the town's most reliable producer is J. Wegeler Erben. But Östrich has other assets, not the least of which is one of the most congenial small hotels on the Rheingau, the Hotel Schwann. An attractive, timbered house with Renaissance gables, the Schwann affords cozy oak-paneled dining rooms, and a delightful terrace for warm days. Snails and game, especially partridge served with a remarkable sauce of game stock, Madeira, paprika, and cream, are perhaps its best specialties. Another commendable one combines pieces of veal, tomato, and bacon on a skewer. The Schwann's wine list is small but outstanding, and one may stay overnight in comfort.

*Hattenheim. So far, with a few exceptions, we have not mentioned the names of outstanding Rheingau producers whose names on bottles spell infallible quality. In addition to the vineyards held by the German state (*Staatsweingut*), always indicative of quality, special attention should be paid to bottles bearing the names Langwerth von Simmern, Graf von Schönborn-Weissenthied, Fürst Löwenstein, Graf Eltz, and the Schloss

Reinhartshausen. Nearly all are proprietors in Hattenheim and its neighboring village of Erbach.

Nestled at the base of a little valley behind Hattenheim is one of Germany's oldest and greatest vineyards—so prestigious that, like Schloss Johannisberg and Schloss Vollrads, it uses only its own name on its labels, spurning mention of the town. This is the state-owned Steinberg, consisting of some sixty walled acres, the work of the Cistercians in the twelfth century. Perhaps the most appropriate place to taste Steinbergers is in the little gatehouse *weinstube* of the Kloster Eberbach, a magnificent Gothic monastery of the same era, in whose cellars many Steinbergers are made and aged. After visiting the lovely monastery, one may partake of simple food and superb wines. The fare will be inexpensive, but many of the wines will not. Here we offer a word of advice: Steinberg produces more than twenty thousand cases in an average year, and there is an inevitable variation in the quality of the wines. The best rule of thumb is to stick to the *Kabinett* price class, or higher. The term *Kabinett*, incidentally, was coined at Steinberg during a period when the incumbent Duke of Nassau kept his best wines in a cabinet. Steinbergs are noble wines, strong in flavor and character, but there are other vineyards of Hattenheim that produce wine of exceptional lightness, with their own individual tanginess and charm. If one is careful to be guided, in general, by the names of producers given above, one can hardly be anything but delighted with them. Among the most reputed vineyards are Mannberg, Nussbrunnen, Wisselbrunnen, Pfaffenberg and Engelmannsberg, but there are many others of almost equal quality.

Erbach. The greatest vineyard of Erbach is Marcobrunn, another name often found alone on its labels. Virtually all the finest Rheingau producers own slices of this great vineyard, whose wines possess such unusual balance and fruitiness. At one time Hattenheim laid claim to Marcobrunn, in a boundary dispute that all but rocked the Rheingau; on the country road that parallels the main road, just below the vineyard itself, one will find a famous red sandstone fountain, built to mark the border between the two towns. The names of Erbach's other vineyards are legion: Steinmorgen, Brühl, Siegelsberg, Hohenrain, to name but a few.

Kiedrich. An attractive village, with a charming Gothic church, Kiedrich lies back from the river in its own valley. Wines from the vineyards above the town are most typical of the Rheingau, with lively bouquets and unusual freshness. Kiedrich's most notable vineyards are Gräfenberg, Wasserrose, Turmberg, and Sandgrube.

*Rauenthal. A village also removed from the river and in its own valley. Rauenthalers are more popular with Germans than with foreigners, probably as a result of their comparative fullness and masculinity. The most distinguished individual producer is Graf Eltz, whose wines are only excelled by the *Staatsweingut.* Rauenthal's best and most famous vineyard is Baiken, the most highly taxed piece of vineyard land in Germany. Nor is the quality of its wine far behind the land assessors' valuation. Other superb vineyards are Gehrn, Herberg, Wülfen, and Rothenberg.

*Eltville. One of the special charms of Eltvillers is that they may be as delicate and light as Moselles. The vineyards are among the oldest on the Rhine, the town's name deriving from the Latin *alta villa.* In addition to the *Staatsweingut,* Graf Eltz, and von Simmern, another distinguished producer should be added to the list: J. B. Becker, who makes a magnificent wine from Eltville's best vineyard, Sonnenberg. Other excellent vineyards of the town are Klumbchen, Kalbspflicht, and Taubenberg —but nearly all Eltville's numerous vineyards are good, and even in the lower price brackets the wines are apt to be outstanding.

Walluf (or *Niederwalluf*). Among experts, wines from this town are not always highly rated, but again, those produced by J. B. Becker will be outstanding. The best vineyards are probably Mittelberg and Walkenberg. At Walluf there is a uniquely quiet and simple inn, also called the Hotel Schwann, situated on the river overlooking a tiny yacht basin, with a good kitchen and a fine cellar.

Hochheim. Were it not for the fact that its vineyards are officially so classified, one should not consider Hochheimers as wines of the Rheingau. Hochheim lies almost fifteen miles east of Walluf, beyond the suburban city of Kastel, across the Rhine from Mainz, and it is not on the Rhine at all, but on the Main. Its vineyards constitute an isolated pocket of about five hundred acres sandwiched between orchards and lush farmland. Nonetheless, the wines—full, fragrant, sometimes a bit earthy—are often compared in quality with those of the Rheingau proper. It was the prevalence of Hochheimers in England a century ago that led the British to adopt the term "hock" for German wines in general. Hochheimers were especially popular with Queen Victoria, for whom one of the town's vineyards was named. The Victoria Berg, however, is by no means in a class with the more traditional ones, such as Domdechaney, Kirchenstück, Rauchloch, and Stein.

Many people visiting the Rheingau like to make their headquarters in nearby Wiesbaden, a spacious, airy city, and a thermal spa since Roman days. In a sense, Wiesbaden is hardly a city at all, but a resort. It is filled with parks and broad shaded streets, excellent shops and hotels. Most of the latter tend to be expensive, but Wiesbaden's charm, especially after dark, is sufficient to justify a drain on the pocketbook for a night or two. The two best hotels are the Nassauer Hof and the Schwarzer Bock, the latter with its own thermal swimming pool and—if one does not choose to indulge in the cure in public—thermal water piped into the bathrooms. Yet another hotel—less expensive though more commercial—is the Blum, facing the Kurhaus park.

Wiesbaden's acknowledged finest restaurant is the Mutter Engel, where the fare tends to be international, done with consummate skill. After a few weeks of German cooking, Americans will be both pleased and surprised to find the menu's two "American specialties," categorically described as "steak" and "filet of steak."

Of a warm summer's evening one can do no better than dine on the terrace of the Kurhaus, among the scores of Germans who come to linger there over a three-hour meal with thrice as many bottles, one of which may be Wiesbaden's own Neroberg, her only wine, made within the city limits. Neroberg is not the greatest Rhingau, but the patriotic management will be flattered to have you ask for it. The nineteenth-century quasi-classical Kurhaus, owned by the city, merits a visit anyway, even though it is no longer a place where one takes the waters. Elaborately tiled floors, massive chandeliers, and exquisitely paneled public rooms all render it an example of the best of German style of the last century—a style that in general was not characterized by the best in taste. There is an opera house and a theater, both with creditable companies, under the same roof, as well as what is proclaimed to be the most active gambling casino in Europe, Monte Carlo excepted.

II : *The Rheinhessen and the Rheinpfalz*

Across the Rhine from the Rheingau is a great rectangle of land—predominantly vineyard land—known as the Rheinhessen, or Hessia. Statistically this is one of the two largest wine-producing areas of Germany; qualitatively its only great wines derive from about half a dozen towns. With the exception of Bingen, opposite Rüdesheim, all of these towns are on the west bank, around the corner and upstream from the city of Mainz. The rest of this vast rectangle, contained by the Rhine on two sides, the Nahe River on the west and the Rheinpfalz to the south, produces mediocrity, much of it exported under the label of Liebfraumilch.

The Rheinhessen is the traditional home of Liebfraumilch, the Rheinland's equivalent of Moselblümchen. Rarely if ever seen on a wine list in Germany, Liebfraumilch is nonetheless Germany's most exported wine. It is definitely a put-together concoction, and of those who put it together there are probably no more than a dozen (out of several hundred) who do an outstanding job. Liebfraumilch, at best, is pleasant and soft, usually a bit on the sweet side, and invariably more expensive than it deserves to be. Part of what you pay for is in the name: "Milk of the Holy Mother."

By law Liebfraumilch may come from nearly anywhere on the Rhine, except the inland wine districts of Franconia and Baden and, of course, the Moselle. It is most commonly a blend of Rheinhessen or Rheinpfalz wines, in bad years often containing a trickle of rejects from the Rheingau—paradoxically rendering it livelier by virtue of a bit of Riesling juice, however poor the reject might have been in its own right. In the Rheinhessen the principal grape is the Sylvaner, colloquially called the Oestereicher, on the assumption that it originated in Austria or in the east (*Ost*). Next in line comes the Müller-Thurgau, the cross between the Riesling and the Sylvaner. The Riesling, though highly prized, is grown in relatively small quantity and confined entirely to the best vineyards. Since both the Sylvaner and the Müller-Thurgau, good producers and easy to raise, yield a higher sugar content than the Riesling, Rheinhessen wines often run naturally to more than 11 percent alcohol, as contrasted to an average Moselle at 9 percent or a Rheingau at 10 percent. Despite their alcoholic strength, good Rheinhessens are both soft and racy—wines, as the saying goes, that make and hold friends easily.

Unless one has already taken an excursion by ferry over the head of the Binger Loch from Rüdesheim, an experience that should not be missed if possible, one will need to retrace one's steps to visit the isolated pocket of vineyards at Bingen. For the convenience of all concerned, the authorities would have done better to put the vineyards of Bingen in the same geographical category as the Rheingau, or else to have classified them along with those of the Nahe—the river that, flowing from the north, empties itself into the Rhine at the Binger Loch. The Nahe, incidentally, should not be entirely overlooked. A comparative newcomer among German wine districts, whose labels are not often seen abroad, the Nahe produces excellent wines, though highly variable in type. Its three best wine towns, not too far upstream from Bingen, are Schloss Böckelheim, Kreuznach, and Niederhausen. Should you come across a bottle of Schloss Böckelheimer Kupfergrube made by the *Staatsweingut*, you will do well to take advantage of the opportunity.

The terrain and soils of Bingen, terraced vineyards filled with slate, are reminiscent of the Moselle. But Bingen's wines are neither Moselles nor Rheingaus. The finest come from two hills adjacent to the town: the Rochusberg and the Scharlachberg, this latter meaning "scarlet hill" and so named because once upon a time it grew red grapes. A climb to the top of the Rochusberg brings a view of the Rhine and the Binger Loch almost as impressive as that from the heights of Rüdesheim from the other side. The Rochusberg's best vineyards are Eisel, Schlossberg, and Schwätzerchen, though their wines are not to be compared in quality to those called Scharlachberg from the other hill. Labels of Bingen wines often bear names hyphenated with one or the other of two neighboring villages, Büdesheim and Kempten.

While still on this part of the Rhine one may want to visit Ingelheim, the site of Charlemagne's northernmost bastion, from which he watched the thawing snows of the Rheingau and planted his vineyards accordingly. Viticulturally Ingelheim is best known for its red wines, though in our opinion they in themselves are hardly worth the trip. For most wine-lovers, the true Rheinhessen begins above Mainz, with the towns of Bodenheim, Nackenheim, Nierstein (the most famous), Oppenheim, and Dienheim. Here the vineyards, the best planted to Rieslings, overlook the river from steep but unterraced hillsides, the vines growing in red soil mixed with soft, brick-colored slate. Facing east, the vines are restricted to the rays of the morning and midday sun, but the grapes benefit enormously from the heat of the wide river, and the growing season is long. The prized Rieslings, for example, are rarely harvested before November.

Despite the great names, it must be admitted that there is a sameness to most of the towns of the Rheinhessen; and it is easy to pass rapidly through them almost without noticing. Nierstein is probably the most colorful. Its wide and shaded quay, where barges and river craft are tied alongside, tempts one to pause, and the unpretentious Rhein Hotel on the quay may be recommended for a respite. Though the inn's kitchen is undistinguished, the cellar is filled with a goodly supply of honey-colored Niersteiners, the softest and most alluring of all the Rheinhessen, with the pungent fragrances of fresh melons. One will not soon forget the joys of a bottle of one of Nierstein's greats—Rehbach, Glöck, Hipping, or Auflangen—consumed *sur place*. Nierstein is also the seat of one of the Rheinhessen's traditionally great producers, the firm of Franz Karl Schmitt. Two others to be recommended are Heyl zu Herrnsheim and the ubiquitous but always dependable *Staatsweingut*, all of whose names on labels of the Rheinhessen invariably spell quality.

The best vineyards of two other of these famous wine towns, Nackenheim and Bodenheim, through which one will already have passed on the road from Mainz, are Bodenheimer Ebersberg, Kahlenberg, and Rettberg—and Nackenheimer Rothenberg, Fenchelberg, and Stiel. In nearby Oppenheim look especially for Auslesen and Beerenauslesen from vineyards named Kreuz, Goldberg, and Kröttenbrunnen. The best of Dienheim, the last of the greats, is Goldberg.

Some twenty miles and thousands of vines upstream the Rheinhessen ends with the city of Worms, viticulturally notable for a small walled vineyard that surrounds an ugly church in the very center of the city, the Liebfrauenkirche. Traditionally this tiny vineyard—whose two principal owners are the large firms of Langenbach and Valkenberg—is responsible for the generic name of Liebfraumilch. It appears that in some past century the wines of the Church of the Holy Mother of Worms, whose vineyards produce two thousand cases a year at best, must have been a good deal more desirable than they are today and failed to meet the demand. Thus a name was created for common wines from other parts of the Rheinhessen that would carry the same association.

Wines from the Liebfrauenkirche, Liebfrauenstift wines, as they are called, are the only ones in the entire Rheinhessen that by German law may not be blended and called Liebfraumilch, should the producer desire it. To be quite honest, it might be better if they were. Grown on the flat, fertile soil common to this hot and humid pocket of the Rhineland, they tend to be strong and coarse in flavor, with overtones that remind one of pine needles.

Above Worms the valley bed is richly alluvial, far too fertile for raising good wine grapes; nor was it, until comparatively modern times when this section of the Rhine was finally diked and controlled, a very happy place for humans, either. From Basel to Worms the capricious river twisted and turned at will, chasing man from his villages and fields, leaving in its wake stagnant oxbows and swamps where crops had once flourished. Waterborne commerce was anything but successful. One reads of attempts to pull barges upstream to Basel, forty horses or ninety men to a single barge, with both man and beast wading waist deep through the muddy floods. In general river commerce was a one-way affair, by means of boats specially constructed to navigate the treacherous rapids, and built so they could be readily dismantled in Holland and sold for lumber.

In our continuing search for great wines we must turn about a dozen miles inland to that section of the Rhineland called the Rheinpfalz, colloquially known as the Pfalz or (in English) the Palatinate, a name bestowed by the Romans after the Palatine, one of the seven hills of Rome. One can only think the Romans must have been hopelessly nostalgic, as there is little resembling a Roman hill to be found anywhere around. From the Rheinhessen to France on its southern border, the Pfalz is a flat plain elevated a few hundred feet above the Rhine, and split down the middle from north to south by a range of hills called the Haardt mountains—an extension of the Vosges of Alsace. The Rheinpfalz has much to remind one of Alsace. Although the largest producing wine region in Germany, it is filled with orchards and field crops, quaint villages and twisting roads.

Like the Rheinhessen, the Pfalz is predominantly a land of Liebfraumilch and *konsumwein* (*vin ordinaire*, both white and red), with its only important vineyards concentrated in a small area, specifically a handful of towns lying just east of the range of hills, all linked by a road that has been known for generations as the Deutsche Weinstrasse. Hardly forty miles long, this road and its towns are divided into three sections, the Unter-Haardt, Mittel-Haardt, and Ober-Haardt, the latter being closest to France. But by far the most celebrated of the three is the Mittel-Haardt, measuring only ten miles along the Weinstrasse and containing the four greatest villages.

The Pfalz has the warmest climate of any viticultural region of Germany, and the lowest rainfall; especially in the Mittel-Haardt, it is endowed with a red soil that at first glance one would think far too rich for the wine grape, particularly the Riesling. On close inspection, however, one finds it filled with minute granite chips and stones, comparable to many another great vineyard land. This soil and the temperate climate render the wines of the Mittel-Haardt even more alcoholic than those of the Rheinhessen. What they lack in softness they make up in pronounced tastes and fragrances, and the great ones have the reputation of being better in poor years. In fact, the bigger the year, the more their charm and character disappear. This is simply part of the regression one observes in the Riesling and many other grapes of northern Europe as one proceeds south— or tries to grow them in warmer places, such as Italy or California. The noble grapes of the northland feed on adversity. Under seemingly ideal conditions, without adversity, their juice contains less acid and more sugar, an imbalance leading to a less distinguished wine.

What most distinguishes the Pfalz from other regions of Germany and northern Europe is not so much the high quality of the wines of the Weinstrasse as the number of grape varieties used by its progressive growers. Under the German so-called two-thirds law, a wine called "Riesling" need only contain two-thirds of Riesling juice. In other parts of Germany the best producers spurn such a habit and pride themselves on pure products. Whereas the growers on the Moselle or the Rheingau stick to the Riesling, producers in the Pfalz are continuously experimenting with new combinations or crosses of grapes that may be blended to improve their wines. The Riesling is, of course, the acknowledged best, the Sylvaner the most widely produced, and the Müller-Thurgau the standard variety for blending. Yet nowhere else in Germany will one find so many other grape varieties or crosses not only used for blending, but often appearing in bottles under their own names. One of the most successful is the Muscat, the principal variety being the high-producing Mario-Muscat, yielding a thick, musty wine in its pure state, but adding much body to a blend. Another is the Gewürztraminer, principally known to the world nowadays as an Alsatian plant producing a highly fragrant and spicy wine. In the hands of a good Pfalz producer, especially if he has made it into an Auslese or a Beerenauslese, the results put the Alsatian versions to shame. Yet another is the Scheurebe, like the Müller-Thurgau a cross of Riesling and Sylvaner, the basic difference being that with the latter the Riesling is the female factor, whereas with the Scheurebe it is the botanical father. Although the Scheurebe's principal use is for blending, wine made in the Pfalz from the Scheurebe alone sometimes locally brings a higher price than a Riesling. For our own palate, we find it difficult to believe; yet we must admit that this acrid wine with its almost offensive bouquet skillfully blended with the Riesling, effectively exaggerates the best qualities of the latter, while erasing all its own bad ones. Perhaps one of the finest Pfalz wines one will ever drink will be a Beerenauslese made from this particular blend.

For the record (and that only) the Pfalz also produces a large proportion of Germany's red wines, distinctly watery and inferior products, usually blends of the Spätburgunder, the Burgundian vine we have already met at Assmannshausen, and another red grape called the Portugieser, whose origin is unknown even to oenologists. In contrast to their distinguished white neighbors, however, they merit little attention.

Although he may experience difficulty in finding or identifying the great vineyards, the wandering oenophile will find much to intrigue him in the countryside and quaint villages and towns of the Pfalz. The first wine town of importance one meets when traveling the Weinstrasse or the Mittel-Haardt is Kallstadt, whose best-known vineyards are Horn, Annaberg, Nill, and Saumagen. Kallstadters are not the greatest wines of the Weinstrasse, but sample them, at least, and note their contrasting personalities to those tasted hitherto. The village of Kallstadt is no exception to the rule for Pfalz towns. It is full of ancient timbered houses and cobblestone alleys, and peopled by folk who love wine above all else. One should not overlook the popular Weinstube Henniger on the principal street, managed by the same family for three hundred years. It does a land-office business of serving good food and the best in local wines by the glass, to a continuous flow of customers who, like oneself, may have patiently waited half an hour or so to find seats at the long refectory tables. At its lowest ebb the mood at this centuries-old restaurant is anything but staid, and as the evening wears on, whether one intends it or not, one finds oneself swept up into the inevitable songful cameraderie. Wines served in giant goblets pass in a continuous flow from bar to table, washing down a variety of specialties of the house: snails, ham, the ubiquitous sausage, local fish and game. Venison, incidentally, is one of the Henniger's masterpieces. Regrettably, the establishment has no rooms, but for those who would tarry, across the street is an ancient inn, also a famed *weinstube* in its own right, the Weincastell Weissen Ross.

Bad Dürkheim, the town that follows, is a popular resort, and certainly the most pretentious and sophisticated town on the Weinstrasse. Even better known in Germany for its curative waters and its gambling rooms than for its wines, the latter are nonetheless of a very high class, comparing favorably with the finest of the Pfalz. Like so many German wine towns, Bad Dürkheim seems to be widest awake in the small hours, when its *weinstuben* close. Thus, if you need a lodging with peace and quiet for more than half the night, investigate the Hotel-Garten Heusser, a comfortable establishment in the suburb of Seebach. It serves breakfast only, but at least you will be in a mood to digest it. A good, albeit simple, restaurant is the Vier Jahreszeiten, run by the local wine cooperative.

One should never quit Bad Dürkheim without having visited the Naturweinschenke or Dürkheimer Fass, a wine-tasting house (also serving meals) whose facade is a gigantic wine barrel, or *fass*, with a hypothetical contents of nearly two million liters. Advertised as the "World's only Restaurant in a Cask," the Dürkheimer Fass is German corniness at its corniest. Every September the Fass becomes the setting for the annual *Wurstfest* (sausage fair). At a recent festival lasting five days, two hundred and fifty thousand liters of wine, along with an estimated one hundred and fifty kilometers of sausages, were consumed. The Fass may not supply you with Dürkheim's best—from vineyards such as Hochness, Michelsberg, or Spielberg—but there is no better place to find and try for yourself a Scheurebe or a Mario-Muscat or a Müller-Thurgau in their pure state.

Another famous restaurant near Bad Dürkheim, also in the Seebach suburb, is the Weinstube Zum Käseburo (the Cheese Bureau). This curious name derives from its once having been the tax office of the Electors of Heidelberg, in the days when the fiefs paid their tithes in cheese. Virtually unchanged since the fifteenth century, at which time it was an inn run by Benedictine sisters, the restaurant's wine list is excellent and its culinary attainments worthy of the legend, however improbable, that here was the birthplace of that always welcome variation on the omnipresent schnitzel, *Cordon Bleu*—a veal cutlet slit down the middle and filled with slices of mild cheese and ham before cooking.

Over the next few miles we pass through the four towns of Wachenheim, Forst, Deidesheim, and Ruppertsberg. This is the acknowledged finest section of the Weinstrasse. Lest the reader become panicked in the sea of labels emanating from these towns, here are a few words of clarification. Like the Côte d'Or in Burgundy, nearly all the great vineyards of the Weinstrasse are split among many owners, which frequently leads to good, mediocre, and truly bad wines all bearing the same vineyard name on their labels. The name of a reliable producer is therefore an indispensable guide. Three classic producers of the Pfalz have for many decades been referred to as the "Three B's"—the first and most famous being the late Dr. von Bassermann-Jordan, who before his death was probably the most respected vintner in Germany. His vineyards are still ably managed by his son. The other two members of the celebrated trio are Dr. Bürklin-Wolf and Reichsrat von Buhl, whose wines are hardly less distinguished. Of almost equal fame are two producers who identify themselves on labels simply as Drs. Deinhard and Pioth—and there are others, too, such as Wilhelm and Heinrich Spindler, Josef Reinhardt, and the Koch-Herzog Erben. Any of these names on bottles mean quality.

Wachenheim wines are especially noted for their body and finesse. The town itself is dull and affords little temptation to stay and investigate, but the names of any of its great vineyards— Böhlig, Goldbächel, Rechbächel, Gerümpel, and Bächel are probably the best—are sufficient to embellish any wine list.

Experts disagree on which of the two towns that follow— Forst and Deidesheim—is the greatest of the Pfalz. Both produce wines of much distinction, subtly combining both sharpness and steeliness on one hand and polish and breeding on the other. Many of Forst's best vineyards are virtually within the town itself, and reputed to be among the most highly taxed in Germany. The extraordinary quality of their wines is thought to be partly the result of a unique black basalt outcropping that appears in the soil of the Weinstrasse at this point, along with the fact that all Forst's vineyards benefit from the proximity of a nearby quarry whose rubble is periodically and painstakingly strewn over them. Of the several dozen great or near-great vineyards, the following are the most important: Jesuitengarten, Freundstück, Kirchen-stück, Ziegler, and Kranich. Jesuitengarten, wholly owned by the estate of Bassermann-Jordan, is generally considered one of the world's greatest.

Ruppertsberg's best vineyards are Hofstück, Hoheberg, Nuss-bein, and Gaisböhl. Again, this is a village devoid of charms, especially in contrast to Deidesheim, whose narrow streets, brownstone houses, and ancient Rathaus all make it a fascinating place to stop. Its impeccable wines are: Dopp, Grain, Grainhübel, Hohenmorgen, and Kränzler. Lunch or dine at Deidesheim's superb inn, the Gasthof Zur Kann, run by a Frenchman whose secret ambition, it seems, is to prove he can prepare German dishes better than the Germans themselves. Undeniably, he succeeds. In addition to memorable food, you will drink some of the Pfalz's best, served inexpensively in carafe.

I I I : *Alsace*

Centuries ago a French king (supposedly Louis XIV), standing for the first time on the heights of the Vosges overlooking the plain of Alsace, overwhelmed by the beauty of what he saw below, is said to have burst out with "What a wonderful garden!" Alsace is a garden land indeed—a continuation of the lush Weinstrasse, yet more so. About the only way of knowing one has left the Weinstrasse and reached the Alsatian Route du Vin is when one passes through a curious triumphal arch, bilingually called the Wein Tour, and has been given the perfunctory blessing of a French customs officer in a dialect incomprehensible even to one knowing both French and German. Among other linguistic transitions, one will soon observe the term *weinstube* giving way to *winstub.*

To the west the gentle Haardt mountains blend into the bald-pated Vosges; the style of the little villages—timbered houses with overhangs, squares filled with fountains and gay, potted flowers—remains Germanic, but their quaintness, if anything, intensifies. The broad green valley that is Alsace is still that of the Rhine, even though one tends to lose sight of the fact: the distance between the Vosges and the German Black Forest, beyond the Rhine, is barely twenty miles. It is filled with small tributaries draining the mountain passes, most of which empty into Alsace's only river, the minuscule Ill, which rises far to the south near Basel and paces the Rhine almost the entire length of Alsace, finally joining it at Strasbourg.

The vineyards of northern Alsace, clinging to the foothills of the Vosges, are not ones to produce great wines, so we may divert our course a little to the east, passing through a lovely flat, almost semitropical countryside devoted to hops and tobacco, cabbages and corn. Halfway between the border and Alsace's capital city of Strasbourg, one might well wish to indulge in the hospitality of the Hostellerie Écrevisse in the town of Brumath. The Écrevisse is an isolated gastronomic Mecca to which Germans and French alike travel for miles, and, especially on weekends, it is a good idea to find a seat in the simple dining room before the crowd arrives. The fare is excellent—but we will save our praises for others even more deserving. There are comfortable rooms, far less expensive than their equivalent in the capital.

Although parts of Strasbourg are as bustling and confused as any modern French city of its size, other sections of it are endowed with a quiet charm. The city is a kaleidoscope of contrasting French and German culture, architecture, and gastronomy. Its one-spired Gothic cathedral, among the most beautiful of its kind in all France, towers hundreds of feet above streets filled with ancient Germanic houses. The quarter known as la Petite France, where two canals flow past square towers protecting the ancient city, might be found in an old town on the Loire or the Cher.

As the gastronomic capital of Alsace, Strasbourg is distinguished for its German dishes with a redeeming French touch, or vice versa. Its *foie gras*, its succulent onion tarts and fish prepared in all conceivable fashions are, one and all, unrivaled. Some of the local dishes for which it is famous have a distinctly peasant origin, such as roast goose stuffed with sausage meat; or Beckenoff, a ragout of pork, lamb, and potatoes stewed together in an earthenware pot; or its own version of sauerkraut, served with powerful portions of sausage, ham, pork, and sometimes goose. For desserts there are the traditional Kugelhupf, a rich cake with raisins and Kirsch, and innumerable other little cakes flavored with anise or other spices. Alsatian cookery is noteworthy for its overabundance of calories: Strasbourg chefs are apt to garnish almost everything except *foie gras* with *foie gras*; and rare is the dessert, whether it be elaborate cake or delicate fruit tart, that is not hidden beneath a welter of whipped cream. Undoubtedly this is why one finds in Alsace so many powerful *eaux-de-vie*, or so-called *digestifs*, which most Alsatians habitually sip after their gargantuan meals. The Alsatians will make an *eau-de-vie* out of anything at the drop of a hat. Along with the fragrant Framboise, distilled from raspberries, or Kirsch from cherries and Prunelle from plums, some of the more esoteric are Myrtille (blueberries), Gratte Cul (wild roses), Houx (Holly berries), Coing (quince), and the medicinal Enzrane or Gentiane (from the forest flower). If one likes marc, a distillation of the leftovers after grapes are pressed (usually an acquired taste for non-Europeans) the finest and most aromatic is marc de Traminer, from one of Alsace's two best wine grapes. All of these fiery but subtly flavored *eaux-de-vie* (except marc, essentially a brandy) are served ice-cold to bring out the bouquet, which would be lost if they came to the table, like Cognac or Armagnac, at room temperature.

Among the best, and certainly the most conveniently situated hotel in Strasbourg is the Maison Rouge on the Place Kléber. It has the convenience, in this busy city, of an underground garage beneath the Place itself, and is within walking distance of all of Strasbourg's superb restaurants. Of these, one of our favorites over the years is Au Gourmet sans Chiqué, only a block or two from the Place Kléber. Au Gourmet sans Chiqué is just what the name implies: superior food without sham or chicanery. Which is not to imply that the chef-owner has denied himself indulgences in décor. The walls and shelves of this little establishment seem to hold nearly everything that has ever seized his fancy; the results of which being almost as pleasing as anything that appears from the kitchen. One undeniable culinary masterpiece is the *truite maison*, for which the chef gives partial credit to a former guest, the late king of Norway. *Truite maison*—basically not uncommon in Alsace—is a sautéed trout, burned off with a glass of brandy or *eau-de-vie* and kept warm while a sauce of heavy cream, pepper, and salt is thickened in the same pan in which the fish was cooked. After visiting this, his favorite restaurant in Strasbourg, a number of times, the king finally got around to making his brilliant contribution: a few drops of Worcestershire to enliven the sauce, and the whole topped with sliced sautéed almonds. The suggestions were adopted—and no one should make the error of dining at Au Gourmet sans Chiqué today without trying the rechristened *truite maison au roi de Norvège*. Another masterpiece of the house, also involving almonds, is *crêpes maison*—light pancakes filled with sliced blanched almonds, which have been mixed with butter and sugar. Finally, they are flambéed at the table with Grand Marnier. With your trout have a Riesling from J. Muller of Bergheim; with the crêpes, a Gewürztraminer, preferably a sweetish Réserve or an Auslese.

Two other excellent restaurants of Strasbourg, where the gastronomic philosophy is anything but *sans chiqué*, are the Valentin-Sorg, in the penthouse of the city's only skyscraper, and Au Crocodil, also near the Place Kléber. Especially at the former one will find *haute cuisine Alsatienne* at its finest and most caloric. Less ostentatious and more reasonably priced is the Restaurant Zimmer, old-fashioned and traditional. The Zimmer is a favorite of the Strasbourgers themselves, particularly when in need of a hearty Sunday midday meal. Here is the place for regional or country dishes: *coq au riesling,* chicken in a light cream sauce with a wine base, or the omnipresent *choucroute garnie,* in portions large enough to feed the whole family. If one has the capacity for it, *choucroute* is best washed down with quantities of a good Alsatian beer, such as Kronenbourg (France's best), or a neutral wine, perhaps an Alsatian Pinot Noir—the usual name for the best of the local *rosés.*

No European wines are more the result of history and circumstance than those of Alsace—or owe more to the spirit and courage of the people who have made them over the years. The cultivation of the wine grape in Alsace is assumed to have begun with the Romans, who arrived, by way of the Rhône, in the first century of this era, shortly after yet another contingent of Romans settled on the Moselle. Thus the origin of Alsatian vineyards coincides roughly with those of the Rhineland, and comparably their grapes are all indigenous northern types. Under the Merovingians, and later the influence of the Church, Alsatian vineyards grew in numbers, and as time went on, their fame spread down the Rhine valley, even to England across the Channel. What should be emphasized is that Alsatian wines, despite their French nationality, are (and always have been) wines of the Rhine. Only in name are they French wines, and indeed until the years following Alsace's liberation in 1918, Alsatian wines were hardly known throughout the rest of France at all. In olden days this little province was economically blocked from France by the Vosges, and France itself—being viticulturally self-sufficient—had little need for its wines, much less craved their Rhenish tastes.

Few parts of Europe have been so ravaged and devastatingly overrun as Alsace, or have changed hands so many times. During the Thirty Years War its towns and vineyards were plundered and flattened in turn by Germans, Swedes, Spaniards, and many others, including the French. After the Franco-Prussian War, Alsace again became German territory. The period that followed was perhaps its most trying. From 1870 to 1918 every attempt was made by the Germans to degrade Alsatian nationalism, which in effect took the form of loyalty to France. German was made the compulsory language in the schools; street and place names were Germanized, and all possible was done to erase Gallic tradition. As for the wines, Alsatian vintners were forced to replace their superior grapes with inferior, high-producing ones, such as the Chasselas and the Elbling, and the products of Alsatian vineyards were channeled to cheap German markets—even though, paradoxically, Germany has never made enough good wine to fill its needs.

In 1918 the Alsatians found themselves free again, but with their traditional viticulture all but lost sight of. Their best vines were gone—and as with Burgundy after the Revolution, all the famous pieces of land for growing them had been divided and subdivided among many owners. For a while the task of putting things back together seemed impossible, especially with governmental assistance concentrated west of the Vosges. Finally a handful of enlightened vintners took the matter in hand and set the rules for future Alsatian viticulture—rules that broke with the tradition of French or other European wine-making yet turned out to be the saving of Alsace. This break was to abandon the concept of naming wines for a particular piece of soil: Alsatian wines were thenceforth named varietally, after the grapes themselves, enabling each producer to contribute his grapes to town or village cooperatives, and encouraging a return to Alsace's traditional or "noble" grapes.

It has taken the Alsatians many years—interrupted by World War II, during which many of their vineyards and villages were once again sorely devastated—to reach a point where their wines are nowadays not only appreciated in France itself, but also gaining in foreign markets. Today, with thirty thousand acres of grapes under cultivation, Alsace produces almost one-tenth of France's wine. More important yet, vineyard names are now appearing on labels, the *sine qua non* of quality. Within the past few years many of the traditional vineyards have been put together under one ownership, and in most instances planted to grapes of a single variety.

Among the best Alsatian vineyards are Kaefferkopf and Brand in Ammerschwihr; Sporen, Clos des Amandiers, Clos des Murailles, Clos des Capucines, Clos des Sourcières, Clos des Maquisards, Au Moulin, and Schonnenberg, all in Riquewihr; Mandelberg and Brand in Mittelwihr; Clos de Zahnacker and Clos Sainte-Hune in Ribeauvillé, and Ganzbronnel in Barr. Usually these vineyard names will be accompanied by the name of the grape, or in cases where a blend has been made by crushing several types of "noble" grapes from the same vineyard, the Alsatians have reverted to an ancient appellation, the term *Gentil*. This, in effect, is the highest appellation for a blend. Next in line comes the word *Edelzwicker*, meaning wine made from "noble" grapes drawn from different vineyards. The word *Zwicker* is something else again: an "unnoble" blend, or *vin ordinaire*.

More than nine-tenths of all Alsatian wines are white. The finest rosés are from the Pinot noir grape and are usually so labeled. Lesser ones are called *vin gris* or Pinot *rosé*, from the Pinot meunier. Some *rosés* fall into the category of light reds, such as a wine called Pinot Rouge, which should be treated like a *rosé* and chilled. Legitimate reds are all but nonexistent and definitely not worth bothering about: the chances are that one will not meet them. Only the white grapes are entitled to the term "noble"—and by no means all of them. When the official *Appellations Contrôlées* were first applied to Alsace in 1961, the Riesling, the Gewürztraminer and its less fragrant cousin the Traminer, the Muscat, and the Pinot gris or Tokay were classified as "noble"; the Sylvaner and the Pinot blanc (Klevner) as "fine," and the lowly Chasselas, a survivor of the German occupation, as "ordinary." The two latter are names rarely seen on a label and are usually used for blending. The Chasselas is the common base for Zwicker.

In the hands of good producers, the Riesling and Gewürztraminer make the wines of the greatest character. The former are somewhat coarser and less fragrant than the average Rheingau

Riesling, but often nearly comparable to those of the Pfalz. Gewürztraminer, a development of the more common Traminer (the word *Gewürz* means "spicy") is one of the most fragrant and unusual wines of all France. When made as a Spätlese or an Auslese (the Alsatians usually label them *Réserves*) it becomes Alsace's most individualistic wine. Tokay, no relation to Hungary's famous wine, may be entirely pleasant, though lacking in acidity. Sylvaner is the most popular—the (white) Beaujolais of Alsace, or the wine for everyday drinking. It is apt to be a little watery, with a subtle bitterness that is not unpleasant. Muscat can be almost as fragrant, in its own way, as Gewürztraminer; both are best served as dessert wines, although they also belong among the very few wines of the world that harmonize with pork or ham.

Alsatian wines, like the wines of the Moselle, come in tall green bottles or *flutes*. In terms of alcoholic content (and quality) there are two appellative classifications: *Vin d'Alsace*, meaning a wine that need not be more than 8 percent; and *Grand Vin* or *Grand Cru* or *Grande Réserve*, all of which must contain no less than 11 percent. The name of a good producer is important. In our experience, five of the best are: Dopff et Irion and the firm of Hugel in Riquewihr; Willm in Barr; the Domaines Viticoles Schlumberger in Guebwiller; and J. Muller in Bergheim. It is well to know that there is another firm named Dopff in Riquewihr, as well as one that goes by the name of Schlumberger in Ribeau-villé.

The superior vineyards of Alsace begin at the town of Barr, about fifteen miles southwest of Strasbourg. As one passes down the Route du Vin, one sees them rising gently a thousand feet or more into the foothills of the Vosges, these hills now higher and more majestic than the Haardt range that served as a backdrop to the Pfalz. The soil covering these foothills varies enormously. At the top it is too chalky and dry for fine wines; at the bottom it is heavy clay and stones, producing coarse wines. The best vineyards are found halfway up the slopes, which is said to be one reason so many of the wine villages are perched well above the valley floor, or partway up their little side valleys. Almost without exception, every one of these villages is a delight—Barr, with its Hôtel de Ville, or town hall, commanding a tiny, triangular public square; Mittelwihr, whose every doorway seems to lead to a flowered courtyard surrounded by shadowed balconies. Dambach's single street is one of sagging, moss-covered roofs—presided over at either end by fortified towers. High above Barr on a crag of the Vosges is the convent of Sainte-Odile, built in the eighth century by the father of a child whose sight was miraculously restored. Sainte-Odile still functions, and its nuns run a simple hostelry for pilgrims and religious tourists.

Among the few castles of the Vosges not in a state of ruin is Haut-Königsberg, a tremendous fortification on a spire of the Vosges above the village of Keintzheim. Seemingly unassailable, it was once conquered and ruined by the Swedes when they invaded Alsace during the only major foreign war that Scandinavian nation ever fought. In 1900, after nearly three hundred years of neglect, Königsberg was rebuilt and occupied by Kaiser Wilhelm II. Nowadays it is a museum, its contents regrettably illustrating more the affluent bad taste of its restorers' era than its former feudal glory. One may wager that if Haut-Königsberg had ever come to the attention of the late William Randolph Hearst, it might well have been transported stone by stone to some mountainside overlooking the Pacific. The castle is reached by a long and tortuous road, but the trip is well worth it. Few panorama can rival the sight of the Black Forest looming behind the distant Rhine, with the verdant plain of Alsace in the foreground below.

Two of the more intriguing towns on the Route du Vin, both wine towns of wide renown, are Ribeauvillé and Riquewihr. Following the pattern of so many Alsatian wine towns or villages, Ribeauvillé is limited to a single street, fortified by towers at either end, following the course of a little mountain stream as it winds through the valley. Three miles or so up the valley, beyond the town, is one of the best inns in Alsace, the Pépinière. Viewed from the road below, the Pépinière is anything but inviting, distinctly lacking in the usual earmarks of a well-run hostelry—

an impression that a confident management has elected to combat by simply painting on the wall the phrase "To hesitate is to regret." Once inside, one well understands how one could have regretted. The rooms at the Pépinière are adequately comfortable; the food has few peers in rural Alsace. Two notable specialties are *escargots au Muscat*, snails served out of their shells in a simple sauce of butter, white wine, and parsley, and as a contrast, *tournedos 1900*, an improvisation on *tournedos Rossini* so fanciful as to have driven the gourmand-composer of *William Tell* out of his mind with gluttonous rapture. In addition to some of the best Alsatians, the cellar holds a few rare Burgundies at bargain prices, along with nearly the entire gamut of Alsace's multitudinous *eaux-de-vie*: Myrtille, Sureau, Gratte Cul, Houx, Coing, Quetsche, and the rest.

Midway between Ribeauvillé and Riquewihr is Hunawihr, whose wine cooperative was one of the first to gain a reputation after 1918 and to this day maintains the highest standards. Even though wines from cooperatives are usually suspect, those of Hunawihr are an exception. Hunawihr was badly mangled during the last war, and a good part of it rebuilt in modern dress; in fact, little remains of the old village but its fountain and an eleventh-century fortified church, picturesquely set on a hill outside the town in the middle of the vineyards.

So many town or village names of Alsace end with either "wihr" or "willer" that one is bound to speculate about the origin of these suffixes. One far-out theory in Alsace is that "willer" goes back to Roman days, deriving from "villa." A far more plausible explanation is that both terms meant a source of water. Since every Alsatian village appears to have been built around its fountain, we incline toward the second theory. Riquewihr, the jewel of Alsace, also has its fountain, placed at the top of its sloping cobblestoned street, so that one has only to carry downhill. Once a fortified town, Riquewihr seems miraculously to have escaped all the devastations of its neighbors; in fact the village is in a remarkable state of preservation.

It goes without saying that Riquewihr is a good place to stay away from on weekends, for there will be few seats in the restaurants and no peace from the hundreds of milling tourists that are delivered, with clockwork regularity, by puffing buses that pull up outside the ramparts. But Riquewihr happily leads a double life. On weekdays this little bit of redistilled Alsace is transformed once more into a leisurely village, where the housewives cluster in doorways whispering gossip, and their long-nosed Alsatian dogs once more have the run of the street.

Despite the tourist trade, Riquewihr has few restaurants worthy of mention. The one that gives the impression of being the most authentic is the Hotel-Restaurant Schmidt, near the lower end of the village. Here one may lunch or dine well on local dishes: chicken or duck cooked in Riesling, or the Schmidt's particular version of *choucroute*, which is put over a flame at the table and baptized with a bottle of Champagne. The wine list, obviously, is predominantly made up of the best of Riquewihr itself.

It is just possible that after an hour or so you will find Riquewihr's ultra-perfection a bit cloying; we therefore suggest, as an alternative to the Schmidt, the Hotel-Restaurant Aux Armes de France at Ammerschwihr, about ten miles south on the Route du Vin. Like Riquewihr, Ammerschwihr is a famous wine village. Regrettably most of the town was destroyed during the last war, and except for the Armes de France, the town is a little bleak. However, you will be anything but disappointed in the simple upstairs dining room of this old-fashioned inn, presided over by a truly superb chef. Except in Marseilles you will never be served the like of the *soupe aux poissons*; nor finer *escargots* this side of Dijon. Among the chef's many unusual creations there is *saumon braisé au Pernod*, salmon baked with Pernod. Even though the idea may not appeal, we simply say: try it. *Volaille sautée au vinaigre* is another, though perhaps not quite as original: sautéed pieces of chicken in a sauce of chicken stock reduced with chopped tomatoes and a little garlic, a shallot or two, white wine, and pepper—subtly enlivened at the end with a touch of vinegar, and thickened with butter. Few French inns can claim such attentive service, or such reasonable prices.

Yet another restaurant within easy range of the Route du Vin has gained a reputation among French gourmets, since its founding not too many years ago, that is little short of astronomical. This is the Auberge de l'Ill, at Illhaeusern near Sélestat, managed by two exceptionally talented (and commercially astute) brothers. There is a charming garden on the river's edge where one may lunch or dine in good weather, and a kitchen with few peers or rivals in the realm of *haute cuisine*. The Auberge is what one might call a "one-trip" restaurant. The fantastic *prix fixe* menu— one commences with *brioche au foie gras*, passes on to *saumon soufflé*, thence to venison *Saint-Hubert*, and so forth, far past the hour of responsibility—remains virtually unchanged from day to day and year to year, which can hardly be said of the state of one's pocketbook following a single visit. To make matters worse, the Auberge stocks all the best of those rarely seen bottles from the Domaines Viticoles Schlumberger, wines that in the opinion of many people are the greatest that can be made from Alsatian grapes.

The most famous segment of the Route du Vin, which began at Barr, ends with the city of Colmar, the traditional wine center of Alsace and the seat of one of the oldest and best viticultural schools in Europe. Set in a strategic position, to command the valley, the city has been important, both militarily and economically, since the days of Charlemagne and his son, Louis le Débonnaire, both of whom frequently occupied its imperial residence. Colmar's center suffered appreciably during World War II, but its side streets without any question contain some of the most decorative and typically ornate houses in Alsace; an ornateness that would be downright ugly in any other sphere of art except folk architecture, or any other part of the world but Alsace. The world-famous Unterlinden Museum, housed in a thirteenth-century Dominican convent, is noted for its unique collection of Alsatian art and antiquities, the most notable being the enigmatic Rétable d'Issenheim by Alsace's only great painter, known today by the name of Mathias Grünewald. At the other end of the artistic scale, there is the mummified head of a certain fifteenth-century bailiff of Alsace, reputed to have been a thoroughly despised man who met his end at the chopping block. The executioner's blade is realistically displayed as an adjunct to the same exhibit. Colmar's best restaurant, coincidentally, is named the Maison des Têtes, in a lovely gabled house built in the early seventeenth century. Its traditional Alsatian dishes are done with taste and skill; here is the place to say good-bye to your favorites among them, as well as to try the cellar's specialty, Edelzwicker, the blend of "noble" grapes that often brings a pleasant surprise.

I V : *The Upper Rhine and the Bodensee*

To follow the Rhine further upstream, we leave the Route du Vin at Colmar and cross a fertile alluvial plain in the direction of Basel. Half a dozen miles from the river, we descend to a low plateau planted with corn and vegetables, curiously devoid of villages or other signs of civilization. We are now in that part of the valley, which, until the turn of the century, was so subject to the river's dangerous caprices that few people dared to make it a permanent home. Even today, with the Rhine harnessed and canalized with a series of stout dams and locks stretching from Basel to Mainz, the owners of these fields seem disinclined to settle on their land. Generations of bitter experiences have taught them the river is not to be so trusted.

At Basel one finds the Rhine has turned yet another corner and is flowing from east to west as it approaches the city. Basel is the meeting place of three nations—France, Germany, and Switzerland. Each country owns part of it, with the international boundaries anything but logical. One should be prepared to meet a customs house around almost any corner, and it is not impossible to cross the city in what one thinks is a straight line and land up again in the country one has just left. The local language, called Schweizer Deutsch or Basler Deutsch, is an appallingly rapid, gutteral jargon totally defying comprehension by most foreigners.

Basel's traditional hotel is the Drei Könige (or Trois Rois), which overhangs the Rhine at a sharp bend. Beneath its windows white swans glide to and fro in the eddies, and a sharp-prowed cable ferry, about the size of a large rowboat, carries foot passengers to the shaded quay on the opposite bank despite the proximity of two bridges. Many a crowned head has slept at the Drei Könige, adding to its long tradition of elegance and romance. Our favorite restaurant in Basel is the Donati, a short distance downstream near the bridge that leads to the German section of the city. The Donati is an international establishment with an Italian touch—a refreshing change in gastronomic emphasis after a protracted diet of German and French cooking.

Above Basel, the Rhine, now bereft of its river traffic, has shrunk to the size and semblance of an ordinary river. Swift, opaquely green from the mountain streams that feed it, it is filled with reefs and boulders and whirlpools. The tableland of the valley shifts from one bank to the other: alternately one passes through orchards and pastureland, followed by heavily forested sections—the foothills of the Black Forest—which descend steeply to the river's edge. Many of the towns are delightful: Säckingen, for one, whose hexagonal cathedral tower dates from the sixth century; some miles up the river, from the heights of the mountain road one sees Laufenburg, a medieval village on a rocky promontory jutting out into a bend in the Rhine.

Yet another is Waldshut, whose fortified tower straddling the main street is reminiscent of Alsace and the Rheinpfalz. At Waldshut one should cross the river to the Swiss side and follow the country road closest to the Rhine. This is the shortest and most colorful route to the celebrated Rheinfall, a phenomenon of nature that draws thousands of Swiss, Germans, and tourists from all nations each year. The Rheinfall is the Niagara Falls of the Rhine. Boiling through a mass of rocks and erosion-sculptured turrets, the river spills seventy feet in the space of as many yards; into a round basin where riverboats once pulled up to receive the wine casks dragged by oxen around the falls. Goethe once sat for three days in contemplation on the basin's edge.

The closest view of the Rheinfall may be had from the Schloss Laufen, a remodeled castle perched on the heights directly above, incidentally housing an excellent restaurant known as the Restaurant Français. As you watch the raging waters below, you will be served a fine meal, with an opportunity to sample the wines of the nearby Swiss canton of Schaffhausen, the northernmost vineyard region of Switzerland. Schaffhausen's reds—especially those labeled Steinberger Blaurock, Rheinholder Stadt Schaffhausen, and Korbwein Rheinau—are held in high esteem by the Swiss. Like so many products of the Pinot noir made away from Burgundy, they fall into the category of *rosés* rather than reds. One will find them fragrant, fruity, and refreshing, especially if one goes along with the local custom of drinking them young and cold. Both Schaffhausen and Stein-am-Rhein, particularly the latter with its main street of painted houses—murals depicting the history of the house or its occupants—are worth a visit.

Bodensee wines, sometimes referred to as wines of the Lake of Konstanz, are the unsung heroes of German viticulture. Officially classified as wines of Baden (a small, insignificant district on the western edge of the Black Forest), they are usually heard of as "interesting little wines that never travel." The characterization is anything but fair. Bodensee wines, if the truth be told, are much more than "interesting" and certainly not "little." As to whether or not they travel, they are in such demand locally that probably no one has ever seriously tried to export them. The Bodensee district is extremely small, the best of it consisting of an even smaller section of hillside vineyards surrounding Meersburg on the eastern shore, opposite Konstanz. Most of the vineyards are under the control of a division of the *Staatsweingut*; and many of the wines are made from grapes only afforded second rank in other parts of Germany but which excel on the warm, humid shores of the lake. The Müller-Thurgaus of the Bodensee, for instance, are mild and soft; a Meersburger Rülander (Pinot gris) in the hands of winemasters of the *Staatsweingut* is round and well balanced, in contrast to its bland, acid-deficient counterparts of the Rheinhessen or the Pfalz. The Traminers are delightful, and the best Meersburger Rieslings compare favorably with any Rieslings made in Germany except the Rheingau or the Moselle. The only two exceptions to the rule are the Sylvaners, watery and bitter, and, as one might expect, the reds from the Spätburgunder or Pinot noir. The best-known vineyards are Haltnau, Fohenberg, Lustgarten, Gaisbuhl, Bengel, and Lerchenberg.

In summer Meersburg and the surrounding lake towns are besieged by tourists, but happily few of them seem to find their way to the simple restaurant on a back street of the lower town, the Weinstube zum Becker. In the upstairs dining room of this modest establishment, the best that Meersburg affords, one may enjoy a well-prepared meal, far from the madding crowd. The list of local wines is representative of the finest. Remember those of the *Staatsweingut*.

In all probability one will have spent the previous night— before crossing by ferry to Meersburg—in Konstanz, a city magnificently set in a cradle of mountains on the western shore of the Bodensee. When Konstanz was taken by the Romans in the third century, its inhabitants were lake dwellers who occupied a fortified island offshore. Some centuries later this island became the site of a Dominican monastery, in modern days transformed into one of Germany's loveliest hotels. It is impossible to mention Konstanz without recommending a night at the Hotel Insel, or at the least a drink on its terrace overlooking the lake, and an inspection of the remarkable frescoes on the walls of the old cloister depicting Konstanz's, and the Insel's, history.

Also an island, but on the eastern shore of the lake, facing Konstanz, is the city of Lindau, once an important Roman fort. So irresistible have been Lindau's charms for tourists that it became necessary to build yet another city on the mainland to accommodate the visitors. One does best to enter the town on foot. Many leisurely and amusing hours may be spent among

its winding streets, some of them too narrow for an auto-
mobile. There is an excellent hotel, the Reutemann, not far from
a quaint harbor with a fortified lighthouse, but one should not
expect a room during the season without a reservation, much less
a seat at the popular casino-restaurant, the *Spielbank*. Lindau's
local wine, Hoyerberger, is exceptionally high in acid, though a
nice accompaniment to Bodensee trout. We confess we have
never tried it with another more sophisticated local specialty,
Sumser schnitzel—slices of veal stuffed with bacon and topped
with scrambled eggs. The Lindauers themselves down Hoyerberger in enormous quantities, with or without food, claiming
that no amount of it ever produces either an after- or side-effect.

In the watershed of the Upper Rhine, which drains more than
two-thirds of Switzerland, the Bodensee is an important holding
reservoir, a natural flood-control factor against spring floods that
might otherwise cause immeasurable havoc downstream. The
Rhine, which leaves the Bodensee at Konstanz, enters at its
southern extremity near Bregenz, where a small corner of Austria
occupies the shoreline. The next and last vineyards of the Rhine
are to be found about thirty miles upstream, in the minute
principality of Liechtenstein, which has a population of twenty-
one thousand, a standing army of ten, and a police force of
twenty-six. Long ago part of Austria, the principality prudently
changed its status to that of an independent state in a customs
union with Switzerland, which also handles its foreign policy.
Liechtenstein reserved certain rights, allowing it to issue its own
stamps (once the principality's main source of income), as well
as to offer liberal banking facilities to the rest of the world. Its
chief of state, the prince of Liechtenstein, an art collector of
note, lives in a fairytale castle on the hill overlooking the capital,
Vaduz, seemingly oblivious to the fact that his sixty-two-square-
mile country nowadays boasts assets estimated at more than 300
billion Swiss francs, divided among almost ten thousand foreign
corporations—one to every two native citizens.

Along with its stamps, Liechtenstein has always been proud

of its wines, which take the names of the country's only two towns worthy of the name, Schaan and Vaduz. It cannot be said that either Schaaners or Vaduzers, reds largely made from variations of the Pinot noir, are notable as wines of the Rhine; though one of them, Schaaner Abloss Bordella, from an Italian grape, faintly *spritzig* or sparkly, possesses an unusually fragrant bouquet.

If one wishes to stay in Liechtenstein, there are several choices of inns. One is the Hotel Réal in the capital, comfortable but by no means luxurious, where one rubs elbows with the international bankers; another is the Sonnenhof, a converted preboom villa above the town, amid the vineyards. For ourselves, we prefer the seclusion of the latter.

To reach the source of the Rhine, one crosses it through a covered bridge leading from Liechtenstein to Switzerland and follows the valley. One passes through the town of Bad Ragaz, a spa famous in the eleventh century, where it was once the practice to lower the patients on ropes two hundred feet into a gorge below, that they might benefit from the blood-warm mineral waters. Above the town of Chur the Rhine divides: from our road we see the Hinterrhein coming in from the south, draining a great valley leading to the St. Bernard; ahead is the Vorderrhein, leading to the headwaters and the Oberalp pass. After Flims, in prehistoric times the site of a gigantic landslide that forced the Vorderrhein to change its course many miles to the south, the valley narrows to steep pastureland, and we are soon above the timberline of the Oberalp, one of the most challenging passes in all Switzerland. For a long time now the little mountain brook below has been lost to view, but just before reaching the pass there is a glimpse of the Rhine once again, a mere trickle in an otherwise dry bed of rocks, nearly nine hundred miles, as water flows, from the Hook of Holland and the sea.

I I I

The Rhône

I : *From Its Glacier to Geneva*

Just after leaving the summit of the Furka pass, barely a score of miles as the crow flies from the Oberalp and the source of the Rhine, one rounds a sharp bend of the road and comes face to face with the Rhône's glacier. Seen thus from above, the Rhonegletscher looks all but alive: a somnolent, treacherous mammoth, crouching in its mountain valley. In the everchanging mountain lights, its cragged shape continuously coruscates with pastel hues: by day it is alternately blue and green; with the rising and setting sun, a firelike red, and with dusk, the monster's icy blood is stilled to a pallid gray.

If records of a few hundred years ago are to be believed, the Rhonegletscher must once have been an even more awesome sight. Twice its present size, it filled its entire valley, exuding a torrential flow that dropped in cascades almost two thousand feet to the floor of the chasm. Although today the Rhonegletscher has shrunk to half its former dimensions, it still remains one of the most impressive sights of the Swiss Alps and is the only Swiss

73

glacier of any size that can be reached without an arduous climb. A convenient plank bridge has been built from the road, and a tunnel, for soft-soled tourists, carved into the glacier's face leads to its eerie depths.

To accomplish what the raging river does in a matter of minutes, one spends a good half hour descending in corkscrews to reach the village of Gletsch, a bleak mountaineer's settlement serving as a base for the Furka pass, as well as for the equally hazardous climb over the Grimsel leading north to the Swiss cities of Interlaken and Luzern. Below Gletsch the Rhône rollicks gaily along on the start of its journey to the Mediterranean, its valley sometimes verdant and dotted with neat squares of pasture and religiously tended garden plots, giving way all of a sudden to narrow, uninhabited canyons of jagged slate and rock. In the course of the first thirty miles, from canyon to village to canyon, the river drops more than three thousand feet before leveling out into that part of Switzerland called the Valais ("the Valley"), generally considered her finest vineyard district.

Often called Switzerland's Côte d'Or because of the excellence of its wines, the Valais is a geological hothouse. For a brief sixty miles stretching from east to west from the town of Brig, at the northern end of the Simplon pass constructed as a military route to Italy by Napoleon, the valley is dramatically protected on either side by high mountains. Thus sheltered from winds and rains, it is the most arid agricultural section of Switzerland, as well as the one with the most temperate climate. Its terraced vineyards, reminiscent of the Moselle, climb the steep sides of the limestone mountains, sometimes to altitudes of a thousand feet or more above the valley floor. To irrigate these vineyards the Swiss long ago conceived a system of mountain waterways called *bisses*, canals originating in the glaciers above, which spread out along the mountainsides. After watering the vineyards, these *bisses* eventually empty onto the fertile bottomland of the valley. For the Valais is not only famous for its wines: it also produces the finest apples and pears in all Switzerland. The

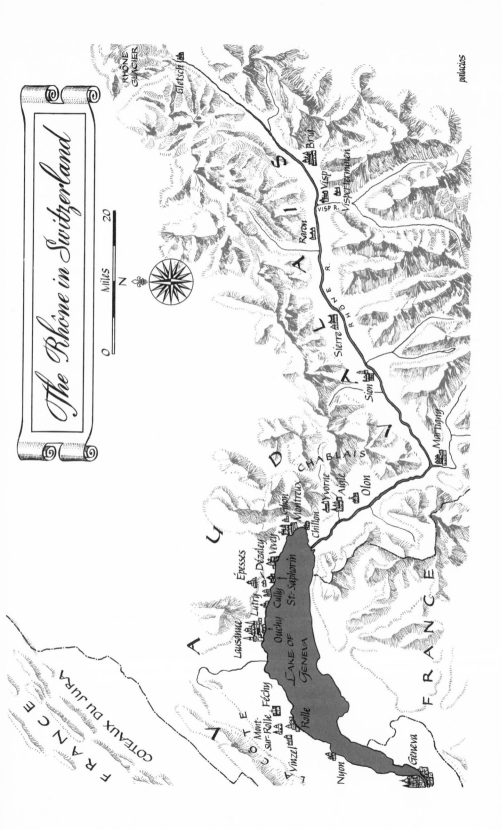

The Rhône in Switzerland

latter, by the way, are the source of one of Switzerland's best *eaux-de-vie*, pear brandy, variously called Pear Wilhelm, William, or Wilhelmine.

The first vineyards of the Valais to appear in any number are to be seen just below Brig, on the left bank of the river overlooking the town of Visp, at the junction of a river draining the slopes of the Matterhorn. Not far from Visp, up a hazardous mountain road that today ends disappointingly in a barnyard, is the site of the celebrated vineyards of Visperterminen, the highest vineyards in Europe, at an altitude of thirty-six hundred feet above sea level. Today the vineyards of Visperterminen are all but extinct, but there remain a few scattered mountain communities in Switzerland that still make the curious type of wine for which Visperterminen was once famous: *Vin du glacier*. Made from an indigenous grape called the Païen and aged in larchwood casks, which give it a peculiar piney taste somewhat resembling Greek Retsina, it can only be found in the tiny bistros and lodges of high mountain villages. Because of the intriguing name, virtually everyone who ever hears of it wants to drink it. In our opinion a questionable pleasure, and certainly not worth a long climb.

Switzerland produces only a small proportion of the wine it drinks, and a great majority of this is white. Indubitably the finest wine of the Valais is white Johannisberg, a blend of the Riesling and the Sylvaner. The name is obviously cribbed, but no matter. As with California, just don't expect a Rheingau. Johannisberg of the Valais is a pleasantly fragrant, delicate wine with a good body, even though its quality may vary considerably, depending upon its proportion of Riesling juice. Unfortunately the Sylvaner is easy to raise and a more prolific producer than the shy-bearing noble grape of the Rhineland; hence the temptation of poorer producers is to stretch the mixture. At least three wine-makers of the Valais won't let you down: the Clos des Chevaliers in Salquenen; and Gilliard and Mont d'Or in Sion.

With the exception of Johannisberg and a few other minor whites, the grape mainly used for whites throughout Switzerland

is the Chasselas, in actuality a table grape that reputedly originated in Burgundy. A notable failure wherever grown as a wine
grape in nearly every other country of the world, the Chasselas
somehow excels on Swiss soils. In the Valais both the Chasselas
and its wine go by the name of Fendant—the most popular and
ubiquitous white of the Valais and one which, when made by
good producers, will not disappoint you. Soft and pleasant,
Fendant smells and tastes remarkably like a freshly cut melon.
Its red counterpart in the Valais is known as Dôle, a blend of
Gamay and Pinot noir that by law must consist of 51 percent of
the latter. As might be expected, Dôle—both in fragrance and
taste—bears a marked resemblance to Beaujolais, the essential
difference being a sweetish flavor, especially as an aftertaste,
resulting from the limestone soil of the Valais' lofty vineyards.
Even though a purist will stick to a legitimate Beaujolais, a good
Dôle—with usage—has a way of growing on one, especially with
Swiss food. Another frequently seen red is Goron, in effect a Dôle
containing a greater percentage of Gamay than meets the law.
Goron often suits a purist better.

Valais producers are strong on trademarks, or what they call
"fantasy wines." Fantasy wines, unlike California generic wines,
are orthodox blends, but one can only report that most of them
are to be avoided, especially by foreign palates. Unfortunately
the presence of so many of them on wine lists tends to be con-
fusing, hence a basic knowledge of the names of some of the other
legitimate wines of the Valais, however rare, may be helpful in
separating sheep from goats. One of these legitimate wines is
white Malvoisie, a sweetish wine with a nice aroma. Arvine,
Amigne, and Humagne are all dryish whites, made from grapes
thought to have been brought by the Romans when they first
settled the Valais in the second century; yet another of a similar
origin is red Pinot Noir. Swiss Pinot Noir, when given a half
dozen or so years in the bottle, is worthy of attention: it may
develop into a near equal of a good or even great Burgundy,
with the fragrance of raspberries one might find in a Musigny,
and perhaps the lovely dark color of a Chambertin. But well-aged

Pinot Noir is rare, owing to the sad Swiss tradition of drinking all their own wines young (obviously the result of never having had enough to go around). One will be hard put to find it.

Despite its beauties of nature, the Valais is regrettably not filled with bewitching towns or tempting places to stop for a meal. The best restaurant in the Canton's capital of Sion, for example, is the Bergère on the Avenue de la Gare, entirely adequate for a satisfying meal, but nonetheless an establishment such as one would rapidly pass up in either France or Germany.

Aside from its romance as the historic northern terminus of the Simplon, Brig is essentially a busy railroad junction, with little charm to offer but its bulbous-spired Stockalper Palace in the middle of the town, a latter-day "château" that in its prime was the largest private residence in Switzerland. Even so, the Stockalper's history is worth a sentence. It was built by a local burgher who became so ostentatiously opulent (perhaps Switzerland's most heinous social crime) that his fellow Valaisians finally drove him into exile in Italy. Sierre is the commercial capital of the upper Valais and also marks the border between the French and German populations; Martigny is the wine capital of the lower part.

Sion alone has attractions for the visitor. Its old section, crowned by two spirelike hills visible up and down the Valais for miles, is virtually unchanged since the Middle Ages. In the fourth-century bishopric atop one of the spires, one finds Roman tombstones amid Corinthian columns and the remains of grape-pressing devices of a civilization long gone. Logically, the inner ramparts of this fortified monastery also contain the former bishops' private vineyards, still planted to Burgundian vines.

In contrast, the region of the Vaud, lying along the sun-drenched shore of the Lake of Geneva, is one of the loveliest parts of the entire globe. At Martigny, the Rhône makes a sharp right-angle turn and heads in a northwesterly direction for some twenty miles down a narrow gorge toward the Lake of Geneva.

For a time one follows a wild and desolate valley, where cataracts tumble from the mountains and ugly crags and boulders divert the river's course; but it soon broadens to an alluvial plain of rich earth, the Rhône's delta as it empties into the long crescent-shaped lake. On the right, wine villages appear at the base of sun-filled valleys stretching like so many fingers into the mountains. This is the southernmost part of the Vaud, known specifically as the Chablais. Its principal wine towns are Bex, Olon, Aigle, and Yvorne, the two latter being the more important—names, in fact, to remember. Their wines are full-bodied yet crisp and refreshing and, like most whites of this part of the Vaud, carry little of the metallic aftertaste so often typical of the Chasselas.

The Chablais ends with the industrial town of Villeneuve, where the famous "Riviera" begins. On the hills above the resort cities of Montreux, Vevey, and Lausanne are some of the finest vineyards of Switzerland, whose settings are incidentally among the most dramatic and romantic in the world. The best-known villages are Saint-Saphorin, Cully, Dézaley, Épesses, and Villette. Remember that, unlike the system of generic names used in the Valais, Vaud wines are nearly always labeled with the village name, a good majority of them also bearing names of vineyards, even though these are not necessarily an extra mark of quality. One should rely instead on the reputation of their producers, some of which own vineyards in several villages. Three of the most dependable are Fonjallaz, Comtesse, and Deladoey-Desfayes. Some of the Vaud's finest are communally owned. Two world-famous ones are the Clos des Moines and the Clos des Abbayes, the prized properties of the city of Lausanne, wines largely set aside for official functions and rarely found except in the very best restaurants.

The traveler and gourmet will not be disappointed in this part of the Vaud. So numerous are the good hotels on this particular section of the Riviera that to list even the best would be to flounder. As anyone knows, the Swiss are master hoteliers:

any standard guidebook will serve for Montreux, Vevey, or the surrounding area, the comparative excellence of most hotels being dictated only by the indicated degree of luxury and the price. Even so, it is impossible not to recommend our long-standing favorite, the Hotel Victoria at Glion, a thousand feet above Montreux facing the French Alps across the lake. The panoramas from its terrace have few equals and the Victoria's chef served his apprenticeship at Lausanne's celebrated Grappe d'Or. One may sit for hours watching the movements of the little lake streamers below, or the ever-changing formations of the *bataillière*, extraordinary configurations made by the muddy, cold waters of the Rhône as it forces (literally "battles") itself into the warm lake. Directly below is the romantic Château de Chillon, celebrated by Byron in "The Prisoner of Chillon," commemorating the fate of a religious revolutionary in the days of the Reformation. And just opposite the Château is a restaurant not to be outdone: the Taverne du Château de Chillon. Its distinguished proprietor-chef, whose framed culinary honors and awards are so numerous that they crowd the walls, will prepare you some unforgettable *plats*. Among these will perhaps be *moules marinières* and *caneton à l'orange*, the latter served with an impeccably authentic *sauce Bigarade*—a rarity even in Paris. Some of the best wines of the house are offered in carafes. Two that should not be overlooked are L'Orailles from Yvorne and the Dôle made by the Clos des Chevaliers near Sierre, among the best producers of the Valais, as we have mentioned.

From Vevey to Lausanne—whether one be a lover of nature or a lover of wine, or both—one must traverse, at least once, the spectacular hill road through the vineyards, the Route des Vignobles. Even so, no gastronome in his right mind (and certainly not in retrospect) will mind retracing his steps and descending to the lake to visit two jewels: the Restaurant Vieux Moulin near Épesses, and the charming village of Cully. The Vieux Moulin, set by a waterfall near the main road, is managed by the Fonjallaz family, whose vineyards climbing the hills behind have been its property for nine hundred years. Some of the Moulin's specialties are recipes you will want to bring home. *Truite en papillote*, for one, is a baked trout served with a simple sauce of basil, parsley, pepper, wine, and butter. Another is *Spumoni*, in this instance made with white wine, a surprisingly better ingredient than the conventional Marsala. Equally unusual, though perhaps more difficult to reproduce at home, is the Moulin's own version of *tutti-frutti*, called *zaccata*. *Zaccata's* principal flavoring is an exotic mountain liqueur called Marrisquin. Among the management's own superlative wines are Clos de l'Évêque, from a vineyard on the property of the fourteenth-century bishop who founded Dézaley, and another delightful white called Clos de la République. Here, too, may be found the rare Clos des Abbayes and Clos des Moines from the municipal vineyards of Lausanne.

In sharp contrast to the sophisticated Moulin is the Restaurant au Major Davel in the nearby lakeside village of Cully, a place for honest Swiss cooking of peasant origin and for sound local wines. The Major Davel is set in a quiet park jutting into the lake, where swans glide silently amid the reflections of vineyards and mountains. By day the life of the village is among the vines above; at night Cully sleeps like a child. Happily Cully is well hidden (and not obviously accessible) from the busy highway; but those who take the trouble to find it will be rewarded.

Lausanne, the largest city of the Vaud, is actually two cities in one, divided by the railroad. The lower and newer town, the suburb of Ouchy, lies on the lake, a residential resort of ornate formal parks and large houses, luxury hotels, and a full quota of marinas. Once Ouchy was a simple fishing hamlet, a favorite haunt of Byron; but that day is long gone. The older, adjoining city of Lausanne spreads into the foothills above, a complex of steeply winding streets and odd-shaped squares, interlaced by modern thoroughfares. Its fifteenth-century Gothic cathedral, considered the best of its type in Switzerland, is regarded as one of the finest examples extant of the transition between Romanesque and Gothic; the bizarre town hall, built of brick and stone and once the residence of the bishops of Lausanne in the days when they ruled this part of Switzerland, now houses the parliamentary chambers of the canton.

It does not necessarily follow, however, that either Lausanne or Ouchy is ideal for an overnight stop. The second offers little appeal for a traveler in search of old-world culture, and there are many airier and more attractive lakeside resorts on the Riviera. And Lausanne itself is apt to be crowded, though its large hotels will provide for you regally. So will several independent restaurants of unmistakable quality. Undoubtedly the best of these is the Au Grappe d'Or—an "in place" frequented by international celebrities and gourmets alike, with a wine list that includes all the gems of Switzerland and many of France and Germany. For summer dining one should try the Chalet Suisse in a park high above the city; homesick Americans will appreciate the Calèche Carnozet, a few steps up a small street near the station, which imports succulent steaks by air from Kansas.

The last section of the Vaud, between Lausanne and Geneva, is known as La Côte ("the slope"). As the name indicates, the countryside along the lake is here gently rolling, hence the vineyards, rarely terraced, may be worked with machinery, resulting in wines that are less expensive to produce. Unfortunately they do not meet the qualitative standards of the other wines of the Vaud. Even the best of La Côte are light and watery, lacking in character; those poorly made or from inferior villages often carry too much of the metallic tartness of the Chasselas, which at its worst brings forth an almost medicinal-tasting product. Among the better wine towns, many of whose wines are certainly worth a try, are Féchy, Bougey, Vinzel, and Rolle, the last a miniscule lake village comparable to Cully, with a pleasant park by the water and an offshore castle whose walls are lapped by the blue waters. Since the real charm of La Côte lies principally in the lakefront, one should not make the mistake of taking the autoroute from

Lausanne to Geneva, the modern highway which traverses comparatively dull countryside several miles inland.

The Rhône leaves the lake at Geneva, considered by many to be one of the more beautiful cities of Europe. For ourselves, Geneva's charms have always passed us by, though we admit to being an exception to the rule. Certainly by night, we grant that its lakefront, with its widespread League of Nations buildings and all the imposing houses of the diplomatic corps and the affluent, is impressive. But by day, Geneva's glamour—a little like its waning international position—blanches into sterile impersonality. Like Montreux and Lausanne, Geneva has excellent hotels, all adequately categorized in any standard guidebook. Yet for a city that plays host to so many diplomats and sophisticated foreigners from all over the world, Geneva is peculiarly bereft of good restaurants, at any price. An outstanding exception is the Restaurant Béarn, a small, chic place on the left bank of the Rhône, just where it flows from the lake. The Béarn's size and décor will remind you for all the world of one of those fashionable uptown New York restaurants to be found in such numbers between Park and Fifth avenues in the fifties; but we guarantee the food and service will be even better, and the check more realistic. One of the Béarns best dishes is *jambon Henri IV*, slices of ham baked with cream, parsley, Madeira, and morilles. Another is *saucisson chaud*, an unusually delicate sausage cooked inside a *papillote*, or sealed envelope of greased paper. The carafe wines are superb, especially the Fendant from the Valais; after your meal, you should take a leisurely walk along the quay where the olive green Rhône flows swiftly, setting out once again on its long journey to the Mediterranean.

Another recommendable restaurant in Geneva is the Buffet Cornavin, housed in the same building as the station—but not to be confused with the official Buffet de la Gare. At the Cornavin, choose game if possible and wash it down with the restaurant's excellent carafe wines. These are apt to be good Burgundies or Rhônes, at astoundingly low prices. In fair weather a table on the terrace outside will open your eyes to yet another side of Geneva, quite different from the genteel atmosphere of the waterfront: what we might call the Geneva of *"les Grands Boulevards,"* frequented by the Swiss themselves.

I I : *From Geneva to Lyon*

Below Geneva the Rhône flows for a time through a broad and undulating valley, much of it in vineyards yielding wines of little merit. This is the western end of the so-called Côte de Genève, the source of *ordinaires* that usually end up in undistinguished, indigestible distillations. An exception is a small district to the southeast, stretching along the border of the Lake of Geneva and up into the French Alps—the Côte de Chablais. One pocket of the Chablais (not to be confused with the Côte of the same name at the eastern end of the lake, beyond Lausanne) has been given a French *Appellation Contrôlée*: Crépy white has a sharp tang and an unusually clean taste. At its best, it is slightly *pétillant*; it is delicious with fish, but definitely a wine to be consumed near its home—at Évian-les-Bains or one of the other nearby resorts. Made from the Chasselas in the shadow of the Alps, Crépy is logically low in sugar and in poor years almost mercilessly high in acid. Hence all but the very superior vintages are utilized for sparkling wines, to which sugar may be added legally as a part of the usual "Champagne" process. Even so, as sparkling it is by no means the most desirable of France, for basic overacidity is a factor that may never be entirely erased or mitigated.

In its course from the Lake of Geneva to the broad plains of the Bresse and its eventual juncture with the Saône at Lyon, the Rhône does serious battle with the Alps and the Jura. Just beyond the Franco-Swiss border, as it winds through a series of deep gorges hemmed in on either side by the protruding fingers of these two interlocking mountain chains, the river becomes hopelessly blocked in its westerly flow by the Jura and is forced into a wide loop to the south. Not too far downstream is the viticultural section of Seyssel, the center of a scattering of vineyards producing wines called *vins de Savoie*—that ancient province whose ruling house, through the graces of Napoleon III, furnished the last kings of Italy.

Savoie is a land in itself. It has a compelling loveliness; and so provincial and isolated are certain parts of it that they hardly seem like France at all. Its tiny viticultural capital, the town of Seyssel, is no exception. Politically Seyssel is two villages divided by the Rhône, one in the department of the Ain, the other in Savoie, joined by a single bridge. Nothing much goes on here but wine-making, and a more relaxed or sleepier little town could hardly be found. Seyssel's other great attribute is the kind of French inn one dreams about: the Hôtel du Rhône et Commerce on the right (Ain) bank. Small, without outward pretension, consisting only of a dining room and a terrace overlooking the river with a handful of modest rooms above, the Hôtel du Rhône is a delight. It is also a strictly family affair. Madame commands the hotel (and its guests) with charm and efficiency; Monsieur, a chef of the highest order, rules the kitchen. Liaison is made by a group of pink-cheeked little girls who run busily back and forth bearing Monsieur's irresistible creations. His versions of the two local, salmonlike fish—the omble and the lavaret, from the nearby lakes of Annecy and Bourget respectively—represent never-to-be-forgotten experiences. *Lavaret à la Robert*, for one, is poached and then garnished with a sauce made from the fish's own fumet, white wine, mushrooms, shallots, cream, and a little vinegar. Its companion, manifestly, must be the local Roussette de Seyssel from either of the town's two outstanding producers—Varichon et Clerc, or Mollex. The former's proudest is Royale Seyssel; the latter's, Clos de la Paclette.

Although this part of Savoie once reputedly made more wine than Burgundy's Côte d'Or, production has dropped alarmingly over the years. Throughout the region one sees traces of hundreds of vineyards no longer worked, and the officially recognized remnants, on the right bank of the river in the Ain—with the *Appellation Contrôlée* of Seyssel—nowadays consist of only six hundred acres. Seyssel has no large estates, and most of the vineyards are what the French call *morcelés*—a few acres of vines forming part of large farms raising other products.

Savoie wines are rarely found outside the region, and the more's the pity. The whites, especially, are both delicate and full in body, reaching a maximum of 10 percent alcohol and smelling subtly of violets or olives, or both. The best is Roussette de Seyssel, made from the Roussette (or Altesse) grape, whose origin is something of a mystery. According to local legend, the Altesse was brought from Cyprus in the middle of the fifteenth century by a certain Charlotte de Lusignon, alleged ruler of Cyprus, Armenia, and Jerusalem, who married the son of Louis II, duke of Savoie. This myth may probably be discounted. In all likelihood the Altesse (the name has nothing to do with nobility, but originates from the fact that the vines excel when allowed to grow high) is probably the Viognier of the Rhône, imported, no doubt, by the Church.

Regrettably, many of Seyssel's whites are not made from the Roussette or Altesse, but from the Molette, a considerably higher producer, indigenous to Savoie, highly acid and almost undrinkable as a still wine. Like the inferior, off-year wines of Crépy, it is useful for *mousseux* or sparklings. The red wines of Savoie are made from the Gamay grape of Beaujolais, as well as from a distinctly inferior one called the Mondeuse rouge. The best is called Chantagne, a product of the Gamay made in the department of Haute-Savoie. In a good year—about one out of three—Chantagne tastes like a creditable and powerful Beaujolais, rather akin to a Brouilly. Others of the region, predominantly white, are Corbonad, Anglefort, Jacquière, and Montagnieu, the last from the Coteaux de Bugey, where the Rhône has finally eluded the Jura and headed northward once more. All should be drunk as near home as possible.

No lover of good food and quaint towns should in conscience leave Savoie without visiting the attractive town of Annecy, at the head of the lake of the same name, a short drive from Seyssel up the dramatic Val de Fier that drains Mont Blanc. Two towns of France vie for the title of "Venice of France": one is Martigues on the Étang (Lake) de Berre near Marseilles; the other is Annecy, its ancient twisting streets filled with arcades, its minuscule Château d'Ille bridging the swift stream flowing from the lake. The bordering quay is filled with tiny shops and cafés; nearby is the Hôtel and Restaurant Auberge de Savoie, an establishment of considerable gastronomic fame. To reach the hotel itself, one climbs age-worn steps passing through the facade of the neighboring Church of St. François; the restaurant below offers, among other specialties of the region, three outstanding versions of the local lake fish: the lavaret, the omble, and the fera, the last from the Lake of Geneva. *Fera Saint-Germain*, the Auberge's version, is grilled and served with the lightest of Béarnaise sauces. Ideally it should be accompanied by the Auberge's own choice of a Crépy, and the meal finished off with one of those local cheeses for which Savoie is so famous. One of the best is Saint-Marcellin, small and soft, a mixture of cow's and goat's milk, somewhat resembling a Camembert. Yet another, Comté, is hard and slightly gritty. Then there is the creamy Reblochon, well known abroad. But perhaps the best of all—not strictly Savoyard, but shared with the neighboring province of Bresse, is Bleu de Bresse. Bleu de Bresse is not a "bleu" at all (in the sense of a Roquefort), but a delicate and creamy cheese filled with mountain herbs. And lastly, while still in Savoie and speaking of herbs, one should not forget its indigenous liqueur, Chartreuse, made from a secret formula by Carthusian monks of La Grande Chartreuse, not far distant from Annecy itself. Chartreuse is produced in two colors, *jaune* (yellow) and *verte* (green). Like so many liqueurs invented by the Church, it was originally medicinal. We recommend the *jaune* over the *verte*, the latter being considerably more powerful, both in alcohol and medicaments. It rarely appeals to the uninitiated.

For a quiet night's rest on the journey toward Lyon, a stop at the town of Belley will be in order. Visiting gastronomes may well receive considerable stimulation from the fact that this was the birthplace of Brillat-Savarin, who was friendly with the antecedents of today's proprietors of the Hôtel Pernollet and, according to legend, dined there frequently. Assuming the validity of the legend, there can be little doubt that the great man of jurisprudence and gastronomy also slept there. Known for his gargantuan appetite, he had the unfortunate habit of falling asleep during his meal, often needing to be carried from the table. Belley was once an important coaching station between Geneva and the west, and despite much tasteful modernization, the Pernollet still bears the marks of a *relais* or coaching tavern of days gone by. The rooms give on to balconies surrounding an inner courtyard, whose far end was once the stables. The finest wines of Savoie and the Coteaux de Bugey adorn the wine list, and as might be expected, the menu includes not only one but two memorable creations spun around the lavaret. The first is a superb mousse; with the second the fish is poached and served cold, encased in aromatic aspic.

Finally free of the blockading Jura, the Rhône now rounds a sharp bend and flows northward for a time before turning toward Lyon. The slopes on its right bank are those of the Coteaux de Bugey, some of whose wines, especially its Montagnieu, are worth sampling. It is unfortunate that except for a casual bistro here and there, there are no rewarding inns or other establishments to recommend for the purpose. Equally unrewarding is the flat countryside through which the Rhône now winds on its way to Lyon. For those with the time to spare, we heartily recommend leaving the river, and making a detour to the north, through Chalamont and Villars, encompassing part of the ancient province of Bresse—a hauntingly beautiful part of the world filled with ponds and lakes, with incredibly verdant pastures grazed by sleek cattle, whose owners occupy some of the handsomest country manor houses of France.

I I I : *Lyon and The Beaujolais*

The city of Lyon, which lays claim to being the second largest in France, is nowadays everything the claim implies. The sensible

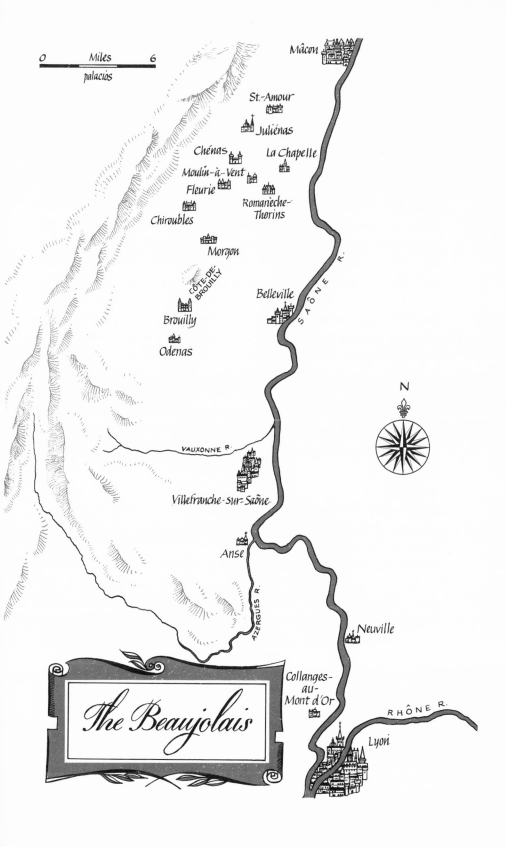

The Beaujolais

time to visit Lyon is on a weekend, when its broad, shaded quays along the Saône, facing the handsome Palais de Justice, are momentarily restored to the charm and tranquillity of yesteryears. Except on weekends, its hotels are jammed with bus-borne tourists in summer and conventions in winter. Twenty years ago Lyon was considered the gastronomic capital of France, and the number of stars accorded its restaurants in the *Guide Michelin* amounted to a veritable galaxy. In those days, nearly every citizen of Lyon was credited with a born instinct for cooking—honest cooking without frills. *Haute cuisine Lyonnaise* has never been the province of sophisticated chefs apprenticed in Paris or Nice or Monte Carlo, but the collective result of strictly personal accomplishments on the part of modest housewives who had gained a reputation for turning out an outstanding dish in the home. In due course some of these talented ladies would set up their own shops—as evidenced by the fact that so many of Lyon's most celebrated restaurants are named for a mother or an aunt or a widow (*Mère, Tante,* or *Veuve*).

Nobody seems able to explain why, but Lyon's gastronomic luminosity has sadly faded. Perhaps the citizens of France's second largest city are today too tired or in too much of a hurry to pause to eat well; or the mass of tourists and convention-goers are led to dine only at the large hotels or one of the several great eating emporiums. Each successive year the *Michelin* strikes a star or two from Lyon's listings, and a generation of Frenchmen has come into being that flatly avers it has never really had a good meal in Lyon. It is a sad truth. Nowadays one may be wined and dined, as a rule, better in the suburbs or in the surrounding countryside than in Lyon itself. Lyon's restaurateurs have foolishly capitalized on their past, gastronomic standards have fallen, and what used to be a beguiling little bistro presided over by a chef—or a mother, aunt, or widow—has become a comparative food mill. One hesitates to apply the word eateries—for after all, France is still France!

Such, for example, has been the fate of the first four establishments listed in the usually dependable *Michelin*: the Mère Guy, the Vettard, the Nandron, and the Mère Brazier. Their food is good, but not that good; their interiors have assumed an impersonal extravaganza, and their former charms lost their savor. The Brazier's out-of-town branch at Col de la Luère, incidentally, ideally situated with a fine view of the Alps and the plains, has more merit than its metropolitan counterpart. Another excellent establishment in suburbia is the Auberge Paul Bocuse at Collanges-au-Mont-d'Or, five miles from town. One can hardly go wrong at this small family-owned restaurant run by a famous chef trained in the best of old Lyon and Paris. Our present favorites in the city, more in the tradition, are La Voûte, Chez Jo, and Chez Juliette. But be forewarned that none of them is inexpensive, and certainly in the case of the former, reservations are in order— both considerations that would have been unthinkable two or three decades ago.

Even though you may be frustrated by Lyon's restaurants and will probably come away feeling your pockets have been picked, you may perhaps at least have surmised how the tradition of *cuisine Lyonnaise* made such an indelible impression on the art of gastronomy the world over. French cooking has often been aptly defined as the "art of using leftovers," but it also involves the lucky circumstance of having at hand the best, freshest and purest ingredients, however elemental. Significantly, Lyonnaise cookery has never been noted for its specialties; its fame, instead, has rested on the availability of the finest chickens (those of nearby Bresse), unrivaled cuts of beef from the renowned Charollais (France's best), fresh fish and crayfish (*écrevisses*) that frequent the brooks and rivers of the region, superb sausages —and the liberal use of the onion, good red wine, and of course insistence on the purest butter. The genius of Lyon lies in preparing these gifts of the land in such a way that their natural flavors are exposed, rather than covered, concealed, or overembellished. Hence even though a *poularde truffée* or *demi-deuil* (a poached chicken with slices of black truffles, painstakingly tucked under its white skin) may sound like an extravaganza, it is the wholesome fowl that takes credit for the glory. Nor could many dishes be more basic than a simple broiled steak labeled *entrecote Charollais*; or a mousse fashioned from the leftovers of a pike (*quenelles*) with crayfish sauce (*à la Nantua*).

Simplicity also characterizes Lyon's local wines—those of the enormously productive Beaujolais region in the rolling hills northwest of the city. For generations it has been a standing joke with the French that the thirst of Lyon, which lies at the confluence of the Rhône and the Saône, is quenched by three rivers: the Rhône, the Saône, and the crimson Beaujolais. The jibe, even though it be directed at the inordinate capacity of the citizens of Lyon, is not entirely far-fetched. There are practical reasons why this mundane wine should be "Lyon's wine." Light and fruity, made from the highly productive red Gamay (a grape long ago banned from Burgundy's Côte d'Or, but peculiarly suited to the granite soil of the Beaujolais) it could never be called truly distinguished. Only at its infrequent best is it perhaps more than France's very finest red *vin du pays*; and few Beaujolais are worth laying down for more than a year, if that. Most of it is best when drunk young—sometimes as youthful as only a few months old. And since so little of it profits from bottle age, its logical market was the surrounding countryside and the nearest large city, which absorbed it with alacrity, by the barrelful.

By virtue of its youthful immaturity, Beaujolais is a heady drink and, incidentally, not always too digestible. Since it lacks finesse, the average Frenchman takes it in unceremonious gulps or long draughts—with ensuing consequences. Passing a table where a large group is seated, you will not always need to look at the labels to know what the wine is: the flushed faces and contagious geniality usually tell the story.

Although a small amount of passable white wine, Beaujolais Blanc, is made in the region—the best is from the Chardonnay grape, grown in the northern section of the region bordering

southern Burgundy—most of the many millions of gallons produced annually are red. Much of this is made in cooperatives,
which, incidentally, welcome visitors to their tasting rooms or
"sheds." These are the wines simply labeled "Beaujolais" or
"Beaujolais Supérieur," the latter a notch higher in quality and
slightly more alcoholic.

The various Beaujolais are not always too easy to distinguish
one from another. The best (known as the *Crus*) derive from
nine classified sub-regions, each with its handful of outstanding
vineyards entitled to add their names to the subregional nomenclature. From north to south these sub-regions are as follows:
Saint-Amour, whose wines are perhaps the softest and smoothest
of all, especially those of its celebrated vineyard, Champs Grillés.
Next come Juliénas (Château des Capitans and Les Mouilles
rank high here) and Chénas, with Les Rochelles, Les Caves, and
Les Verillats. Lying just to the south is Fleurie, its wines as
flowery as its name, two of whose vineyards, Clos de la Roilette
and Chapelle du Bois, are among the most renowned of the entire
region. Close to Fleurie is the most famous sub-region, Moulin-
à-Vent, named for its ancient hilltop windmill and the vineyard that lies beneath it. A wine labeled *Le* Moulin-à-Vent
is naturally far better than one named subregionally just Moulin-
à-Vent. Two other superior wines are Les Carquelins and Les
Burdelines. Moulin-à-Vents are powerful, full wines, and about
the only Beaujolais that it pays to keep in bottle for more than
a year.

The four remaining sub-regions are Chiroubles (Bel-Air and
Le Moulin), Morgon (Château de Bellevue), Brouilly, and
Côte-de-Brouilly. As a general rule, the wines of the Beaujolais
grow coarser and less delicate the farther south they are raised,
and it is a matter of personal taste whether one prefers the
southern ones to their more florid, sprightlier cousins of the north.

After the top classifications of the Crus de Beaujolais, the
nine sub-regionals, comes that of Beaujolais-Villages—wines carrying the name of one of twenty-odd towns of the Beaujolais but

not necessarily included in the glorious nine sub-regions. It is well to remember that a Beaujolais-Villages will not perforce be better than an otherwise unidentified Supérieur, or even a common bottle simply labeled Beaujolais, made by a well-known producer. The most appropriate method for the visitor is to seek out a good restaurant and select the most expensive non-*Cru* on the list. Happily few Beaujolais place much strain on the pocketbook.

The citizens of the Beaujolais are as unsophisticated and charming as their earthy, jovial wines. They are fine cooks, and some of the villages harbor excellent country inns. One good one is the Maritonnes at Romanèche-Thorins, just a step from Moulin-à-Vent. You may not be impressed by its look from the roadside, nor settle immediately into a state of *bien-être* in the sprawling dining rooms. But don't be put off. You will travel far before meeting a better *coquelet au vin* (young chicken stewed, of course, in Beaujolais). Unfortunately the Maritonnes is popular for conventions, and meals and rooms are not always available. We therefore suggest two nearby substitutes. The first is the Relais Robin at Chénas, a country inn with high standards; the second is the Beaujolais at Belleville, a tastefully remodeled bistro on a side street of an otherwise undistinguished town. Its owner-chef will provide you well, and his cellar is stocked with that gem—*Le* Moulin-à-Vent.

I V : *The Côtes-du-Rhône*

Progressing southward from Lyon, the banks of the Rhône hold out four or five isolated vineyard regions, some of them producing certain wines that rival the great ones of Burgundy and Bordeaux. These regions or pockets of vineyards are for the most part widely separated, stretching from Lyon to Avignon, more than one hundred and fifty miles to the south. Their most famous wines are rarely found abroad, even today. Some of them are in too short supply for export; with others, fashion has passed them by. Some vineyards of the Côtes-du-Rhône are traceable to the second

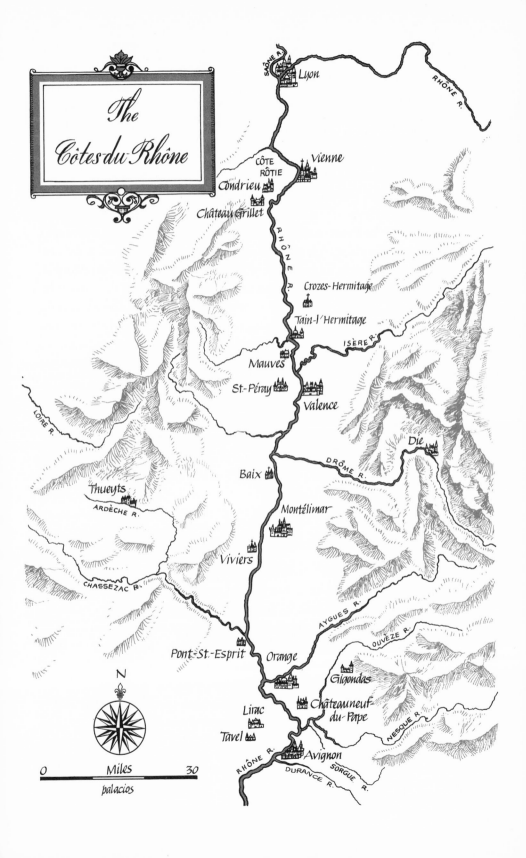

The Côtes du Rhône

Lyon

SAÔNE R.

RHÔNE R.

Vienne

CÔTE RÔTIE

Condrieu

Château Grillet

RHÔNE R.

Crozes-Hermitage

Tain-l'Hermitage

ISÈRE R.

Mauves

St.-Péray

Valence

LOIRE R.

Die

DRÔME R.

Baix

Thueyts

ARDÈCHE R.

Montélimar

Viviers

CHASSEZAC R.

AYGUES R.

OUVÈZE R.

Pont-St.-Esprit

Orange

Gigondas

Lirac

Châteauneuf-du-Pape

Tavel

NESQUE R.

N

RHÔNE R.

Avignon

DURANCE R.

SORGUE R.

0   Miles   30

palacios

century before Christ; all were in existence in Roman times.

The first pocket one meets, producing red wines only, is known as the Côte Rôtie (the "Roasted Slope"), where the vines are spread over two small, high hills behind the village of Ampuis on the right bank. Across the river is the town of Vienne, once a Roman stronghold and a base of operations for Roman conquests in the north. With the exception of a little core of antiquity, Vienne is today a busy place, directly in the path of the heavily traveled truck route between Lyon and Marseilles. The Romans, like the Church to follow, needed their wines, and it seems logical that a good part of the reason for placing their headquarters at Vienne was its proximity to the exceptional wines made across the river, where the indigenous Syrah grape—often erroneously said to be of Persian origin—had been flourishing long before their arrival.

It is entirely possible to pass through the streets of Ampuis without noticing the vines on the two hills directly behind the village. The first of these is called the Côte Brune, which, together with the facing hill, the Côte Blonde, forms a tiny sun-baked amphitheater. Protected by even higher hills to the west, the exposure is in general southeast; the soil is unbelievably stony and poor, the land extremely steep, so that all the vineyards must be worked by hand. Both Côtes are divided traditionally into many small plots with such intriguing names as Les Chaveroches, La Brocarde, La Claperonne, and Le Pavillon Rouge—all distinguished plots of land, though one rarely sees any of these names on labels. The finest Côte Rôties have always been blends from the two Côtes, and superior products are always identified today by the name of a good producer.

As one would expect, there have been abounding jokes since time immemorial about the respective Côtes—comparing the two hills, of course, to women. Wines of Côte Brune are said to possess more lasting qualities; those of Côte Blonde come into fullness sooner and fade sooner. Hence, with women as with the wine, the combination always brings perfection. Close inspection of the two Côtes will reveal that the soil of the Blonde is indeed lighter in color and in texture than that of the Brune. Skillfully blended, and with sufficient age (ten years is a good minimum), Côte Rôtie wines soften into something truly remarkable: fragrant, mellow, and fruity. They have often been called the "Burgundies of the Rhône," and not without reason. But one should be forewarned that even with modern methods of vinification, the Syrah grape—the greatest red grape of the Rhône—is not tamed easily in the bottle, even though in the Côte Rôtie today the blend includes a modicum of the local white Viognier to soften the Syrah's austerity. What they must have been in Roman times is something else again. In one record of that day, they were described as "black and powerful." To this we might add the testimony of Thomas Jefferson, who once passed through Côte Rôtie on donkeyback, and tasted and admired the wines greatly, but noted that one could barely choke them down before they were at least four years old.

Yet another extraordinary little isle now appears, also on the western bank of the river about ten miles below Ampuis. This is Château Grillet, considered by many over the years to be the most outstanding local wine of all France. Containing only four acres, Château Grillet is the smallest isolated plot of land in France with its own *Appellation Contrôlée*. A passing traveler would never know it was there, hidden in a curve of the dirt road leading to the little village of Saint-Michel, which overhangs the river town of Condrieu.

All the oenophiles and experts are probably right: the wine of Château Grillet is certainly most unusual, not to say extraordinary. Made from the white Viognier grape, found only in the regions of Condrieu and Ampuis, Château Grillet is not only characteristically orange-colored, but smells and tastes a bit like fresh oranges. The entire vineyard is owned by a single family, and the production even in the best years is rarely more than two hundred cases. Of all the good or great French wines, Château Grillet also holds the record for not traveling well. The best place to taste it is in Condrieu itself; the second best is at the celebrated Restaurant de la Pyramide, just across the river in Vienne, which hostelry absorbs a goodly proportion of each year's production. In faraway Paris, Château Grillet becomes a mirage; farther afield, worse yet. A few years ago a "gourmet group" in Chicago managed to corner a few cases, where it became the *pièce de résistance* at one of this society's banquets. Thousands of words of praise were written on the subject in the society's reports, but reading between the lines, the event was a Pyrrhic victory.

Along with being a delightful and unusual wine (when drunk at home), Château Grillet is also one of those rare French wines that become seasonally *pétillant*—and healthily so, meaning it has not begun to spoil. Every spring when Château Grillet is brought from the cellars of the Pyramide and opened at one's table, it reveals itself to be slightly sparkling and prickly on the tongue. By midsummer the condition has started to disappear, only to be repeated the following year. The very mention of this mysterious condition, also common to certain Alsatian Traminers and Rieslings on the Moselle, is to risk one's life among academic oenologists or scientists, who find it impossible to believe that the malolactic (second) fermentation can occur in the bottle, cease, and then reoccur. One must simply have faith in one's taste buds, along with the testimony of the venerable wine waiter at the Pyramide. He explains it this way: "When the sap starts to rise in the vines in the spring, the wine in the cellars takes on new life!"

Château Grillet in actuality is only an isolated island in the middle of a much larger area, the white-wine vineyards that go by the appellation of Condrieu. Also made from the Viognier, Condrieu wines bear the same characteristics, though are not quite of the same caliber as those of their famous neighbor. Condrieus are likewise best when drunk near home, and are best of all at one of the pleasantest hotels on the Rhône, the Beau Rivage on Ampuis' riverbank. As the river rolls by and the barges pass on their way from Lyon to Marseilles, you may bask in the culinary glory of a highly competently run Relais de Campagne. The wine list contains all the local gems, including Château Grillet, Condrieu, and Côte Rôtie; the cuisine is outstanding. Two of the specialties are *oeufs en gelée au foie gras* (poached eggs encased in an aspic heavily doctored with port and served on a slice of *foie gras*) and *turbot au Vermouth*. The sauce for this latter consists of coarsely chopped mushrooms and tomatoes, carefully sautéed until tender, in cream whipped subtly into the reduced Vermouth *fumé* in which the fish itself was cooked.

If the superb cooking of the Beau Rivage does not suffice, one may always cross the river to Vienne and splurge at the Restaurant de la Pyramide, by reputation one of the very greatest in France. So much has been written in praise of the Pyramide that perhaps the less said here the better. Go for yourself and see— but be sure your pocket is bulging and your appetite adequate for the task. The distinguished and inventive chef who built up its reputation, Fernand Point, is long since gone, but the place still maintains its traditional standards. There are few places in all of France where that pride and joy of French cookery—*présentation* —is more ingeniously carried out, or better backed up with culinary skill from behind the scenes. The menu is nearly always the same—based today largely on the most acclaimed jewels of the late M. Point's creations over the years—thus the Pyramide tends to be a one-time-only experience. As one food writer aptly put it, the Pyramide "changes the eaters rather than the edibles." You may also stay overnight at a recently built annex belonging to the management, La Résidence de la Pyramide, happily only a short stroll from the restaurant. Prices at La Résidence reflect those of the mother establishment—but then, one may as well die for a sheep as a lamb.

To attain the next oasis of great vineyards of the Rhône, in this case the source of both red and white wines, one journeys downstream forty miles to the town of Tain on the left bank. Here is the home of Hermitages, wines—especially the white ones—

rarely seen abroad. Behind the town rises what is called the Hill of the Hermit—a large, round dome entirely covered with vineyards. Near its top is a lonely shrine, its story (which may well be more truth than fancy) being that a crusader returning from the Holy Land once climbed to what was then an ordinary shrine and, while kneeling in worship, received a vision to remain on the spot and tend the vines of the Lord.

Geologically, the Hill of the Hermit is another excellent example of how little fertility the wine grape requires. The entire dome is solid rock, covered in most places by only a half dozen or so inches of poor soil. What nourishes the vines is not so much the soil. The vines' roots penetrate fissures in the rock, sometimes to a depth of thirty feet or more, for food and water.

The only grape allowed at Hermitage for red wines is the Syrah, which we have met on the Côte Rôtie. The Syrah is unquestionably an indigenous plant, although the legend of the hermit is often embellished to lead one to believe that he brought the plant with him from the Middle East. Red Hermitages are hard and coarse for many years after birth, like those of the Côte Rôtie. It is not only a waste of time but a felony to drink them before they have earned at least eight or ten years in the bottle. When mature, they are fragrant, solid, and satisfying.

All the vineyards or *mas* on the Hill of the Hermit bear famous names, yet one rarely finds a bottle with a vineyard name. Comparable to blending wines from the Côte Blonde and the Côte Brune, tradition in Hermitage has also evolved a method of combining the various *mas* to bring about a perfect wine. For this reason the name of an honest and able producer of Hermitage is of utmost importance, for the Rhône abounds with charlatans. Your best producer must be a local grower and not simply a *négociant* or buyer. In other words, unless the man or firm whose name appears on the bottle can also identify himself as a *propriétaire*, *éleveur*, or *récolteur*—all implying on-the-spot ownership—the bottle should be regarded with suspicion. The mere title of *négociant*, even if his address is the same town as that in which the wine is made, is no guarantee. Some of the best producers of Hermitages (and other Rhônes) are Jaboulet-Vercherre, Paul Jaboulet Aîné, Chave, Sorel, Chierpe, and Cotte-Vergne.

One of the white wines most appreciated by French connoisseurs is white Hermitage, produced in considerably less quantity than the red. It is beautifully golden in color, mellow in flavor, though somewhat lacking in bouquet. What it lacks in fragrance, however, it recovers in body and style and alcoholic potency. It may be drunk young—yet it is also one of the longest-living dry white wines of France. Bottles of it have been opened at fifty years of age and still found in perfect condition. White Hermitage is made from a blend of two grapes: the Marsanne and the Roussanne, vines only found in this section of the Rhône, though the Marsanne has been successfully transplanted to Switzerland, where it has become the source of the wine imitatingly called Ermitage, an undistinguished rarity of the Valais.

The Hill of the Hermit is not the only fount of wine in the region of Tain. Surrounding it on three sides are hundreds of acres of lowland vineyards, perhaps the best known of which are classified as Crozes-Hermitage. The vineyards of Crozes lie in a flat, dull country, and their wines play second fiddle to those of the Hill—although the general public is encouraged to believe that Crozes is a vineyard on the Hill. Needless to say, geography never has endowed the wines of Crozes to make them equal to those of the Hill; and they are at an additional disadvantage by virtue of the fact that the Grenache grape, an easy-growing, abundant producer that we shall meet again at Châteauneuf-du-Pape and elsewhere, is the principal grape of Crozes. Combined with a bit of the noble Syrah—plus the hyphenated magic of the name of Hermitage—it has made many a fortune for many a Rhône *négociant*.

Three other traditional wine-making towns in the area, Saint-Joseph, Mercurol, and Gigondas, are nowadays responsible for even more common and undistinguished reds than Crozes, although whites of Gigondas are exceptions to the rule. Yet for some inexplicable reason we have never found a white Gigondas within fifty miles of its birthplace. The best producer of Gigondas Blanc is the firm of P. Amadieu. Saint-Joseph lies across the river near the town of Mauves, more famous for its apricots than its wines.

On Tain's main street one finds two excellent hostelries, the Cabaret du Vivarais and the Restaurant Chabert. The latter, which we have always preferred, adheres to the traditions of honest French cooking, and lays little stress on interior décor. As far as their wine lists are concerned, you will probably observe that both establishments have been considerably infiltrated by local *négociants*. The best wines of Tain are rarely found at either place. As we have already warned, be sure that your wine comes from a bona fide *propriétaire*, and that the name on the bottle is not accompanied by the words *marque déposée*, indicating a registered trademark. Remember, too, that there are no such titles as *grands crus* or *premiers crus* authorized for the Rhône valley. Any bottle so labeled is bound to be, in one way or another, a fraud, however minor a fraud.

The pleasantest hotel in Tain, the Deux Coteaux, is regrettably what the French call *garni*, meaning it offers no meals but breakfast. Yet there are compensations. Situated at the end of a quiet street, where the town's old bridge is today restricted to foot traffic, the Deux Coteaux overlooks the river and a deserted towpath. Although today the Rhône is dammed for power and navigation on an average of every fifteen miles from Lyon to the sea, in days gone by these towpaths were an integral part of this important route of waterborne commerce, then as hazardous as the Moselle and parts of the Rhine.

Below Tain one begins to sense the pervading atmosphere of Provence. Walled towns appear on far-distant hills; the steep bluffs by the river, sculptured by the elements, resemble vast, manmade fortresses. Buzzards circle the sky, and the plane trees arch over the roads, making cool, dark tunnels. Every town has its square with a game of *boules* in progress. The only wine to be found along this long expanse of the river is Saint-Péray, a sparkling white whose proponents claim it was invented before Champagne. Across from Saint-Péray is the bustling town of Valence, with its famous Restaurant Pic. The Pic, like the Pyramide at Vienne, is a place only for those with large appetites and ample bank accounts. You may taste Saint-Péray here, at its best, and the wine cellar affords some of the best of the Rhône, especially from Hermitage and Châteauneuf-du-Pape. The Pic is yet another one-time-only. It must be visited to be believed; and its memory will linger. For those not yet recovered from the lavish gluttony of Vienne, we advise skipping the Pic and substituting the Hôtel La Cardinale at Baix, some twenty miles down the river on the right bank. Located on an isolated quay, in a building once a cardinal's palace, the Cardinale is quiet, relatively inexpensive, and thoroughly satisfactory.

Sometimes even tourist traps have their special charms. One such is Montélimar, a bit farther yet to the south, the nougat capital of France. For the promotion of its principal product, France's popular candy made from honey, Montélimar has few peers. Nearly everything ludicrously carries the name of Nougat. There is the Café Nougat, the Relais Nougat, a Bar Nougat, a Rôtisserie, and dozens of others. Peculiarly, throughout the entire surrounding countryside, one rarely sees a beehive, or even a bee. Montélimar's ancient hostelry, the Relais de l'Empereur, is worth a visit. There is a secluded, shaded courtyard, a dovecote, a fine kitchen, and a notable cellar. Napoleon once slept here on his way to Elba, along with many another famous man in succeeding years. But l'Empereur has also kept up with the times: not so many years ago the hotel added what it proudly calls an "American Bar."

Many guidebooks warn against a night's stay at Orange, to our mind the most charming of the famed trio of Roman relics in southern France (the other two being Arles and Nîmes). Except for the magnificent city of Aix-en-Provence, there is probably no more fascinating town in all Provence, especially after nightfall. You may well experience a near nervous break-down navigating your car through its tiny squares and incredibly narrow, crowded streets, but once you have found a parking place and a room, Orange of an evening will have been well worth the strain. Few Roman edifices still standing are more impressive than the masterfully proportioned amphitheater, or the triumphal arch built in the first century B.C. Hannibal made Orange his headquarters, while putting his elephants through their paces before their Alpine climb. Many centuries later the city became, for a brief time, part of colonial Holland.

Orange has a very creditable restaurant, and a tolerable hotel. At the Restaurant Provençal, Provençal cooking—subtle in its use of garlic and olive oil—excels. Share it with a bottle of gentle *rosé* from Lirac (a Château de Segriès, if the house has it) or a white Gigondas as chosen by the management, and you will not leave the table unhappy. And since the citizens of Orange—unlike those of most small French cities—never seem to go to bed, we warrant you won't either. The hotel is the Hôtel Arène, so unpretentious that it is difficult to give credibility to the large photograph in the foyer, autographed by none other than Queen Juliana of the Netherlands, a guest during a recent anniversary of the city. The kitchen of the Arène has an undeserved star in the *Michelin*, but there is a good wine list. The hotel's most unusual offering is a marc de Châteauneuf-du-Pape. Tasting like Armagnac, with an aroma of freshly cooked prunes, this particular *eau-de-vie* is truthfully an experience.

A few miles south of Orange one finds oneself in the open countryside of Châteauneuf-du-Pape, whose modern history traces back to the schism of the papacy in the fourteenth century, when a dissident faction of the Church's hierarchy left Rome for Avignon. The great vineyards of Châteauneuf-du-Pape lie atop a gently sloping hill some distance from the Rhône, near the village that the popes centuries ago selected for their summer retreat. Perhaps the most arresting phenomena of this best-known wine region of the Rhône are the stones—stones that are often the size of melons and that so completely cover the surface of the earth that it is difficult to ascertain whether there is any soil at all. As with the slate of the Moselle, these stones hold and reflect the sun's heat; as a result, in the comparatively temperate climate of the Rhône, the grapes become so ripe and full that their sugar content is capable of attaining nature's alcoholic maximum of 18 percent for fermented grape juice. Many wines from Châteauneuf-du-Pape's great vineyards must be blended with wines from lesser vineyards to reduce the alcoholic content, in order to conform to import laws of countries such as the United States, whose legal alcoholic limit for a table wine is 14 percent.

The traditionally great wines of Châteauneuf-du-Pape are red, although a certain number of whites—of far lesser character and quality—are also made. The reds, requiring long maturity, are soft and hearty with great body and a marked purple hue. In contrast to the Côte d'Or or the Beaujolais, where a single grape is specified, the formula for Châteauneuf-du-Pape calls for a multitude. In days gone by no less than thirteen different varieties of grapes entered the blend, a formula no doubt invented by the Church. Happily, certain small estates continue to adhere to this receipt, even though the average Châteauneuf-du-Pape of today is made with only three or four of the original thirteen. Predominant among these is the Grenache, the high-producing, easily grown vine responsible for so many other Rhône wines; others include the Syrah of Hermitage, the Cinsault, and the Mourvèdre. Without doubt today's wines are ready to drink sooner—they also suffer in quality. Fortunately it is still possible to find ones made in the traditional manner. In addition to knowing the names of the best estates—Château Fortia, Domaine de la Nerthe, and Domaine de la Solitude are among the best—there is yet another almost infallible guide: the presence of the coat of arms of Châteauneuf-du-Pape, symbolically representing a pope's miter above two crossed keys. This symbol, blown into the bottle, is allowed only to vineyards following the highest tradition. Châteauneuf-du-Pape was the first important vineyard area of France to promulgate strict local laws governing the quality of its wines. Again, one should be warned that bottle age is vital—eight to ten years is a good minimum. And watch out for the usual tricks of the Rhône: *grand* or *premier cru*. There are none such authorized for the Rhône.

All that remains today of the once fabulous summer palace of the popes is a stark lacework of ruins among the stone-laden vineyards, its profile silhouetted against the sky from many miles distant. Facing each other across the fountain in the village, where the *vignerons* congregate on slack days, are Châteauneuf-du-Pape's two hotels, the Mule du Pape and the Mère Germaine. Not too long ago the cellar of the Mule du Pape was acknowledged to be the finest on the Rhône, and a meal in its roomy second-floor restaurant confirmed the chef's star in the *Michelin*. But both kitchen and cellar today leave something to be desired— perhaps the result of the inn's acquisition by a local wine merchant, albeit a good one. For those who would be content to wash down slightly less elegant fare, with a wider and more democratic choice of wines, we must conscientiously recommend the Mère Germaine across the square, with its airy dining room affording a lovely view of the valley.

With the exception of the two *rosé* wine communes of Tavel and Lirac, about ten miles west of Avignon, the vast vineyard lands between Châteauneuf-du-Pape and the Mediterranean are devoted to common wines. Almost without exception they are nameless in origin (and deservedly so), useful only for blending. At Avignon, with its imposing papal palace whose gardens so dramatically overhang the river, the great growths of the Rhône that commenced in the arid Valais so many miles upstream come to an end—not in a trickle, but in a vinous outpouring of mediocrity. Our particular journey now takes us elsewhere.

I V

The Loire

I : *The Upper Loire*

Not only is the Loire the longest river of France; it is also its largest watershed. Flowing northerly in a great curve from the highlands of the Massif Central to Nantes on the Atlantic, the Loire is almost nine hundred miles long. And when combined with those of its principal tributaries—the Allier, the Cher, the Vienne, and the Loir—the total area of the watershed is considerably more than doubled. Few great wines grow in this watershed, but there is no section of France in which there is to be found such vinous versatility and variation. From the volcanic hill of Corent, overlooking the upper valley of the Allier, to the region above Nantes responsible for Muscadet, there is an almost unbelievable range of types and colors, sweetness and dryness in the wines.

One dramatic way to reach the headwaters of the Loire is from the south, by climbing the Alplike valley of the Ardèche, a tributary of the Rhône. The lower section of the Ardèche, incidentally, is known for its minor wines, called Côtes de Vivarais, pleasant little reds and *rosés* classified as V.D.Q.S. Exemplary ones, locally named *vins d'origine* on the wine list, await the traveler at the sleepy town of Thueyts, whose Hôtel du Nord provides some dishes, such as a *pâté de grives* (thrushes) and *trite au Champagne*, you will be a long time forgetting. Why such a gastronomic oasis as the Hôtel du Nord turns up in such an out-of-the-way village, on so comparatively untraveled a route, is something that one eventually learns not to try to explain about France.

Shortly after Thueyts one turns at the top of the pass through the Forêt de Mazan, a mountaintop cathedral of giant spruces, seemingly undisturbed by the hand of man. Soon one emerges on a high plateau carved every which way by deep, wooded gorges —boiling mountain streams that, after much turning and twisting and indecision, eventually find their way to join as one. One of these streams is posited on the map as the Loire, but whatever geographer saw fit to pick it as such could only have tossed a coin. High above this maze of gorges is a wild and isolated countryside, where the roads lead through barnyards, cattle roam the unfenced hills, and peasants stop to gape at strangers.

For almost a hundred miles the Loire plays a hard-to-get game. For the most part it flows through canyons accessible only to goats and cows. There is a brief stretch near the town of Le Puy where one may follow its meanderings—only to be frustrated again when the river disappears into the Gorge de la Loire, solely penetrated by the railroad. To find the first vineyards of the watershed, it is expedient to jump over, at this point, to the valley of the Allier, the Loire's most important tributary. Just north of the city of Clermont-Ferrand, headquarters of the Michelin rubber empire, one sights the village of Corent, perched high on the slope of a volcanic cone which rises dramatically out of the plain. This is the last spot where one would logically expect to find vineyards, yet the *rosés* produced on the Corent slope—dry and delicately tinged—are among the unsung *vins du pays* of France. Classified as a Vin d'Auvergne, the production is infinitesimal, and nearly all of it is cornered and bottled by the

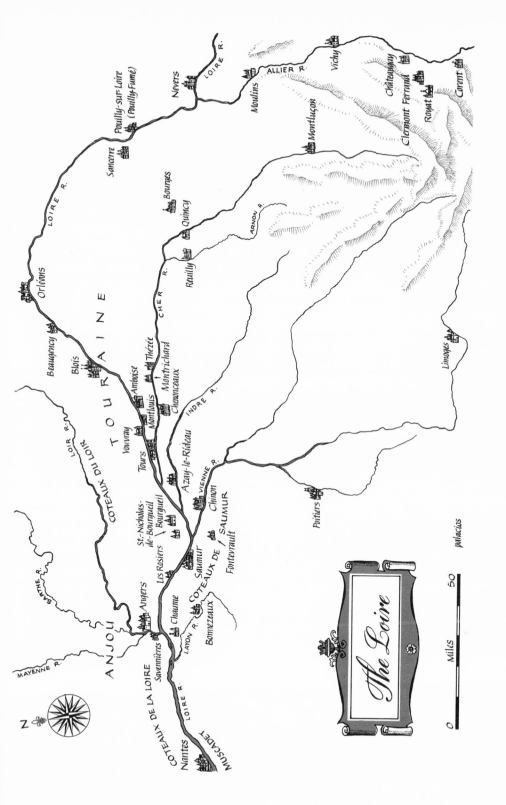

The Loire

Miles
0   50   palaces

N

MAYENNE R.
SARTHE R.
ANJOU
Nantes
MUSCADET
LOIRE R.
Savennières
COTEAUX DE LA LOIRE
Angers
Chaume
LAYON R.
COTEAUX DU LAYON
Bonnezeaux
Les Rosiers
COTEAUX DE SAUMUR
Saumur
Fontevrault
St.-Nicholas-de-Bourgueil
Bourgueil
COTEAUX DU LOIR
LOIR R.
TOURAINE
Tours
Vouvray
Montlouis
Amboise
Chinon
VIENNE R.
Azay-le-Rideau
INDRE R.
Chenonceaux
Montrichard
Thézée
CHER R.
Rueilly
Quincy
Bourges
ARNON R.
Poitiers
Limoges
Beaugency
Blois
Orléans
LOIRE R.
Sancerre
Pouilly-sur-Loire
(Pouilly-Fumé)
Nevers
LOIRE R.
Moulins
ALLIER R.
Montluçon
Vichy
Châteaugay
Clermont Ferrand
Royat
Corent

firm of Rougyron, *négociants* whose seat is yet another wine town, Château Gay, beyond Clermont-Ferrand. Corent also makes a nondescript red and an undistinguished white. One should climb the twisting road above the village and see the fertile coal-black crater at the summit; but about the only way to find a *rosé* de Corent is to make a courageous plunge into the maelstrom of Clermont-Ferrand.

It is beautiful irony that the city of Clermont-Ferrand, the source of the classic *Guide Michelin*, contains not a single restaurant with a coveted *Michelin* star. Equally ironic is the fact that hidden under the lowest of all categories—a simple fork and spoon—is one of the most superb little restaurants in all France, the Auberge de l'Écu de France in the suburb of Royat. One is almost led to suspect that Bibendum's experts save the Auberge de l'Écu de France for their very own. Its owner-chef is nothing short of a master. From the Mediterranean, he can produce a perfect *loup grillé au feneuil* burned off with cognac. Snails, without their shells, are prepared with white wine in an inimitable fashion. The *filet de boeuf Périgordine*, its sauce loaded with truffles and mushrooms, is sheer delight. His cellar contains *rosé* de Corent, of course, and many another rarely found wine. Among others are the wines of Saint-Pourçain, known colloquially as the wines of Vichy, also part of the Loire watershed. Both Saint-Pourçain red and white are fairly coarse stuff, but Saint-Pourçain *rosé* has a rare charm and delicacy, with an unusual bouquet reminding one of freshly peeled apples. One should also try the management's recommended Château Gay: the red and *rosé* are amazingly soft, with a first taste of fresh cherries. The Auberge is no "one-time" place! Were we an editor of the Michelin, we would lunch there daily.

After Clermont-Ferrand one should cross again to the Loire, to its first fountainheads of traditional wines, Pouilly-Fumé and Sancerre. At Nevers the river, which hitherto has been so often lost in dark gorges and circuitous twistings, comes to light, and settles down to the personality that is to characterize it all the way to the Atlantic. It flows smoothly along a gravelly bottom, dotted with small islands and treed dunes, banked by soft willows and poplar groves. Nevers has an impressive ducal palace, and two good hotels: the traditional Hôtel de France, nowadays a somewhat commercialized hostelry at the center of town, and the Auberge de Porte de Cloux, more quietly situated with a view of the city's old ramparts. Although neither is truly outstanding, Nevers is nonetheless a better choice for the night than either Pouilly or Sancerre. The cellar of the Hôtel de France is in itself a good reason for dining there. Here—if they are to be found anywhere—one will drink the best vintages of the upper Loire, including white Pouilly-Fumé.

The vital consideration with the wines of Pouilly lies in the appellations: Pouilly-Fumé or Blanc Fumé de Pouilly on the one hand, and the simple, geographical appellation Pouilly-sur-Loire on the other. The former should mean a wine that is the product of the Bordeaux white Sauvignon grape reputedly brought to the Loire by the Church many centuries ago. Wine with the appellation of Pouilly-sur-Loire, always distinctly inferior, is made from the Chasselas grape, the one we have already met in the Valais and around the shores of Lake Geneva. The Chasselas is an easy-to-raise table grape, not a wine grape. If it may be said to excel at all, it is in Switzerland, definitely not on the Loire. Regrettably, about two-thirds of Pouilly's vineyards are planted to the Chasselas, with the inevitable admixture by unethical *négociants*, labeling them as Pouilly-Fumé. Abroad, too, there are not a few importers obviously hoping that wine labeled Pouilly-sur-Loire will be mistaken for the real thing.

The name Pouilly-Fumé is attributable to the "noble rot" or *Botrytis cinerea*, which in this section of the Loire produces a blue-gray smoke when the grapes are picked at harvesttime, hence the term *fumé*. Despite the fact that the Pouilly-Fumé has been recorded as having been Marie Antoinette's favorite wine, until about twenty years ago it was still little more than a *vin du pays* treasured by the *cognoscenti.* Suddenly the wine became the rage of Paris, thence London, thence New York; today few, if any, minor French wines are so much in demand around the world, with resulting catastrophe. Much wine formerly made and bottled under such vineyard names as Coteaux de Loges, Loge aux Moines, and Côte Rôtie—vineyards that over the years made the traditional best—are now simply bottled as Pouilly-Fumé. Bottles from only one famous vineyard are still seen everywhere: Château de Nozet. Unfortunately, it is not the wine it once was, even though in occasional years one receives a certain nostalgic promise from one of its bottles. With the exception of the well-kept vineyards of the Château de Nozet most of the vineyards of Pouilly, lying downstream from the village, give the impression of neglect. There is little more depressing than vines whose owners appear to be simply milking them for what the name is worth.

The otherwise dour village of Pouilly, a one-street affair punctuating Route Nationale No. 7 from Paris to the south, has one highlight: the Hôtel-Restaurant L'Espérance. It affords a pleasant summer terrace overlooking its own small vineyards, with the river beyond; the wine of the *propriété* is, of course, featured on the list of the house. Once again one is tempted to raise the question, "Where are the Pouilly-Fumés of yesteryear?" But fortunately at L'Espérance you may at least feast yourself. One indispensable specialty, which we have rarely, if ever, seen better executed, are *croquettes Jurassienne,* deep-fried cheese sticks put together basically from a classic Mornay sauce with an extra charge of cheese and nutmeg, thickened with egg yolks. The perennial *brochet au beurre blanc,* the classic pike of the Loire poached and served with a sauce of whipped butter, shallots, and either wine or vinegar, or both, is delicious. Yet another dish, something of a surprise to find on the Loire, is *coquilles Saint-Jacques "Marchand de Vin,"* sautéed scallops incongruously (but harmoniously) accompanied by a rich red-wine sauce. If you happen to spend the night at L'Espérance, be sure of a room that does not give on arterial route No. 7.

About fifteen miles downstream, and several miles back from the river on the left bank, is the medieval town of Sancerre, high on its hill above the Loire. Here are wines, made of the Sauvignon, equal to what Pouilly-Fumés once were. Sancerrois soils are chalkier and better-drained than those of Pouilly, and the ensuing wine is drier and zestier. In poor years, one must admit it can be entirely too acid. Happily for Sancerre, the Chasselas grape is not allowed under the *Appellation* laws, hence the district is free of the practice of surreptitious blending. A very limited quantity of Sancerre *rosé* is also made, an unusually dry wine produced from the Pinot noir.

The best towns of the Sancerrois are Bué, Chavignol, and Sancerre itself; the best traditional vineyard is that of the Château de Sancerre. The vineyards climb the conical hill on all sides, the finest being on the south slope. The Chavignol vineyards are to be found up a small valley some miles to the west—well-groomed vines lined neatly along the rolling, chalky hills. Although less astringently dry than many others of the Sancerrois, Chavignols seem never quite to compare in purity or finesse: they have a curious flavor—a taste of raw grapiness—foreign to French wines as a whole.

Two other minor satellites, belonging to the same cluster as Pouilly-Fumé and the Sancerrois, are the vineyards of Quincy and Reuilly, off to the west in the valley of the Cher. Small and relatively unimportant areas, their wines bear a close resemblance to their two more celebrated sisters. They, too, are made from the Sauvignon, or Blanc Fumé grape; and both (especially Reuilly) are even drier than the wines of the Sancerrois. One rarely finds either more distant than Paris.

I I : *The Middle Loire*

After passing Sancerre, the Loire sweeps gently eastward, gathering momentum before rounding the great curve that leads past Orléans and Blois. Few grapes—and certainly no great wines

—grow along its banks until it has reached its confluence with the Cher many miles to the southeast in Touraine. Yet if one is as much traveler as wine enthusiast, it would be foolish to bypass the fascinating city of Orléans. Its monumental Gothic cathedral with its three unique rose windows, the handsome arcaded streets, and all the memories of Jeanne d'Arc render Orléans a must. Nor should you miss the mounted statue of the Maid in the principal square, a present from Nouvelle Orléans, Louisiana.

The city's most desirable hotel is the Arcades on the Quai Cypierre. The Arcades lacks a restaurant for anything but breakfast, but that is small matter. A few blocks up the quai on a narrow side street, you will find the Auberge Saint-Jacques. Two standard dishes at the Saint-Jacques are of irrefutable quality: first, the classic *brochet au beurre blanc* of the region; the second, *caneton a l'orange (bigarade)*, prepared with a skill rarely duplicated. The wine list, besides being thoroughly comprehensive, contains more than just a few unusual Loire wines, such as the management's own selection of the luscious Bonnezeaux from Anjou, virtually impossible to find in Angers itself. One's only criticism, in fact, might be the absence of the two traditional red *vins d'Orléans*: Saint-Jean-de-Braye and Beaugency, both strong, coarse wines made from the Cabernet franc of Bordeaux (here called the Breton). Though both live more in history than the present, and there is no reason to believe that either was made better several centuries ago, their potency has been forever memorialized by the words of a courtier during a visit to Orléans by Charles I of England, who wrote home that "the wines of this place [Orléans] are so strong that we are sworn not to let His Majesty drink them."

Descending the river from Orléans (passing Beaugency on the right bank) one begins to see why the Loire watershed is known as the most versatile of France. Its banks for many miles back are covered with vines; yet only about one-third of all the wines are entitled to an official appellation. The balance is simply raised for local consumption, in most cases reaching only the peasant's own cellar. Even the French government has admitted failure in estimating the viticultural production of the middle and lower Loire.

Many of the grapes in this part of the Loire are not officially authorized, though most are worth noting, since their names, or alternate names, are often seen on bottles that turn out to be surprisingly good, however quasi-official the label may be. In Touraine alone there are at least a dozen. The most famous is, of course, the Chenin blanc, the official and traditional source of Vouvray, and the great grape of Anjou. The Chenin blanc goes by several names. In Touraine it is called the Pineau de la Loire; on the Cher to the south it is the Gros-Pinot. Another grape coming into prominence is the white Sauvignon, probably a closer relation to its Bordeaux counterpart than the Blanc Fumé of Pouilly and Sancerre. On the Cher it is known as the Surin, and in the hands of one or two producers it makes a superbly fragrant wine. One may see either name on labels. Yet another white, of comparatively inferior quality, is known as the Menu-Pineau, from faraway Arbois near the Swiss border.

Among the red grapes, also used for *rosé* wines, are Bordeaux's Cabernet sauvignon and Cabernet franc, the latter known in Touraine, as in Orléans, as the Breton, after an abbot who planted a vineyard on the Loire for Cardinal Richelieu. The Breton is also called the Veron, the Bouchy, or the Bouchet, according to locality. Other successful red grapes are the Gamay from Beaujolais, the Malbec from Bordeaux (here called the Cot), and the Pineau d'Aunis, a plant indigenous to the Loire and used only for *rosés*. A complete list of these grapes would be futile. For the wines of this section of the Loire, suffice it to say that the most important are white Vouvray and Montlouis; and among the reds, Bourgueil, Saint-Nicolas-de-Bourgueil, and Chinon.

The Cher parallels the Loire, joining it below Tours. In our hop-and-skip travels across the Loire watershed, we recommend you cross over to this ambling little river, in itself a miniature Loire, with its gravelly bottom and tiny islands overgrown with willows. In the vicinity of Thézée, one will commence to notice the special geology peculiar to Touraine and upper Anjou, so important to the making of the local wines. The basic pattern, which continues intermittently for miles downstream, consists of a narrow alluvial strip along the water's edge, with overhanging chalky cliffs. Above the cliffs, stretching for many miles back from the river, are the gently rolling lands upon which the vines thrive. In prehistoric times these cliffs of the Cher and the Loire were used as cave dwellings; today they have become dwellings for the vintners, backed by vast, cool storage cellars carved out of the chalky rock. One passes many a curious abode built into the cliffs, the front rooms housing the family and the rear quarters devoted to the aging of wines.

Jules Romain has called the Loire "the boulevard of kings and a gallery of masterpieces." One does not wish to belittle the glories of Blois or Chambord or Amboise—yet the so-called great châteaux of the Loire are by no means the only ones of attraction. Along with the kings of France, members of the lesser nobility also built their country places in Touraine, sometimes in better taste than their rulers'. Many of the more charming of these are to be found along the banks of the little Cher, at Selles, Saint-Aignan, Thézée, Montrichard, and Chissay. Since the last three towns are also wine centers, one may well wish to linger and sample vintages not to be had elsewhere. We recommend in particular the simple Hôtel Bellevue at Montrichard, on the banks of the Cher where it flows beneath an ancient Roman bridge. Persuade the management to prepare a *canard sauvage bonne femme*, wild duck with a sauce of its own *fumé*, blended with onions, tomatoes, and carrots, or the traditional pork dish of Touraine, *porc aux pruneaux*, slices of pork with prunes in thickened, cooked-down cream. For a local wine we are especially partial to a Sauvignon of Thézée, if possible from Thézée's best producer, Ricard et Baron. If pressed, the management of the Bellevue may also be able to produce a bottle of marc de Touraine, a fragrant *eau-de-vie* made from the Chenin blanc, or the Pineau de la Loire, however you wish to call it.

A few miles further downstream is the Cher's most celebrated château, Chenonceaux, among the most exquisite in all France. Approached through beautifully kept gardens, this lovely building romantically straddles the river. Its most romantic period in history was associated with Diane de Poitiers, the mistress of two successive kings of France, François I and Henry II, his son. In days gone by Chenonceaux was also the source of a well-known *vin du pays*, the production of which has recently been revived by its present benefactor. It may be bought by the bottle at the gate of the château, largely as a curiosity, for it offers little challenge to its neighbors.

In the tiny village nearby one will also find two good inns, the Ottoni and the Bon Laboureur. Though both have merit, we tend to favor the second, with its shaded courtyard and comfortable cottages in the garden. One will be happy here, even though the cuisine is not above average, nor the wine list remarkable. But one may at least have a good bottle of Vouvray, the wine of Touraine.

The wines of the Vouvray cluster—one should include not only Vouvray itself, but likewise Rochecorbon and Montlouis on the left bank—begin just above Tours on the Loire itself, only a stone's throw from the Cher. Vouvrays are probably the least predictable and most variable wines of the Loire. Depending in large part on the vintage year, they may be dry, sometimes to the point of unpleasant acidity; or semisweet (*moelleux*); or sweet (*liquoreux*) almost to the same degree as a Sauternes or a Beerenauslese. Additionally they may be made as a still wine; or a natural sparkling, when they are called *pétillant*; or as *mousseux*, with a sparkle comparable to Champagne. For our own personal taste, it is in the second (and rarest) form that a Vouvray excels.

As a still wine, Vouvray is usually released within two or three years, if dry; if *moelleux* or *liquoreux* and of a good year, it will be kept far longer in one of the deep caves along the river—for Vouvray is one of the longest-lived white wines of all Europe. Vouvray *mousseux* is subjected to a second fermentation in the bottle, and is traditionally considered the best French sparkling wine next to Champagne. Like the rest, it may be either dry or semisweet, this latter being the type most exported. The *pétillant* also goes through a second fermentation in the bottle, but a lesser one, producing almost imperceptible bubbles and a subtle bite. Perhaps the most reliable producer of Vouvray is the firm of Monmousseau, but there are other more widely known ones, such as the Château de Montcontour and Ackermann-Laurence.

The conventional stopping place for a superb meal and a bottle of Vouvray is the Hôtel Choiseul at Amboise, a sleepy town a few miles up the Loire, whose partly destroyed château was built by Charles VIII. His successor, François I, persuaded no less a personage than Leonardo da Vinci to move to Amboise and assist with his own additions to the complex. Leonardo fell in love with Amboise and lived in a nearby house until his death. At the Choiseul on the quiet Quai Violettes (heavy traffic travels the other side of the river) one may enjoy an excellent meal from a kitchen that specializes in fish from the Loire, and a cellar stocked with Vouvray and red Bourgueil. But perhaps by this time you may have experienced your fill of the ordinary run of French inns and wish for something different. In this case we can strongly recommend a night at the Hôtel Château de Pray a few miles upstream, situated in its own park. The proprietors of this century-old establishment have succeeded admirably in preserving charm and antiquity, along with inconspicuously providing modern conveniences. The *cuisine* is not what could be called *grande*, but that may be a refreshing change in itself. A stay at either of Amboise's hostelries is preferable to the ordeal of plunging into the busy city of Tours, which since World War II is no longer either a gastronomic mecca or a place of much charm.

Down the river from Tours one passes through the principal red-wine districts of the Loire—the source of wines that, once again, live more in history than in the present, even though the production of some of them is considerable. Consumption is almost entirely local, and few bottles are saved long enough to do the wines real justice. Even in Paris one rarely sees a red Bour-

gueil or a Saint-Nicolas-de-Bourgueil, much less a red from
Chinon or a Champigny, the last perhaps the most highly regarded today. All four wines are made from the Cabernet franc,
the "second" red grape of the Gironde, and the source (when
used alone) of very hard wines indeed. On the Loire the Cabernet
franc produces vintages that, especially with the Bourgueils,
possess exceptionally exotic fragrances, such as of raspberries
and violets. But when the glass is brought to the lips, one soon
realizes that such wine is only worth drinking after at least ten
years of aging. A drinkable bottle, of sufficient age, is nearly
impossible to find even at the best of the few good local inns.

It was at Chinon on yet another tributary of the Loire, the
Vienne, that Jeanne d'Arc first met the dauphin, after waiting in
prayer for two days in the town below, before being allowed in
the castle above. The castle, once the seat of Cardinal Richelieu,
is now a ruin, and the town itself offers small attraction. But a
few miles southwest, up a back road, stands the simple farmhouse
of Rabelais, overlooking the valley where this celebrated stumble-
bum tended his vineyard, facetiously named La Devinière.
Rabelais had a proclivity for the stout red wines of Chinon and
also for its taverns. Chinon still abounds with tales of how the
defrocked reprobate, riding back to La Devinière after his favorite
tavern had closed, habitually awakened the honest folk of the
countryside by shouting his irreverent songs, punctuated by
belches.

Like all reds of the Loire, a good many years of age in bottle
is required for a Chinon red before mellowness sets in. Chinon
also has a rare and not overly distinguished white made from the
Chenin blanc, and a *rosé* with a strong and metallic taste that is
no competition for the soft *rosés* of Anjou further downstream.

III : *Anjou*

The name of Anjou has been familiar to wine-lovers abroad
longer than any other wine of France, tracing back to the days

when the Plantagenet kings of England were also dukes of Anjou, and Anjou wines traveled more to England than to Paris. Later, when Bordeaux wines—again because of Plantagenet rule— became the favorites in England, the Anjou trade turned to the Dutch, who sent ships far up the Loire to obtain its priceless gems. It is a shame that today so few of these excellent wines reach foreign shores.

Anjou technically begins at Candes-Saint-Martin just below the confluence of the Vienne and the Loire. Here the Loire, a river that has never appeared to be in much of a hurry anyway, noticeably slackens its pace, and even though the geological pattern of chalky cliffs rising above the river's banks continues, the valley now takes on a feeling of greater space and less intimacy. The principal wine sections of Anjou are known as *coteaux*: the Coteaux de Saumur, extending from Touraine to the city of Saumur; the Coteaux de l'Aubance (perhaps the least distinguished of all), and the Coteaux de la Loire, below Angers, the source of most of the traditionally finest white wines. To these must be added the Coteaux du Layon, lying along the banks of the river Layon, which wends its way to meet the Loire from the south.

Entering Anjou through the Coteaux de Saumur, it is worth one's while to detour a few miles inland to the village of Fontevrault on a hillside commanding a vast expanse of vineyards. In the eleventh-century abbey of this little town is one of the few remaining kitchens of France tracing back to the Middle Ages, with cooking bins large enough to roast a whole ox on a spit, and room for dozens of cooks to prepare banquets for hundreds. Here also is the chosen resting place for four Plantagenets: Henry II, Eleanor of Aquitaine, Richard Coeur de Lion, and Isabelle of Angoulême. A few decades ago the British suggested that the tombs be moved to a more apppopriate and frequented resting place, Westminster Abbey. But the French turned down the proposal. Before leaving Fontevrault one should have a meal at the town's tiny restaurant, L'Abbaye, an unassuming little café whose outside is hung with Pils Beer signs and other advertisements, indistinguishable, even to an experienced eye, from a good many thousands of corner *bistros* of France. Since it is enormously popular in season, it is well to arrive at the Abbaye either early or late. The cuisine is well above average; the cellar affords typical wines of lower Touraine and the Coteaux de Saumur.

Just below Fontevrault, again on the river's bank, one passes rapidly through the principal wine towns of Parnay, Champigny, Souzay, and Dampierre. These, along with Chacé and Brézé, constitute the cream of the Coteaux de Saumur. Best known of all is the commune of Parnay, the seat of the Château de Parnay, owned for many years by a certain M. Cristal, a pioneer of French viticulture in the last century, who developed many grapes and blends of grapes foreign to the Loire—with resultant remarkable wines. Unfortunately the advent of the *Appellations Contrôlées* brought a commercial halt to these constructive activities, and the wines of the Château de Parnay are now being made from the Chenin blanc and the Cabernet franc. Even so, in Clos Cristal, the estate's proudest label, one will find a white wine with a unique dry steeliness, provided one happens on the dry version. Its red opposite number of the coteaux is Champigny. Considered by experts to be the finest red on the Loire, Champigny has a persuasive fruitiness and a velvet quality that is most unusual for a wine made from the harsh Cabernet franc. Among other virtues, Champigny does not require quite as many years as other Saumur reds to become truly enjoyable.

Many wines of the coteaux, especially in poor years, are made into sparkling Saumur (*mousseux*), sometimes unflatteringly referred to as "poor man's Vouvray." Vouvray derives entirely from the white Chenin blanc; but Saumur *mousseux* often contains a certain amount of the juice of the Cabernet franc, gingerly pressed so as not to extract any of the red color. The result is a basically coarse wine, the faults of which producers seek to overcome by bottling it with a considerable *dosage* of sugar, comparable to a sweet Champagne. We do not frown entirely on Saumur *mousseux*; it may suit some tastes better than Vouvray, or even Champagne itself.

Saumur was once a leading wine port for British and Dutch ships carrying the wines of the Loire. Today its primary bid to fame is what remains of a famous French cavalry school and a celebrated equestrian museum. The principal hotel, the Budan, aside from its situation on the lovely broad expanse of river, leaves a good deal to be desired: an old-fashioned, nowadays commercial establishment, whose kitchen does little justice to the written menu. We amend this criticism, however, by adding that rarely will one find a better version of the famous *beurre blanc d'Anjou*, the standard accompaniment for local shad, pike, or salmon. Here is the Budan's formula: to about four tablespoons of combined dry white wine and vinegar, very slightly reduced, one beats (literally, aerates) little by little over a very slow fire the equivalent of a quarter pound of butter. At the end one adds some very finely minced shallots and some pepper. The result is as fresh and piquant a sauce as can possibly be imagined.

Certainly preferable to the Budan is a remodeled manor house some eight miles down the Loire, the Hôtel Prieuré Chênehutte —or in yet another echelon, the Jeanne de Laval, across the river at Les Rosiers. Here is a truly well run inn with a superb chef and an exemplary wine list, containing nearly all the best of Anjou. The monumental collection includes a Château de Parnay and a Brézé, as well as three traditional "greats" of the lower Loire: La Roche aux Moines, Quarts de Chaume, and Bonnezeaux. The last two are dessert wines, made in the Coteaux du Layon to the south: that all-but-forgotten wine district responsible for some of the most delightful sweet wines of the world.

The Layon, which joins the Loire just south of Angers, is a tiny, ambling stream flowing through a countryside of drumlin hills, quite dissimilar to the flat plains of Touraine and the Coteaux de Saumur. Along the valley's southern slopes, and in the protected pockets of its hills, are nature's hothouses for vines.

Regrettably, very few of the classic *liquoreux* are made today, though some may still be found in the commune of Bonnezeaux, at Thouarcé, and somewhat farther downstream at Chaume, whose most famous vineyard, the Quarts de Chaume, has the honor of its own *Appellation Contrôlée*. These are wines that Rabelais, who favored them next to those of his native Chinon, described as having "a fragrance that spreads itself like a peacock's tail." More delicate than a Sauternes or a Barsac, with a subtle bouquet akin to wild honey, their alcoholic content in the best years can rise to 15 percent, with enough residual sugar remaining to render the wine very sweet indeed.

In Rabelais' day, all the legendary wines of this part of Anjou were made sweet—a practice that continued until comparatively recent times. Within the past few decades, however, public demand for sweet wines has dwindled, and early in the course of this trend the Anjou producers, whose wines were not particularly well known abroad, began picking their grapes sooner, thus eliminating the excess sugar. The commercial results, unfortunately, have not been outstanding. The presence of residual sugar in the wine augments the flavor of the Chenin blanc, and the lack of it leads only to mediocrity.

No one should leave Anjou without tasting a Quarts de Chaume. The word *quart* means "quarter." At one time in its history this particular vineyard became the property of a doctor obviously too busy to supervise the vineyard himself. Dividing it into quarters, he leased each quarter to promising wine-makers, reserving the right to buy the produce of whichever part he selected in a given year. Nowadays, wine from the part generally acknowledged to produce the best is labeled Château de Bellerive. Other well-known towns of the Coteaux de Layon, now chiefly making dry wines, are Rablay, Faye, and Saint-Aubin-de-Luigné.

As one works one's way down the Loire, comfortable accommodations and gastronomic discoveries become more and more scarce. Almost the last center for creature comforts is the city of Angers, the capital of Anjou, which lies not on the Loire itself, but several miles to the north on yet another tributary, the Mayenne. A sprawling town with handsome wide boulevards, Angers is an ideal place for a night. Here, from the great castle whose bulbous towers are capped with alternate layers of black and white stone, the counts of Anjou once reigned. One of the descendants, Henry, who was king of England on the side, locked up his conspiring wife, Eleanor, in one of the towers. Several centuries later, an unrelated Henry, Henri III of France, for reasons wholly unknown commanded the massive château to be razed to the ground. Happily his death intervened and the building was saved for posterity. One of the most famous tapestry museums in France is at Angers, and it will quicken the heartbeat of gourmets and gourmands alike to learn that Curnonsky, that self-appointed prince of French gastronomy, was born here. His memory is well perpetuated by an admirable restaurant, Le Vert d'Eau, a comparative newcomer. Le Vert d'Eau, of course, specializes in dishes of the region (principally fish), but it acquits itself well in other fields. In the former category, one may wish to try one of the most recondite of all Angevin dishes, eels with prunes.

Traditionally the best hotel of Angers is the Hôtel d'Anjou, on the corner of one of the principal boulevards, with its restaurant and bedrooms facing the airy Place de Lorraine. Our own recommendation, especially after a dinner at Le Vert d'Eau, is the more simple Hôtel Croix de Guerre, up a peaceful side street.

Even more famous in history than the *liquoreux* wines of the Coteaux de Layon are those of the Coteaux de la Loire, on the right bank below Angers. The wines of the Coteaux de la Loire are drier than those of Layon, steely, and comparatively light in bouquet. In certain ways they resemble those of Pouilly-Fumé and Sancerre, except that one will readily perceive a nobility about them: even when poorly or carelessly made—as some are today—they are anything but *vins du pays*. In the annals of French viticulture, they rank just below the wines of Bordeaux and Burgundy.

To find the Coteaux de la Loire, one must leave the beaten track immediately after Angers and follow the riverbank to the village of Épiré; this village, along with Savennières and La Poissonière, constitute the three principal wine communes. Here is the beginning of the delta of the Loire. Islands and towheads increasingly torment the river's progress, forcing its flow through marshes and shallow channels. Along the shore the pattern of chalk cliffs that we have seen for so many miles upstream gives way to gentle slopes; the villages are filled with quaint country houses, their lawns spreading down to the river's edge, many of them recalling days of a greater prosperity and trade. On the plateau above, the vineyards, too, are indicative of better days. Amid massive, ancient vine stalks, one sadly notices wide gaps in the rows of vines, where those that have died have not been replaced. Yet with all its decadence, this is one of the more fascinating parts of the entire river.

Savennières' two most celebrated vineyards are La Coulée-de-Serrant and La Roche aux Moines, wines that in past days have been favorites of the kings of France, and to this day are served at the Élysée Palace. The two vineyards are adjacent and both extremely small—the Coulée-de-Serrant being less than ten acres. Convenient signs guide one down a little lane to where the monastery of La Roche aux Moines contemplates the Loire from a bluff, with La Coulée close by. Since this tiny acreage is controlled by a single owner, its wines are more reliable; those from La Roche, with a dozen or more owners, are more variable. Another nearly comparable wine is that of the Château de Savennières, whose vineyards are conscientiously maintained by the president of the local wine syndicate. In Épiré one should look for the Château d'Épiré and Chamboureau.

The last wine to be made along the banks of the Loire is Muscadet. Muscadet, in a sense, belongs in the same category as the multitudinous *rosés* of the Loire. It is a dry little wine, rarely acid, with a piquant charm when young—a wine that the French themselves say "may be drunk to quench one's thirst." Popular both in France and elsewhere, one especially good reason being its modest price, Muscadet is a relative newcomer to the Loire. The best of it is made from a grape brought from Burgundy in the eighteenth century, colloquially known as the Melon, no longer seen in Burgundy itself. The Melon was apparently imported in desperation by vintners in the vicinity of Nantes to replace red grapes killed in the disastrous winter of 1709—a winter, it is said, so severe that the sea froze along the coast at the mouth of the Loire. As a wine Muscadet has not been improved by the practice of mixing it with the juices of yet another grape, the Gros Plant, a cousin of the Folle blanche, whose acid juices are used for the distillation of Cognac. Certain producers in the Nantais make a wine from the Gros Plant alone, happily so labeled. Muscadet comes from the western reaches of the Coteaux de la Loire, as well as from an area across the river in the Sèvre-et-Maine.

V

Burgundy

I : *The Côte d'Or*

"Were it not for the grape, we would starve!" It may seem like
stretching the imagination to include Burgundy in any book
having to do with wines and rivers, yet there is a key to the one-
time presence of water in this common saying of the Burgundians
themselves. Burgundies are not the wines of the Saône, the winding stream to be found some twenty miles or so off to the east—
any more than the wines of Chablis, Burgundy's northernmost
section, may be called the wines of the tiny trout stream, the
Serein. There is little doubt, however, that the finest grape land
of Burgundy was once lapped and eroded by a prehistoric sea—
creating a geological condition from which, in a sense, it never
recovered. The Jurassic soil, as the geologists term it, is a chalky
clay mixed with stones and rubble, high in iron and minerals, and
to this day lacking the usual coating of fertile topsoil. Until the
last century many of the vineyards were still filled with boulders
and rocks; only comparatively recently have they been thoroughly
cleared, to facilitate cultivation of vines. This otherwise unpro-

ductive land, most especially the narrow ribbon of it known as the Côte d'Or (the Golden Slope), lying along the eastern edge of an ugly range of hills, is nearly ideal for the wine grape.

It has never been established exactly when Burgundy's vineyards were planted. Most authorities guess that the wine grape flourished on the gentle slopes of the Côte d'Or long before the Romans arrived. There is ample evidence that the Romans themselves nurtured the industry, perhaps to a point of overindulgence, for not too many centuries afterward Rome ordered the destruction of all the vineyards in Gaul, seemingly pointing its finger directly at the Côte d'Or. In legend this was attributed to the fact that the vineyards of Gaul were competing with the vineyards of Rome. But an alternate explanation seems to make more sense: the emperor, Domitian, simply wanted more grain planted on the open land of the province, the better to feed the legions. Rome was obviously misinformed on the acreage and geology of the barren Côte d'Or. But no one heeded the order, anyway.

Over the years, Burgundy, the hot-headed little duchy that once expanded its power as far north as Holland (until it was finally absorbed into France by Louis XI) has become known as the source of several of the world's very finest wines. But it was not until comparatively recently that Burgundy—the wine— meant more in the eyes of the public than the crop taken from a small ribbon of vineyards south of Dijon, until the French Revolution the closely guarded property of the nobility and the Church. Nowadays the term *Burgundy* connotes wines from as far north as Chablis and as far south as Macon and Beaujolais. Like their aggressive ancestors, the Burgundians are born promoters, who have managed to stretch the magic of the name to every possible geographical limit.

The gate to the Côte d'Or, the heart of Burgundy, is the city of Dijon. It is here that one will probably wish to stay, although there are excellent hotels both at Beaune, halfway down the strip of famous vineyards, and at Chagny, at its end. Dijon has much

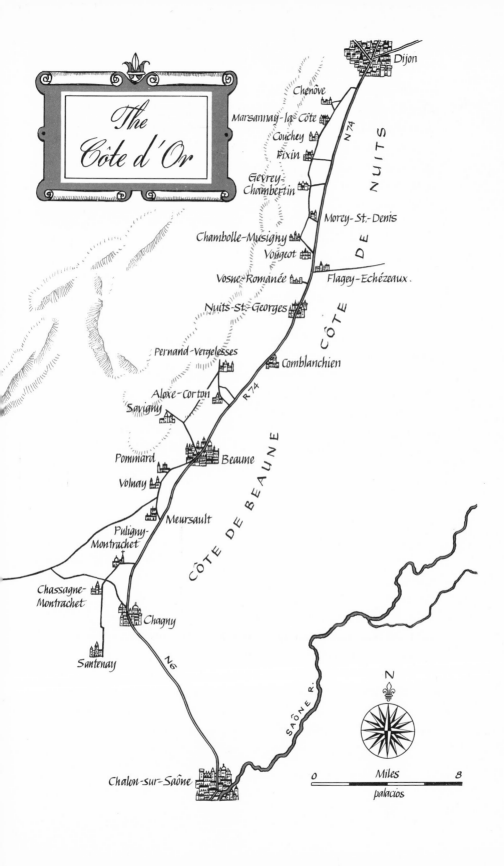

The Côte d'Or

Dijon
Chenôve
Marsannay-la-Côte
Couchey
Fixin
Gevrey-Chambertin
Morey-St.-Denis
Chambolle-Musigny
Vougeot
Vosne-Romanée
Flagey-Echézeaux
Nuits-St-Georges
Pernand-Vergelesses
Comblanchien
Aloxe-Corton
Savigny
Pommard
Beaune
Volnay
Meursault
Puligny-Montrachet
Chassagne-Montrachet
Chagny
Santenay
Chalon-sur-Saône

N 74
R 74
N 6

CÔTE DE NUITS
CÔTE DE BEAUNE
SAÔNE R.

N

Miles
0   8
palacios

to recommend it: its cathedral, its rococo parks, and the palace of the dukes of Burgundy on the half-moon Place de la Libération, whose provincial elegance is reminiscent of Nancy's Place Stanislas. The ducal palace contains a most remarkable kitchen, a vast room with fireplaces on all sides, where roasts were prepared for feasts that sometimes included several hundred guests. For the dukes, owners of the great vineyards of the Côte d'Or, were connoisseurs of food as well as wine. Not infrequently the feasts involved fifty or sixty courses, spread over a banquet that stretched out for several days.

Burgundian love of food is still reflected in the famed Foire Gastronomique held every autumn—an occasion that, if one is fortunate enough to be in Dijon at the proper time, one will not soon forget. With the whole city seemingly turned into a great festooned kitchen, one soon overlooks the promotional origin of the occasion: to prove, of all things, that Dijonnaise cooking was better than Lyonnaise! The proof, of course, is in the pudding, and Dijonnaise and Burgundian specialties are notably rewarding —even though they are principally concentrated on snails, ham, and mustard.

Burgundian snails have two important functions: to eat, and to be eaten. For centuries Burgundian snails have been encouraged to devour the grape leaves at a time when the grapes themselves need more sun. When the snails' work is done, the Burgundians catch them, boil them fiercely for hours until they may be pulled from their shells, and then stuff them back again with a delectable mixture of butter, parsley, and garlic. A snail's flesh has a subtle flavor, too subtle sometimes for many people to appreciate; but as a vehicle for hot garlic butter, it has few peers.

The Burgundians prepare their ham in endless ways. One of the simplest but best known, served as an hors d'oeuvre, is *jambon persillé*—bits of ham and parsley in aspic jelly. Yet another is *jambon braisé sous la cendre*, or *à la crème*: ham slices cooked in cream, the latter enlivened with mustard. The dish comes to your table still encased in an envelope of heavy waxed paper that has prevented it from being overcooked or charred in the oven.

Dijon's mustard is universally celebrated, and certainly the most famous of all is that produced by the Dijon firm of Grey-Poupon, sold in decorative little pots. French mustard, made with vinegar, is perishable and lasts only a short time after being exposed to the air; but few people the world over are ever inclined to dispose of one of Grey-Poupon's flowered and besnailed canisters. During the Foire Gastronomique the windows of Grey-Poupon on the Rue de la Liberté will be filled with a collection of antique mustard jars, approaching the size of small amphorae, heirlooms of this family-owned firm. Many is the tourist who has coveted these exquisite antiques for lamps, only to be told by the polite clerks that if the jars were for sale, the price would be several million francs.

Despite the Foire and the city's gastronomic tradition, Dijon is singularly lacking in great restaurants. On the Place de la Libération, opposite the ducal palace, is the restaurant Pré aux Clercs et Trois Faisans. In days not so long gone the Trois Faisans was so highly considered that Parisians on their way to Switzerland used to make a special detour to visit it, and likewise to visit the Pré aux Clercs, a separate establishment housed nearby. But a merger and a change of management to a certain extent has eclipsed these glories, even though the now-combined cellar remains one of the best in town. Today one often resorts to the restaurants of the hotels, of which there are three. By far the most pretentious is the Hôtel de la Cloche, facing the principal park. By contrast, the Chapeau Rouge, situated in the older section of the city, is hardly an equal in terms of airiness and modern comforts, but its restaurant is undoubtedly the best in Dijon, entirely deserving of its star in the *Michelin*. The cellar, too, is more representative of Burgundy's best producers. The fact that the Lions meet at the Cloche and the Rotarians at the Chapeau Rouge may or may not be significant; our recommendation, in any event, is that one sleep with the Lions and dine elsewhere. For this latter purpose we have a particular penchant for the restaurant of the tiny Hôtel du Nord, on the rue de la Liberté. For honest cuisine at reasonable prices, it should not be overlooked.

A bit of persistence with the management should serve to unearth some elegant, well-aged bottles.

The strip or ribbon of the Côte d'Or extends for some thirty miles south of Dijon and is today divided into the Côte de Nuits and the Côte de Beaune. Years ago there was also the Côte de Dijon, now a suburb of the expanding city; once there were attempts to name the southern extremity of the ribbon the Côte de Blancs, this being the main white-wine-producing area. At its broadest the ribbon is less than a mile; at its narrowest, sometimes only a few hundred yards. At one point this stratum of viticultural gold disappears entirely, near the villages of Comblanchien and Corgoloin, where a massive quarry and factory appear to mar the tranquillity of the vineyards. Below Corgoloin it pops up again, the dividing line between the Côte de Nuits and the Côte de Beaune.

Paralleling the ribbon on its eastern flank is Route Nationale No. 74, a three-lane artery frequently referred to as one of the most hazardous pieces of highway in France. As one drives southward on it, there are vast expanses of vines both to the right and left—vines that to the uninitiated and unknowing all look the same. Yet those on the right are among the most famous names in France, while the vineyards on the left—each and all—have never been heard of. We may assume that perhaps even before Roman days No. 74 was an oxcart demarcation between the good and the mediocre. The wine villages, rather unappealing little hamlets, lie off to the right. You may well wish to avoid the hazardous No. 74 and follow the back road that links the villages, nowadays promotionally labeled the Route des Vins—except that a better orientation of the various vineyards is gained by risking life and limb and sticking to No. 74.

One leaves Dijon through the suburb of Chenôve, once an important wine-making town of the old Côte de Dijon. Today, with difficulty, you may succeed in finding a few patches of vines, side by side with artichokes and turnips, in the backyards of Chenôve, but Chenôve's principal contemporary fame rests largely on the largest winepress in France, colloquially named "Big Maggie," after a fifteenth-century duchess, Marguerite, in her day an important local grower. Close by is the village of Marsannay-la-Côte, itself also fast becoming a suburb, although at present still the source of the Côte d'Or's only creditable *rosé* wines, products of the Pinot noir. Marsannay's scarcer white, usually called Chardonnay de Marsannay without a vineyard name, is of better quality, even though it ranks low on the scale of the half-dozen rare whites made on the Côte de Nuits. Few wine-lovers of the world, including many experts and even some Burgundians, are aware that two of the Côte de Nuits' finest whites are produced in small quantities in the nearby town of Fixin: Clos des Marcs d'Or Blanc and Clos de la Perrière. The former may at least be had in Dijon; the latter, unfortunately, is entirely limited to private consumption.

At Fixin, a quiet village whose only real attraction lies in its arrestingly simple manor house, we come to the finest of the three great groups or clusters of vineyards of the Côte de Nuits. The first group may loosely be called the Chambertin cluster, centered around the great vineyard of that name. For the second, the lodestone is the Clos de Vougeot, though the characteristics of its wines spread as far north as Morey-Saint-Denis and Musigny, and as far south as Vosne-Romanée. The third cluster is centered at Nuits-Saint-Georges. The comparative subtleties of the wines of these three clusters, all of which lie within a stretch of ten miles along the famous ribbon, are only to be marveled at. Bear in mind that all three use the Pinot noir grape, the traditional and prescribed red grape for Burgundy (except for Beaujolais), and that all the wines are grown on the same stretch of soil, with the same appropriate southwest exposure. They are irrefutably red Burgundies of the same type, yet they are as different from one another as a Moselle and a Rhine wine, or a Côte Rôtie and a Châteauneuf-du-Pape. The wines of the Chambertin group, long-lived and highly tannic when young, must be categorized as masculine; the fragrant ones of Musigny, Vougeot, and Vosne-Romanée are indisputably feminine. Those of Nuits-Saint-Georges and its neighbors, in the eyes of connoisseurs, anyway, are more earthy. Even at their best they seem to lack the sublimity of the others: they taste and smell more like an ordinary mortal's wine.

Within the three clusters there are, of course, even wider subtleties of comparison—too many, perhaps, to deal with here. But for a fairly realistic assessment of relative merits, one may study the list of classifications made in 1936 by the *Comité des Appellations d'Origine*, the group that undertook the unpopular and back-breaking task of dividing all the vineyards of the Côte d'Or into *Grands Crus* ("great growths") and *Premiers Crus* ("first growths"). One will observe that in the Chambertin group there are twelve *Grands Crus*; in the Musigny-Vougeot-Romanée group, nine; whereas in the Nuits-Saint-Georges there are only *Premiers Crus*. On labels the *Grands Crus* are entitled to an *Appellation Contrôlée* of their own, without the name of the commune; whereas the *Appellation Contrôlée* of a *Premier Cru* requires mention of a town name. The actual words *Premier Cru* are not required—it being implied that the vineyard name and the communal name automatically indicate the status. Or if the words *Premier Cru* appear alone, the wine has then become a blend of two or more *Premier Cru* vineyards, and identity with a particular piece of property is lost.

This system of classification may seem cumbersome and rather illogical, yet, once one understands it, it becomes a fairly accurate guide to quality on the Côte d'Or—provided one realizes, in addition, that all but a very few of the best vineyards are owned by one individual or grower. Hence, quality has two horns: it depends on the vineyard's name and the classification, as well as on the integrity and skill of the producer. The regulation that allows blends from *Premier Cru* vineyards from the same commune also has its distinct advantages. It allows for continuity of quality from year to year under the label of a good producer, something that would be impossible if the name of a certain vineyard were always required. This holds particularly true in

Chablis, the northernmost section of Burgundy, where the caprices of weather may be devastating for some vineyards, but not for others, depending not so much upon their situation in the valley of the Serein, as on chance.

Before the advent of the *Appellations Contrôlées*, local classifications on the Côte d'Or called for the best vineyards being called *Têtes de Cuvée*, followed by *Premier Cuvée* and *Deuxième Cuvée*. Sometimes the former term will be seen on a label—usually placed there by some diehard Burgundian whose *Tête de Cuvée* vineyard did not make it into the *Grand Cru* class. As with the celebrated Bordeaux classification of 1955, the 1936 Burgundy reshuffling produced many soreheads and diehards. Among the most vociferous of these over the years have been the adherents of the Clos des Lambrays, a vineyard in Morey-Saint-Denis whose *Tête de Cuvée* status was not promoted to *Grand Cru* rank along with the three other great vineyards of the commune, the Clos de la Roche, the Clos Saint-Denis, and the Clos de Tart. Hell will probably freeze before the Lambrayans cease and desist. Nor are they entirely without company.

At this point we must once again take time out to clear away the confusions surrounding Burgundian names—confusions that have beset wine-lovers for years. For the average wine-lover, entirely too many Burgundian wine or place names are hyphenated. The only truthful explanation of this situation is that it arose from the practice of exploitation. Not so many decades ago all the communes of the Côte d'Or had one name, such as Gevrey, Chambolle, Vosne, Puligny, Chassagne, and so forth. History does not record the identity of the promotional genius who thought up the idea of combining the name of a commune with that of its best vineyard. But the resulting confusion has turned out as intended, and thousands of unknowing wine-drinkers have been cleverly led into thinking, for example, that a bottle labeled Gevrey-Chambertin (the lowest appellation for any wine or blend of wines from this commune) is the real thing. Comparable are wines labeled Chambolle-Musigny (from the commune once known as Chambolle, its most famous vineyard being Musigny), Vosne-Romanée and Aloxe-Corton, as well as Puligny- and Chassagne-Montrachet. Contributing to the confusion is the comparable practice of hyphenating the name of a world-famous vineyard to a lesser neighbor. Montrachet, for example, has four; white Corton, among the *Grands Crus*, one, but with the red *Premiers Crus*, a dozen (not all listed in our appendix). Le Chambertin in turn has eight, including Chambertin-Clos de Bèze, Mazis-Chambertin, Griotte-Chambertin, Latricières-Chambertin, Ruchottes-Chambertin, and Chapelle-Chambertin. These are definitely not Gevrey-Chambertins. The only solution, unfortunately, to this diabolical system of hyphens is to commit the list to memory.

Anyone wishing to discover the best Burgundies must also memorize the names of the good producers, variously known as *négociants, propriétaires*, or *éleveurs*. At the time of the French Revolution all the vineyards of the Côte d'Or were sold at auction, piecemeal, unlike those of Bordeaux, and regrettably have never been restored to one ownership. Chambertin and its neighbor Chambertin-Clos de Bèze—which taken together represent approximately seventy acres—are a case in point. The two vineyards are owned by more than two dozen people, each with his own demarcated rows (or row) of vines. The motivation of these owners varies enormously—many sincerely attempting to produce the finest wine possible, others being interested only in the investment or prestige. Often the management and wine-making is left to incompetents or frauds. Herein lies the fallacy within the phrases often seen on the labels of Burgundies: "Estate-bottled," *"Mise en bouteilles à la propriété"* or *"Mise dans nos caves."* The terms were conceived to compete with the château-bottled nomenclature of Bordeaux; but for purely practical reasons, the implied procedure could not possibly be carried out in Burgundy. Many vineyards in France have their own adjacent cellars, but in Burgundy no one has ever set up a cellar adjacent to his particular rows of vines; hence no Burgundy wine could ever be bottled "*à la propriété*" unless one loosely interprets the terms to mean a cellar of the same ownership—somewhere in one of the villages of the Côte d'Or. More likely than not, the wine will have been fermented, aged, and bottled in Beaune or Nuits-Saint-Georges, Chagny, or Santenay.

A few hundred yards down the country road from the village of Gevrey-Chambertin, we come upon the Clos de Bèze, formerly the property of a Benedictine abbey that once controlled most of the vineyards in Gevrey. One tract they did not control was a neighboring field owned by a peasant named Bertin, on which he cultivated turnips. According to the story, a rival religious order subsidized Bertin to rip up his turnips and plant vines. The field has kept the name of Champs de Bertin—but the wine has exceeded the Clos-de-Bèze in fame. Rich, full-bodied, and notably long-lived, it has no peer among its neighbors. Chambertin was Napoleon's favorite, always on his table during peace, reputedly always in his caravan in time of war. It was the wine he took on his ill-fated campaign to Russia, and the wine that kept up his spirits while the shattered remnants of his army struggled home after the worst military defeat in France's history. In all likelihood, Chambertin was the wine that kept him company on Elba.

Passing Latricières-Chambertin on the right, the next finest (after the Clos-de-Bèze) of all the hyphenated Chambertins, the road winds into the village of Morey-Saint-Denis. Its two best vineyards, the Clos de la Roche and the Clos-Saint-Denis, are difficult to identify unless one knows exactly where to look. Both belong to the Chambertin group: virile wines, long in maturing and never as soft as those grown immediately to the south. This demarcation of type actually takes place within the village itself. Beginning with the Clos de Tart and the large vineyard of Bonnes Mares—shared by both Morey-Saint-Denis and Chambolle-Musigny—we enter the group or cluster of vineyards so often described as "bottled velvet and satin." Here are wines of unbelievable smoothness, with overtones and fragrances that recall flowers or redolent fruits. The most famous lie beyond the village of Chambolle, a typical little wine town overlooking the great Musigny and Burgundy's largest vineyard, the Clos de Vougeot.

The massive and monumental Château de Vougeot—formerly part of a Cistercian monastery—is nowadays the property of the Burgundian promotional organization, the *Confrérie des Chevaliers du Tastevin*, and a must for any passing tourist. Another must, provided one is able to gain admittance, is one of the fabulous *Chapitres* periodically staged by the organization in a remodeled cellar of the Château. With the local chevaliers presiding in colorful orange and red robes, members and their guests are treated to a four-hour banquet, washed down with a half dozen wines specially selected from the Côte d'Or. Needless to say, few of them derive from the hallowed acres of the Clos itself, whose several dozen owners deem them far too valuable for such frivolity. For centuries the wines of the Clos have been considered among the most desirable in all of France, and, in the days of the Cistercians, they were divided into three distinct classifications. Those of the vineyard's superior upper third were known as the *cuvées des papes* and reserved for church dignitaries. Wines from the middle third were known as the *cuvées des rois*; those from the lower third, that part of the vineyard which borders Route 74, belonged to the *cuvée des moines*, dispensed to the monks themselves and the common man. In the fourteenth century a certain abbot sent a number of casks of what must certainly have been wine from the *cuvée des papes* to Rome and was shortly thereafter rewarded by being made a cardinal.

To Frenchmen of today the Château de Clos de Vougeot has the status of a national monument—its wines, regardless of any relative merits, are considered fit for the gods, and French regiments passing on Route 74 are traditionally brought to a halt, to salute. Bordering the Clos on the west are superb vineyards of Échezeaux, whose wines in the hands of some producers are of almost equal excellence, though the name, which when properly pronounced sounds like a sneeze, over the years has constituted a considerable marketing deterrent outside of France.

Two of the rarest (and finest) white wines of Burgundy are made in respective corners of the Clos de Vougeot and Musigny: Clos Blanc de Vougeot, and Musigny Blanc. Easier to come by in New York or London than in their native habitat, perhaps not quite as fragrant and luscious as the wines of Meursault or of one of the hyphenated Montrachet communes to the south, they are nonetheless fine examples of the products of the noblest of all white grapes, the Chardonnay, the vine prescribed for all the best vineyard land from Chablis to Macon.

The southernmost vineyards of this famous cluster lie on the gently sloping hillside behind the village of Vosne-Romanée: six vineyards that nowadays constitute subdivisions of a tract once called Romanée. In piecing together relics found in the vicinity, archaeologists conclude that it must once have been the site of a Roman camp, but little else is known of its history until the Middle Ages, when it was the property of the Prieuré de Saint-Vivant, after which one of the vineyards, Romanée-Saint-Vivant, is named. Saint-Vivant itself occupies the comparative lowland, closest to the village, and its wines—while good—are probably the least desirable of all. As one climbs the slope, next in line is Romanée-Conti—certainly the most celebrated in the eyes of the world—with La Romanée behind, Richebourg to the right and La Tâche to the left. And down the middle, between La Tâche and the others, is a strip barely a dozen yards wide, appropriately called La Grande Rue, the source of superb wines that are somewhat inexplicably classified as *Premier Cru,* among its five *Grand Cru* sisters.

There are few wine-lovers who have not heard of Romanée-Conti, even though few have tasted its wine. Indistinguishable from its neighbors without a guide, this tiny four-acre tract came into prominence during the reign of Louis XV as the focus of a court feud heard all over France, when it became coveted by both the king's mistress, Madame de Pompadour, and his closest advisor and cousin, the Prince de Conti—sworn enemies and rivals for the royal ear. By craft and chicanery the prince finally gained ownership, immortalizing himself by attaching his name to the vineyard. But in a broader sense la Pompadour won in the end. She out-wiled the prince in the court and forced his retirement to a life of letters and mysticism.

Today Romanée-Conti and most of the original Romanée vineyard are owned by a combine that calls itself the Société Civile de la Domaine de la Romanée-Conti. Their cellars, situated at the rear of the village, bordering Saint-Vivant, are among the most hallowed spots in all of the Côte d'Or, and fortunate is the visitor who is able to produce an introduction and receive an invitation to taste these wines in cask.

Good hostelries are rare between Dijon and Beaune, but we have no hesitation in recommending a visit to an unprepossessing little restaurant called La Toute Petite Auberge, near Vosne-Romanée on Route 74. Here, bordering the busy highway, one may partake of an excellent, though simple, meal, and draw from a well-selected cellar of wines of the Côte de Nuits. The Auberge, incidentally, is a favorite lunchtime rendezvous for many of the distinguished growers thereabouts, who obviously see to it that the cellar is amply stocked with their own.

The last town in the Côte de Nuits is Nuits-Saint-Georges, a bustling place where many of the best-known vineyard owners of the Côte de Nuits have their cellars. Just below the town one should leave the highway and follow the farm road that runs through the ribbon of vineyards, now reduced in width to almost nothing. Even though the vineyards of the cluster are only classified as *Premiers Crus*, they produce notably excellent wines— distinguished for their vitality rather than softness, robustness rather than elegance. The most famous plot, of course, is Saint-Georges itself, though we have our own favorites, among which are the nearby Cailles, Vaucrains, and Perrières. Near the end of the Côte, just before it disappears into mediocrity, is the Clos d'Arlots, best known for its white wine; just beyond, the Clos de la Maréchale, whose wines are often seen abroad, marks the end of the group.

Beaune, the principal town of the Côte de Beaune—the southern division of the Côte d'Or—was once a fortified town, conceived in a great circle. Many of its ramparts and bastions still stand, flanked by a generous moat nowadays regrettably dry. Beaune is the true wine center of the Côte d'Or and the place of business for most of its merchants. Hidden beneath its narrow twisting streets is a maze of tunnels that once linked the defenses of the town, latterly turned into wine cellars.

Beaune's principal architectural gem is its fifteenth-century Hospice, or almshouse, an amazing Gothic structure with an incongruous Flemish touch. Still in use as a charity hospital (although a modern plant has been added next door) the ancient building was originally the gift of Nicolas Rollin and his wife, Guigone de Salins. A chancellor of Burgundy at the time of Philippe le Bel, Rollin had previously distinguished himself almost entirely by the high taxes he had imposed on the populace. His sudden generosity led to a celebrated remark by Louis XI, who commented wryly that since Rollin had stolen so much from the poor, it was only fitting that he give some of it back.

Rollin and his wife also endowed their hospital with vineyards, thereby starting a precedent that over the years led to donations totaling almost ninety acres along the entire range of the Côte de Beaune. Every November, in the great hall of the Hospice, the wines are offered at auction—an event attended by buyers and wine experts from all over the world, with the prices sometimes making headlines in the Paris papers. With a lack of orderly coordination that could only take place in France, two auctioneers, by no means working in concert, shout at the audience from two different sides of the room, while aides mill around and mingle with the crowd to make sure that all bids are successfully understood above the tumult. A third auctioneer is in charge of the taper or candle that theoretically, when burned to its end, halts the bidding. Yet how many an aspiring buyer has his hopes dashed! If the auctioneers decide they can squeeze a few hundred additional francs from the crowd, a second or sometimes even a third taper appears from somewhere, lit and ready to burn to its socket. To soothe the tempers, a great banquet is given that night in the cellars of the Hospice—the beginning of a three-day *fête* in which the *Chevaliers du Tastevin* and other wine organizations figure.

The wines of the commune of Beaune, the spot where the ribbon of the great vineyards spreads to its widest, are among the most dependable of the entire Côte d'Or. As a local saying has it, "There are no bad wines in Beaune." In a sense this is true. Beaune can boast no very great wines, or any *Grands Crus*, but her wines are fragrant, earthy, and consistently good, meant to be drunk and not rolled around the glass by connoisseurs. With the exception of the comparatively rare Clos des Mouches Blanc, made at the southern extreme of the commune, they are all red.

Greater wines, including one of Burgundy's most famous whites, Corton-Charlemagne, are made north of Beaune in Aloxe-Corton. The wines of this commune, whose vines did not escape the attention of the Emperor Charlemagne, are rugged and long-lived, and especially delicate with adequate aging. One might call them the Chambertins of the Côte de Beaune. Just north of the town standing amid the vines one will see the stately lines of the Château Grancey, the seat of the Côte d'Or's most venerable vintner, Louis Latour, and behind, bordering the woodland, the celebrated vineyard of Corton itself, with its dozen hyphenated cousins—the Clos du Roi, Perrières, Bressandes, among others—occupying the middle ground. Only Corton itself and the white Corton-Charlemagne are designated as *Grands Crus*, but the differences among all these great wines are barely perceptible. Behind Aloxe-Corton, in the communes of Pernand-Vergelesses and Savigny are comparable, though less well-known, vineyards. Wines labeled Vergelesses should not be overlooked.

One will lunch or dine far better in Beaune than in Dijon—in fact, the meat and drink one is afforded here is nothing short of superb. Just outside the ramparts is the Hôtel de la Poste, now run by the third generation of a famous family of innkeepers. On fair days we recommend the shaded terrace. The food is expensive, but worth it; the cellar, of course, is exemplary. Yet another establishment, slightly less in the traditional vein of old French inns, is the Restaurant du Marché in the town itself, close by the Hospice. The Marché's cellar, if anything, is even more versatile than the Poste's. But there are many other places to choose, suited to all pocketbooks. Much like the wines of Beaune—there being no bad ones—there are few unworthy eating places.

Just south of Beaune, a road branching to the right leads one through the twin villages of Pommard and Volnay, the fame and popularity of whose light-colored, albeit red, wines trace back to the Huguenots. Many of the inhabitants of Pommard and Volnay, who were forced to flee France when Louis XIV revoked the Edict of Nantes, sent home for their native wines, spreading their virtues far. Even the best Pommards and Volnays are only classified as *Premiers Crus*, though in our opinion many of them deserve a higher ranking. They are sprightly and charming, with a lightness that goes hand in hand with their color. Several generations ago these wines were light-colored almost to the extent of being *rosé*, because of an accepted practice of the day of adding a certain quantity of white juice. Although local vintners stoutly deny that the practice continues, the fact remains that many of the wines are suspiciously pinkish. This is not to say they are any the worse for what might be unorthodox methods of vinification, for one will travel a long way before finding better wines than an Épenots, a Clos Blanc, or a Commaraine from Pommard, or a Caillerets or a Clos des Chênes from Volnay.

After one has crossed the little river of Meursault one is in the colloquially named Côte des Blancs, the section where the finest white Burgundies are concentrated along a five-mile stretch of land. The village of Meursault, the largest settlement on the Côte de Beaune other than Beaune itself, with its shaded squares and fourteenth-century church, is by no means lacking in charms, though most writers on the subject (including ourselves) seem to overlook these in their impatience to get to the derivation of the commune's name. Certain ancient records have it that the area was once mysteriously known as *muris saltus*, Latin for "mouse jump." Paragraphs have been written advancing the theory that the great vineyards in Meursault are so closely packed together that they are, as it were, a mere mouse's jump apart— hardly remarkable, since most great vineyards in the Côte d'Or are contiguous. Another theory, somewhat more plausible, is based on the fact that the little river is so narrow that the Roman legions referred to its ford as a mouse jump. We ourselves adhere to a third. In other historical records Meursault is referred to variously as *mure caldus* and *muris saltus*. *Caldus* may be translated as chalk, and *saltus* is only one scribe's error (or jump) away from *salsus*, salt. *Muris salsus* would mean salty bank or wall of earth. It is a curious fact that many wines of Meursault carry a subtle trace of the taste of salt.

In any event, it is difficult to forget or overlook names in Meursault. One of the first vineyards one meets after entering the Côte des Blancs is colorfully named Gouttes d'Or—"drops of gold." Nothing could better describe the appearance of its flowery, deep-yellow wine. Genevrières, another of the great vineyards, produces wines that bear an unmistakable spiciness—as the name implies, akin to juniper. The two best vineyards, however, are Charmes and Perrières, the latter traditionally a *tête de cuvée* of the commune before the new classification lowered it to a *Premier Cru*.

The countryside of the Côte de Blancs is more rolling than that of the northern part of the Côte d'Or, and just before entering Puligny-Montrachet the ribbon of great vineyards makes a sharp rally to the right, up into the highlands toward the hamlet of Blagny. Few vineyard names of Blagny are ever seen on bottles, nor are they well known outside of Burgundy. But a bottle labeled Meursault-Blagny should contain a white wine of superior quality. Blagny also produces a red wine, comparable to a good Volnay, that is rarer yet.

Puligny-Montrachet and Chassagne-Montrachet, the two next communes, share the great vineyard of Montrachet; hence the hyphenations. The name Montrachet probably derives from Mont Rachet, meaning "bald hill." Here is the source of the most touted white in Burgundy—often referred to as the greatest dry white wine in the world. The word "hill," one will agree, is a bit far-fetched; actually, these sacred acres occupy a gentle rise of land, probably once indeed "bald" in its infertility before grapes were planted, from which one may easily survey the hyphenated cousins, Bâtard, Chevalier, Bienvenues-Bâtard, and Criots. Of the four, the wines of Chevalier are the indisputable best, though none equals the liquid gold of Montrachet itself, which at the hands of its best owners (some of whom are far more competent than others) carries a unique soft beeswax flavor, along with the body of a Greek goddess. There is little doubt that the wine of Montrachet epitomizes all that man or nature can draw from the Chardonnay grape. Bear in mind, then, that the finest Montrachet comes from a handful of acres belonging to the Marquis de Laguiche, also the owner of an almost equally valuable part of the vineyard of Morgeot in Chassagne. Between the two of them, they probably constitute the finest white wines of the Côte d'Or. Other superior vineyards, close by, are Pucelles in Puligny, and Caillerets, Boudriotte, and Maltroie in Chassagne. Not everyone knows, incidentally, that Chassagne produces almost as many good red wines as white—wines that, along with those of the neighboring commune of Santenay, represent tremendous value by virtue of public ignorance about them. Heavier in color and body than those of Pommard and Volnay, they may be likened to the Cortons grown to the north.

With Santenay, whose best-known vineyards are red Gravières and La Comme, the ribbon of "greats" once again disappears below the surface, this time not to be seen again. We recommend one short detour of a few miles to the east to the town of Chagny and a restaurant with few peers, the Hôtel Lameloise. Part of the network of the Relais de Campagne, the Lameloise is hardly inexpensive—but well worth it. In all of Burgundy there are no more delectable snails; and we additionally recommend the specialty of *truite pochée*, a trout poached in white wine anointed with a sauce of butter, cream, and shallots. Although the Lameloise is but a stone's throw from Chassagne, Puligny, and Meursault, the best of its cellar—both red and white—comes from the Côte Chalonnaise in southern Burgundy. Among the reds, the patron's choice of Mercurey is a delight; with your trout, you should have the soft white Vieux Château of Montagny.

I I : *Chablis*

In view of the amount of wine consumed by mankind, one never ceases to be astounded by the relatively infinitestimal acreage actually devoted to the raising of the wine grape. Chablis is an outstanding example. Any visitor approaching Burgundy's northernmost white-wine region is in for a surprise. One literally stumbles on this isolated little pocket, a tiny sunken oasis of grapeland surrounded on three sides by broad upland fields, on the fourth by a low range of hills forested by brush and scrub oaks. The finest vineyards, the eight so-called *Grands Crus*, are all clumped together in an area that barely consists of a hundred acres; about two dozen lesser *Premier Cru* vineyards dot the nearby landscape, together constituting an added acreage of only a few hundred more. Beyond these are scatterings of vineyards making inferior wines labeled simply as Chablis or Petit Chablis. Then there is the tiny village (with nothing to offer but its inn), split in two by a beguiling stream with the fitting name of the river Serein ("serene") that winds languidly through the narrow valley. This, in essence, is all there is to Chablis, whose wine is known, drunk, and prized the world over—not to mention all the innumerable exploiters of its name, and the flood of degrading imitations.

The fame of Chablis wines spread to certain quarters of the world as early as the thirteenth century, when an enthusiastic itinerant monk recorded them in his journal as "having the color of spring water and an exquisite fragrance that fills the heart with joyous assurance." For the best Chablis, made in one of its rare good years, the description holds to this day. Its secret is its soil, a substance of almost pure chalk said by geologists to be an exposed fragment of a subterranean stratum known as Kimmeridgian chalk, the result of prehistoric fossil deposits created when the entire area was covered with water. This Kimmeridgian stratum, limited around Chablis to an area of about fifteen square miles, only rises to the earth's surface in two other spots: Champagne and the cliffs of Dover. This soil—perhaps more difficult and taxing to a wine producer than any other soil on the face of the earth—is responsible for the uniquely dry, "flinty" wines, as well as for their subtle bouquet realistically described by local vintners as smelling like freshly cut or chopped mushrooms.

The grape of Chablis is the white grape of Burgundy, the Chardonnay, brought by the Cistercians from the Côte d'Or in the twelfth century when they founded an abbey at Pontigny, about ten miles distant from Chablis down the Serein. Apparently this particular contingent of Cistercians, who called their grape the Beaunois after their native Beaune (a name that still sticks in Chablis), were exceptionally eager colonizers of the wine grape, for at one time their vineyards stretched all the way from Tonnerre, on the canal de Bourgogne, to Auxerre on the Yonne. In succeeding years the wines they produced, known then as Vins d'Auxerre, were the first Burgundies to be drunk in Paris. Wines and other goods in that day traveled largely by water, and those of Tonnerre, Chablis, and Auxerre logically made their way down the Yonne and the Seine and eventually across the channel. It is a recorded fact that one importation was made to England as early as 1212, for the delectation of King John.

Like the wines of the Côte d'Or, which before the days of the *Appellations Contrôlées* were subject to adulteration and blending with inferior products from the Rhône, Chablis' wines have not always come exclusively from Chablis. Evil days fell on Chablis and its neighbors when the vineyards were hit by the phylloxera at the turn of the century, somewhat later than in other districts of France. When the problem of this crippling blight was finally solved by the importation of disease-resistant roots from America, most of the vineyards of the region were grafted with high-producing, poor-quality species of grapes, such as the Melon, now responsible for Muscadet, and the Côte d'Or's second white grape, the Aligoté. The traditional Beaunois, upon which the reputation of Chablis had rested for nearly one thousand years, was all but forgotten; in effect, Chablis became just another white wine. Worse yet, the quasi appellation of the day was stretched to cover any wine produced between Auxerre and Tonnerre. This situation might well have led to the total eclipse of one of France's greatest dry white wines, had not a group of Chablis growers taken matters into their own hands. Backed by local oenologists, a crusade was initiated to limit the appellation of Chablis to wines grown only on the chalky, Kimmeridgian soil, and produced exclusively from the Beaunois, or Chardonnay. This battle between purists and opportunists raged for thirty years and was not finally settled until the advent of the *Appellations Contrôlées* in 1938.

Today the wines of Tonnerre and Auxerre take different names, and only the best are classified as V.D.Q.S. Few of them are worth the trouble of ferreting out, with the exception of those from the ten-acre vineyard of La Channette at Auxerre, once the property of the Benedictines. Red, white, and *rosé*, all made from either the Chardonnay or the Pinot noir, they have somehow been overlooked by the *Comité des Appellations d'Origine*. Yet— on reflection—there might be some subconscious method in the *Comité*'s madness. By a certain stretch of the imagination, a Channette *rosé* could be called a Pink Chablis—an entirely legitimate reason, if there ever was one, for keeping it out of the limelight!

Frequent early, killing frosts—along with a soil so fragile that it is continuously washing down the slopes and thus must be hauled back to cover the vines—make Chablis a harassing place for its vintners. Great or very good years in Chablis occur on an average of two or three in a decade; in some seasons the crop is a total loss. The only factor that benefits the producer is that the

Beaunois vine is usually long-lived in its Kimmeridgian surroundings—often producing well until forty years of age. The wines,
also, are capable of maturing for many years in the bottle. Ten to
twenty years for a great vintage of a *Grand Cru* is not old. Its
color may have changed from the delicate green of "spring water"
to a golden yellow, but it will in all likelihood not be the result
of maderization, as in most other white wines. A bottle of a 1953
or a 1959—or even a 1947 or a 1949—is still apt to be a great one.
Chablis can be unusually high in alcohol, as well as in acidity.
Both qualities are inimical to oxidation.

One night in 1940 this isolated little village, more than a hundred miles from Paris and well removed from any military in-
stallations, was the victim of a flight of Italian bombers, which,
for reasons that will never be known, saw fit to jettison its load.
Nearly the entire village was destroyed, except for one important
legacy: the tradition of Chablis' only hotel, L'Étoile. L'Étoile
is a distinctly undistinguished edifice, both within and without:
an Hôtel de la Gare (without the gare) where one might expect
to uncover a traveling salesman or two, and inedible fare. In the
slack off season one will need courage to push one's way through
the deserted foyer in the direction of the kitchen, perhaps to find
the family at supper. But only a pair of guests suffices to animate
the place. Within the hour the gloomy dining room will have
come to vibrant life, with Madame presiding over neatly uni-
formed little waitresses, and Monsieur chanting happily in the
kitchen. One begins, obviously with *sole au Chablis*, and ends
with a specialty of the house, *soufflé à l'orange*, a creation miraculously devoid of egg yolks, flavored with a few drops of Grand
Marnier, and baked in the orange's own shell. And contrary to
the frustrations nowadays to be experienced in Beaune, Dijon and
Bordeaux, L'Étoile's cellar will actually provide you with the
best years of nearly all eight *Grands Crus* and the two dozen
Premiers Crus, most of which are grown within strolling distance
of the hotel itself just across the Serein.

Royan

PHARE DE
CORDOUAN

POINTE DE GRAVES

GIRONDE R.

MEDOC

St-Estèphe

Pauillac

St.-Julien

HAUT
MEDOC

Margaux

Moulis

Contenac

CÔTES
DE BLAYE

Blaye

CÔTES DE
BOURG

Cubzac

POMEROL

Pomerol

Libourne

St-Emilion

ST.-EMILION

DORDOGNE R.

City of
Bordeaux

PREMIÈRES CÔTES DE BORDEAUX

Léognan

GRAVES

GARONNE R.

ENTRE-DEUX-MERS

Cadillac

Podensac

Barsac

SAUTERNES

Langon

Bordeaux

N

0   Miles   25

palacios

V I

Bordeaux

I : *The City*

The ideal approach to Bordeaux is by sea, the route of traders since long before Roman times. Coming by sea, one passes the Phare de Cordouan, a looming lighthouse on an offshore rock that has guided mariners for many centuries through the hazardous waters off the Pointe de Grave, and thence into the tidal Gironde.

The Gironde is a magnificent river. Almost five miles wide at its mouth, it teems with traffic of all descriptions: freighters awaiting their pilots, ferries plying to and fro across the choppy waters, fishing boats readying themselves for sea or for the tricky voyage upstream. For the trip up the estuary from Pointe de Grave to Bordeaux, innocent as the water's murky surfaces may appear, requires courage and luck for any navigator. The Gironde's ever-changing currents and unpredictable shifting sands have always been a plague to mariners, and many are the craft that have been trapped by its treachery.

The land on either side of the Gironde is low and flat, particularly the peninsula to the south known as the Médoc. Sailing up the river, from a crow's nest atop a tall mast one may see the Atlantic twenty miles distant. Until the eighteenth century, when the ingenuity of Dutch engineers was enlisted to drain them, great areas of the peninsula were useless marshland. Today they are pasture and vineyards, basking in the sun and the broad river's reflected warmth. About halfway up the estuary, one notices that the land has attained a height of a few dozen feet above the river. It is here that most of the greatest vineyards of the Médoc lie, on the gentlest of slopes leading down to the water's edge. As you contemplate this dull and sleepy coast, you are surprised to learn the names of the little villages, names of wines famed the world over: Saint-Estèphe, Pauillac, Saint-Julien, Margaux, and many another.

A few miles north of the city the Gironde is joined by its two tributaries, the Garonne and the Dordogne, approaching from the south and southeast respectively. The pie-wedge slice of flat land formed by the confluence of these two rivers somewhat resembles a swallow's tail: hence the legendary name of Gironde, a corruption of *hirondelle*—French for "swallow." This wedge of land lying between the two rivers is called Entre-Deux-Mers— literally, "between two seas." Entre-Deux-Mers is only one example of the awareness of people of ancient times of the presence —and significance—of the surrounding bodies of water. The word Bordeaux, for example, means "on the edge of the water"; Médoc, the peninsula between the Gironde and the Atlantic, is so named because it lies between waters, "oc" being in all probability a corruption of *aqua*. In Roman days the province was known as Aquitania.

Bordeaux, the city which gives its name to one of France's two greatest wine districts, lies up the Garonne opposite the swallow-tail. The Romans, who reached western France about two centuries later than they did their German outposts, developed Bordeaux as a port; but there seems to be no evidence that they attempted to build a Rome of the West, comparable to the elaborate settlements in other parts of Europe such as Nîmes, Arles, and Orange in the Rhône Valley, or Trier on the Moselle.

One will read in many an erudite volume that the Romans brought the wine grape to Bordeaux; but there is no evidence for this. As in Germany and elsewhere, the conquerors undoubtedly encouraged viticulture as a whole, and to hasten production may have brought certain varieties from Italy, such as the spurious Elbling vine they took to the Moselle, to the plague and shame of German viticulture ever since. Inversely, the Cabernets, Merlots, and other Bordeaux grapes that grow today in Italy might well be there because of the favorable impression their wines made on the colonizers.

After the Romans departed, taking their trade with them, Bordeaux fell into an eclipse, until the brief but spectacular reign some centuries later of the Frankish king Dagobert, who made the city his southernmost military outpost, very much as the Romans had done with Trier. Dagobert founded the short-lived duchy of Aquitaine, with Bordeaux as its capital; one of the dukes of Aquitaine, William, was the father of the celebrated Eleanor— that calculating personage who managed in her lifetime to be queen of France by marriage with Louis VI, and later queen of England through a second marriage with young Henry Planta- genet, shortly thereafter to become Henry II of England. As we remember, Henry was also a count of Anjou, and as a result of inheritances and marital ties, he came to control virtually all the western seaboard of France.

Bordeaux remained under English domination for more than three centuries—long enough to establish a lasting trade, not to mention a loyalty and *entente*, which exists even to this day. In fact, when the city was taken by a French army at the end of the Hundred Years' War, the French conqueror, Charles VII, found himself distinctly *persona non grata*, openly mocked by his Bordelais countrymen. The two forts that Charles built to protect the city from future enemies were facetiously dubbed Château Trompette and Château Hâ—the first because the King's builders were forced to summon the recalcitrant workers with blasting trumpets; the second immortalizing the King's dedication speech. As he stood at the rostrum before his assembled subjects, the only word the tongue-tied monarch seemed to be able to come up with was a triumphant "Hâ!"

England remains as one of the choice markets for Bordeaux, especially for "claret" (the British term for red Bordeaux wine), and in no other part of France will one find so much fluent English spoken as a second language by the educated classes. It is still standard procedure for the sons and heirs apparent of Bordeaux firms to be sent to England to serve their apprenticeships: to gain a mastery of the language, and cement economic and social ties.

When, some hundred years ago, Victor Hugo wrote, "Take Versailles, add Antwerp, and you have Bordeaux," he was attempting to describe a provincial city of immense affluence and elegance. Bordeaux is today France's largest and most colorful wine port, but many another industrial activity—oil refining and synthetic rubber, for two—have crept into being, blanketing much of the romance of old. Few of today's ports were conceived to handle a twentieth-century population, and Bordeaux is no exception. Perhaps the best time to recapture its charms is after business hours, when a large part of the population has retired indoors or taken itself to the suburbs. One should walk the Quai des Chartrons, where the modest buildings facing the waterfront are still the seats of the great wine firms, many of which were founded by foreigners as long ago as the seventeenth century—unpretentious houses whose second-floor offices are in effect gracious and expensively furnished drawing rooms created for the transaction of leisurely, unpressured commerce. On the street level are the bottling rooms, with vast storage cellars stretching behind—cellars that have to be at ground level, since any subterranean excavation in Bordeaux immediately fills with water. One should also have an *apéritif* on the terrace of Bordeaux's traditional café, the Café de Bordeaux, contemplating the classic lines of the Grand Théâtre across the square, France's second most active opera house whose facade was the inspiration for Paris' far less inspiring one. The Café de Bordeaux today is a close equivalent of what Paris' Cafés de la Paix and Régence represented several decades ago: the habitual meeting place of this provincial city's aristocratic notables.

After dark one should visit the other principal waterfront street, the Quai de la Douane, the site of many handsome buildings such as the Bourse (stock market) and the Customs House. Between the Quai de la Douane and the Quai des Chartrons is the parklike Esplanade des Quinconces, which the Bordelais boast of as being the largest metropolitan expanse of its kind in Europe. No reminder that Bordeaux is still a great and extensive port could possibly be more convincing than the Esplanade after nightfall. A perennial carnival seems temptingly to be just getting under way about bedtime. The Esplanade's vastness by day always seems dwarfed by the disproportionate sculptures of Montaigne and Montesquieu, and two towering columns commemorating Commerce and Navigation, Bordeaux's demigods. But by night it is something else again: unquestionably the largest and swingingest metropolitan expanse in Europe.

Hidden behind the Esplanade is a small circular marketplace, until recent years the site of one of the finest restaurants of France, Le Chapon Fin. Anyone who dined there in its heyday will never forget the caprice of the Chapon Fin's interior, a medley of potted palms, bizarre little grottoes, and splashing fountains with tropical fish—incongruent surroundings in contrast to its *grande cuisine* and impeccable service, not to mention a cellar filled with treasures of Bordeaux going back over the preceding fifty years. M. Sicart, the owner, an unsmiling little man who greeted his clientele in what was said to be his only suit— an ultraconservative business affair worn the year around—died a few years ago. His demise precipitated the start of an unhappy decline in the gastronomic fame of Bordeaux, once considered on a par with Lyon.

Comparable fates—the passing of dedicated proprietors—have overtaken another of Bordeaux's great restaurants, the Trompette, as well as its one-time best hotel, the Splendid. The Trompette still exists, but under new and indifferent management. Its intimate and attractive dining room is only about the size of a large parlor, and there is a wonderful cellar. The prices are New York prices, the specialties traditional Bordelais dishes, even though they may not be prepared with the exact finesse of yesteryear. Three of the most famous are creations based on *lamproie* (eel), *foie de canard* (duck liver) and *entrecôte* (steak).

The regional cooking of Bordeaux is highly varied. In addition to its use of wine, as would be expected, it also includes such diverse elements as beef marrow; those fleshy, giant French mushrooms known as *cèpes*; mammoth goose or duck livers; oysters from the sea, and lamprey eels from the Gironde. Best known to the outside world, of course, is *sauce Bordelaise*, classic company for steaks or broiled beef, though the French themselves have found it enhances nearly any dish, including fish and poached eggs. But many a knowledgeable gastronome, until he has visited Bordeaux, is unaware that there are in actuality at least three legitimate *sauces Bordelaises.* The common *Bordelaise* consists of wine reduced with chopped shallots, thyme, and bay leaf, to which one adds beef stock or *sauce Espagnole,* thickens with a small amount of flour and butter, and finishes with bits of poached marrow. Its alternate version is preferred by the Bordelais themselves, probably because it is lighter and more digestible. Known as *Marchand de Vin,* this is simply wine reduced with some chopped shallots and perhaps an herb or two, thickened at the end by swirling in a bit of butter. A third *Bordelaise* often brings surprise and horror to the countenance of the tourist who has anticipated an unctuous red-wine sauce with his steak. This is a wineless mixture whose origin is buried deep in Bordeaux's gastronomy: bits of poached marrow and fresh chopped shallots, swimming in warm oil and vinegar. The natives of the Gironde adore it.

Another Bordeaux specialty is *cèpes,* saucer-sized wild mushrooms sautéed in butter, flavored with dry white wine. But by far the most prevalent Bordeaux dishes come from the surrounding waters and the sea. Along with local lamprey eels, prepared in a sauce of their own blood and red wine, Bordeaux is famous for its oysters. Once again, visitors from foreign shores may have difficulty at first in adjusting to these. French oysters are more sinewy, with a subtly metallic first taste. The waters surrounding Bordeaux are particularly noted for two varieties: the larger and more expensive *marennes* and the more common *portugaises*. *Marennes* are lovingly cultivated in oyster beds, requiring about three years before reaching their edible adulthood. The *portugaises*, on the other hand, thrive in a comparatively wild state, and are not considered indigenous to the Gironde. Their history, it is said, commenced with a ship from Portugal, which, having been delayed by adverse weather, dumped what the captain thought to be spoiled oysters into the Gironde. The descendants of these fortunate bivalves now cling in profusion to all the rocks surrounding the peninsula.

The Gironde's muddy waters are also good grounds for sturgeon. Caviar de la Gironde is not a qualitative equal of the Black Sea version, but it is considerably less expensive. Bordeaux's caviar industry is only as old as World War I. Before that, no one but peasants ever thought much about the sturgeon.

Yet another favorite in Bordeaux—even though not necessarily unique to this particular part of France—is fresh goose or duck liver, usually seen on menus as *foie aux raisins*: an enormous, whole liver from a force-fed fowl, served with fresh grapes and a sauce containing a healthy dose of Pineau de la Charente— Cognac let down with very sweet wine. To find it in its most authentic form, one should visit the restaurant Dubern on the broad Allées de Tourny, as unconventional an establishment as the Chapon Fin was capricious. The Dubern is first entered as a delicatessen, catering mouth-watering specialties from all over the world. A floodlit tank at the rear contains sullen, staring *écrevisses* (crayfish), next to which are a set of stairs ascending to a second floor with a number of small dining rooms. Only one other restaurant within this gastronomically bereft city rivals the

157

Dubern or the Trompette. This is the Clavel, a somewhat more conservative establishment near the railroad station, the current favorite of the Bordelais themselves. It specializes in its own superb version of *moules marinières* (mussels), known locally as *mouclade*. The Clavel's wine cellar unfortunately leaves something to be desired, in terms of old or distinguished vintages.

Of the three good hotels in the city, the Splendid, the Gascogne, and the Grand, probably the former is still the most recommendable. In any of the three, one may expect comfortable rooms with average hotel food, and wine lists that, however imposing in their size, contain few vintages old enough to drink. If one can manage it, a far more satisfactory place to stay is the Réserve Etche Ona, five miles out of town near the suburb of l'Alouette. The Réserve is not inexpensive, but highly creditable meals are to be enjoyed on its shaded terrace beside a quiet stream, and its rooms are modern and comfortable. Especially during Bordeaux's humid summer months, your sojourn will be worth a somewhat higher check.

II: *The Wines*

Bordeaux lies nearly in the center of the five great vineyard areas of the Gironde. Three of them are on the peninsula itself— the other two are to be found a short distance to the east, beyond the Dordogne. One begins with the distinctly red-wine section known loosely as the Médoc, occupying the peninsula north of the city, bordering the Gironde. To the south and west—the opposite side of the city—is the region of Graves, the source of both red and white wines; farther south yet, adjacent to the Garonne, is the region of Sauternes and Barsac, the land of sweet or *liquoreux* white dessert wines. The other two famous regions, beyond the swallowtail of Entre-Deux-Mers and overlooking the Dordogne, are Saint-Émilion and Pomerol. These two, producing red wines only, have for centuries been called the *Haut-Pays*, the "highlands"—in contrast to the flat, low Médoc peninsula.

It should be borne in mind that these five regions are the traditionally greatest areas: yet collectively they constitute only about one-fiftieth of all the grape land of the Bordeaux district as a whole. Thousands of acres of vines on land of lesser repute flourish in Entre-Deux-Mers, in the Côtes de Bourg and Blaye, and the Premières Côtes de Bordeaux on the eastern shore of the Gironde, and on vast expanses along the banks of the Dordogne. These latter wines, both red and white, rarely bear a label marked by a greater distinction than the simple words *Appellation Contrôlée Bordeaux.*

The classifications, or *Appellations Contrôlées* of Bordeaux wines may seem difficult to grasp at first. It may help basically if one remembers that Bordeaux wines, like most other French wines, are in general graded and classified (and usually resultantly priced) in terms of tradition—which, in effect, means traditional geography. The five main regions mentioned are those that have proven themselves as producers of the finest over the years; within each, similarly, the best areas—and in turn the best specific pieces or parcels of land for growing the wine grape—rate more recondite classifications. Using the Médoc region as an example, here is the progression of *Appellations Contrôlées* for some of its red wines, qualitatively rated from bottom to top:

Bordeaux (meaning the lowest quality of classified red wines. No white or *rosé* wines of the Médoc, incidentally, are allowed a higher classification);

Médoc (any red wine from the entire Médoc region);

Haut-Médoc (any red wine from this more renowned section of Médoc, that part nearer the city);

St.-Julien (a wine from the excellent wine-producing area within Haut-Médoc, surrounding the commune of Saint-Julien— one of six communes so classified);

Château Beychevelle (from a parcel of vineyard land in Saint-Julien, over the centuries having proven itself as the source of very superior wine).

In Bordeaux the traditionally greatest pieces of land are called "Châteaux"—a term that has little or nothing to do with the presence of a country house, in the sense of a château, say, on the Loire. There are indeed many handsome and sometimes historic dwellings connected with Bordeaux vineyards, but they are the exception rather than the rule.

Nearly every articulate Bordelais knows—as his forebears knew —what the best wines are. Partly because of his closeness to the subject, there never seemed much need to list or classify what is, after all, common knowledge; a corollary is that when one is dealing with foreign markets, all the more reason to keep the buyer and consumer as much in the dark as possible. The wines of Graves and Saint-Émilion, for example, were only officially classified a decade or so ago. Those of Pomerol have not yet been legally graded—and a classification of the wines of the Médoc and Sauternes might well have been the victims of this same procrastination had it not been for Napoleon III and his Paris Exposition of 1855. The Emperor logically wanted to show off France's best wares, and commanded an exhibit of the finest wines from Bordeaux, along with an evaluation of what the Bordelais considered their best. In this way there came into being the famous (and widely controversial) classification of 1855, somewhat inexplicably dealing only with wines of Médoc, Sauternes, and Barsac, and overlooking all but one vineyard in Graves, as well as all of Saint-Émilion and Pomerol.

The classification of 1855, which endures to this day despite sporadic efforts to change it, was in its own day an entirely realistic one. The committee appointed for the task—a job that no group appears to have the courage to tackle again—paid little attention to personal preferences, but based its gradings wholly on economic grounds, choosing the sixty-odd wines from the Médoc and twenty-two from Barsac and Sauternes that had brought the best prices over the preceding half century. Because of the high sums it brought on the market, the committee also saw fit to include the wine of Graves' Château Haut-Brion. As mentioned, it remains something of a mystery why the leading vineyards of Saint-Émilion and Pomerol were given no consideration. Several of them—especially Pomerol's Château Pétrus, and Ausone and Cheval Blanc in Saint-Émilion—were certainly eligible. The omission may have been attributable to the long-standing rivalry between Bordeaux and the *Haut-Pays*, traceable to the days of the English occupation when the city's merchants each year successfully contrived to block the shipments of *Haut-Pays* wines to England, until inventories of peninsula wines— Médocs, Graves, and Sauternes—in which they themselves had vested interests, were exhausted.

In the classification of 1855 the Médoc wines were divided into five principal categories or *crus*, beginning with four *premiers crus*, fifteen *deuxièmes*, fourteen *troisièmes*, eleven *quatrièmes* and nineteen *cinquièmes*. (Later, seven *crus exceptionels*, as well as a number of vineyards rated as *crus bourgeois supérieures* were added.) This division of the best into five separate classes has been the source of acrimony and agitation ever since the classification was first made. By far the most publicized individual case has been that of Château Mouton-Rothschild, placed at the head of the list of *deuxièmes crus* instead of among the *premiers*, which latter list was comprised of châteaux Margaux, Latour, Lafite-Rothschild, and Haut-Brion in Graves. The owners of the two Rothschild châteaux were cousins, both members of the famous banking family; and to the proprietor of Mouton-Rothschild, his omission from the top classification was intolerable. Henceforth his labels bore the pouting motto, *"Premier ne puis; seconde ne daigne; Mouton suis."* ("I can't be first; I won't be second; I am Mouton!")

Through good management, the wines of Mouton-Rothschild have improved since 1855—as has their price on the world's markets. Everyone agrees that the château makes wine that often equals and sometimes surpasses the other four; not infrequently Mouton brings, in fact, the best price of all. Seemingly today the matter of where Mouton stands on any printed list is little short of academic, even though the avowed life ambition of the present owner (a Rothschild descendant) is to bring about the inclusion of his wine in an official first class before he dies.

Like the owner of Mouton, practically every Bordelais has his own version of how the list should be written, and thinks—with pardonable license—that his own wine has been erroneously classified. Since 1855 several of the original sixty-odd châteaux have gone out of existence, and the wines of many of them, by virtue of good or bad management, have changed in quality— and undoubtedly will again. Our considered advice to the reader is to forget the list (except perhaps for the first five châteaux) and in general approach all sixty-odd wines as one would members of a great family. Assessment of individual character and quality is then in order. In Appendix C we have given the official list, along with notations indicating which châteaux, in the opinion of a majority of experts, should be placed in higher classifications. But what should be remembered is that many of the experts or owners have their own private fish to fry, especially the Johnny-come-lately owners—for Médoc châteaux are nowadays ten times more valuable than a seat on the New York Stock Exchange, and considerably more prestigious as property. Often a better guide than any of the lists or pronouncements of experts is the price of the wine in a shop or on a restaurant's wine list—reverting back to the criterion used by the committee of 1855.

I I I : *The Médoc*

Before venturing into the so-called Médoc, the fount of some of France's greatest, one or two other specific matters of terminology should be cleared away. The land stretching northward for some eighty miles from the city of Bordeaux to the Pointe de Grave at the peninsula's end is loosely known as the Médoc. Until comparatively recently its northern half was called Bas-Médoc (Lower Médoc), and the half nearer to Bordeaux, Haut-Médoc (Upper Médoc). Some years ago the citizens of the Bas-Médoc, where the vineyard land is distinctly inferior, took it into their heads that the term "Bas" was degrading, inhibiting the sale of their wines. Hence it was agreed that Bas-Médoc should be called simply Médoc; with Haut-Médoc remaining as such. Unfortunately, vintners when labeling their wines do not always follow suit. We repeat: all the great châteaux are situated in Haut-Médoc; but one will see labels where the distinction is not made. The term Médoc is also carelessly used, in print and in spoken word, to refer either to the whole peninsula, or sometimes, most confusingly of all, just to Haut-Médoc.

One other confusion lies in labels of many a château that omits the *Appellation Contrôlée* of Médoc or Haut-Médoc and uses one of the six authorized communal names. As a simple illustration, the wine of Château Latour, one of the four *premiers crus*, is entitled not only that of its commune, Pauillac; it is also a Haut-Médoc; also a Médoc; also a Bordeaux. It could use any of these, but it chooses Pauillac, the most prestigious. Château Margaux, on the other hand, sees fit to label itself simply with the appellation of Haut-Médoc.

Proceeding northward from the city, the six commune names of the "inner" classifications are Margaux, Moulis, Listrac, Saint-Julien, Pauillac and St.-Estèphe. With the exception of only one or two châteaux on the 1855 list (those situated in Listrac and Moulis) most of the great vineyards lie along a thirty-mile stretch of ancient route from Bordeaux to the Pointe de Grave, found on maps as Route D-2. As one follows northward, several significant geological characteristics may be observed. One will notice that the best vineyards, which tend to cluster around the four towns, are on the highest land—land that is none too high, but still higher than its surroundings. Almost invariably, too, the soil associated with the greatest growths is filled with white pebbles. Where the land drops to a lower level, the pebbles disappear. These pebbles have the very same effect as the gray slate chips on the Moselle terrace, or the cobblestones of Châteauneuf-du-Pape, reflecting the sun's heat by day and holding it by night. Geologists tell us they were dropped there by a glacier—the same glacier that also scraped away all the alluvial topsoil of the area, creating the perfect conditions for the wine grape. Farm crops do not flourish in this part of the Médoc.

What one may not observe in passing, however, is the subtle difference in soil that renders the wines softer and lighter at the lower end of the thirty-mile stretch, and harsher but longer-lived as one proceeds northward. The wines of Margaux and its neighboring communes, Cantanac, for example, are reputed for their finesse and soft, velvety qualities. Those of Pauillac and St.-Estèphe, on the other hand, are by contrast high in tannin, hard when young, and unusually slow to mature. These differences are in general attributable to admixtures of clay and chalk versus sand, and variations in iron content. The soil of Margaux, for instance, contains more iron and sand; that of Pauillac, more clay.

Another factor in the variation of the wines may be attributed to the grapes and the individual formulas used by each château. Under the *Appellations Contrôlées* regulations, the red wines of Médoc may be made from six different grapes. These are the Cabernet sauvignon, Cabernet franc, Merlot, Malbec, Petit Verdot, and Carmenère. Of the six, the Cabernet sauvignon—the universal "claret" grape found today from Yugoslavia to Australia—is the basic ingredient, especially in the Médoc. In the blend of châteaux such as Latour and Mouton-Rothschild it may run as high as 80 percent. With others it may divide the honors with its cousin, the Cabernet franc. Both Cabernets tend to be shy producers, and the superior sauvignon, especially, gives a hard wine. This is the reason a certain proportion of the more easily produced Merlot shares in the blend, to give softness and bring about faster maturity. In the vineyards of Saint-Émilion and Pomerol the Merlot takes the place of the Cabernets, with resulting effects: a Pomerol is apt to be mature in ten years, whereas a great Médoc requires twice as long or more of bottle age. The other three Médoc grapes are relatively insignificant. The Petit Verdot lends body to the blend; the Carmenère adds color.

Nowadays the traveler along Route D-2, the ancient Route de Médoc, will have little difficulty in finding the great châteaux, since newly awakened promotional groups in each of the respective communes see to it that they are well marked. Some of the vineyards have erected their own roadside publicity, such as the American-owned *quatrième cru* Château Prieuré-Lichine, one of the first châteaux one meets on the way from Bordeaux. Originally a Benedictine priory (one of the rare instances of Church vineyard holdings in the Gironde), in the years since 1855 Château Prieuré has acquired valuable bits of land from neighbors with higher classifications, and more recently a hyphen with yet another name to glorify its principal owner, whose voice was long one of the loudest to be heard in Bordeaux advocating a revision of the old classification. Prieuré-Lichine's wines are fast to mature, and in exceptional years quite typical, in their softness and delicacy, of wines made in the vicinity. A short distance beyond, one catches a glimpse of the pretty Château Palmer, a *troisième cru*, for years extremely popular in England and once favored by Louis XV. Although·in the first half of this century its wines were not up to par, a change in ownership and management is remedying that.

Château Margaux, whose *premier cru* wines are considered by many to be the most delicate and refined—the word "feminine" is frequently used—of all the Médocs, lays claim to the most imposing building on the peninsula. Formal, almost palatial, with a colonnaded portico and elaborate outbuildings, it is incongruously set amid its expanse of vineyards—its style and dimensions such as one might expect to find in a park along the Loire, or perhaps hidden behind a copse of the Bois de Boulogne. Margaux today is owned by the Ginestet family, well-known Bordeaux wine merchants. Along with its celebrated red wine, the château also produces a certain amount of comparatively undistinguished white, Pavillon Blanc de Château Margaux. For the past five years its owners have adopted the commendable policy of omitting vintage years on the reds when the wines did not conform to their high standards.

Across the road is Château Lascombes, at the present writing a definitely overrated *deuxième cru*, whose vineyards enjoy the highest elevation in this part of the Médoc. Its gray stone château, resembling an English country house, is also owned by a group of Americans. Lascombes is a well-known sight on a shelf in England, even though the wine often carries a mustiness or coarseness that is little short of repulsive. Perhaps a more acceptable wine to the public as a whole is the château's Rosé de Lascombes, one of the few good *rosés* made in Bordeaux. Like the white Pavillon Blanc de Château Margaux, Lascombes' *rosé* may only deserve the *Appellation Contrôlée* of Bordeaux. This is regrettable, since both wines often stand up far better than many other whites and *rosés* of the Gironde entitled to more elegant appellations.

For almost ten miles beyond the Margaux group of vineyards one sees no more pebbly soil, nor vines. Then suddenly, around a sharp curve in the road, one comes upon Château Beychevelle, a large, handsome, and well-kept country house surrounded by its vineyards and its spacious gardens commanding a superb view of the estuary. The name Beychevelle is said to date to the sixteenth century, when its proprietor, the Duc d'Épernon, was Grand Admiral of France under Henri III. To salute the distinguished sea dog, passing ships on the Gironde habitually lowered their sails—the term *baisse-voile* being later colloquialized to Beychevelle.

Château Beychevelle is a large estate whose production of nearly twenty thousand cases a year is considerably higher than that of the average château of the Médoc. So much the better: for its wines are superb. They are tremendously popular in both England and the United States, usually bringing prices far higher than any other fourth growth, and in the opinion of nearly every expert, Bordelais or otherwise, here is a case in which the classifying committee of 1855 unquestionably erred. Beychevelle is a wine of enormous body, fragrance, and individuality—yet the reader should be wary: of all the wines of the Médoc, it is among the slowest to mature.

Beychevelle is by no means the only celebrated vineyard in the Saint-Julien group, which contains more classified great growths than any of the six "inner" communal areas except Pauillac. Just before reaching the village of Saint-Julien, one comes to a foursome of famous châteaux: Léoville-Las-Cases, Léoville-Poyferré, Léoville-Barton, and Langoa-Barton. All four are, in effect, part of the same estate; the first three are *deuxièmes crus*, the last a *troisième*. The imposing Empire Château de Langoa that one passes on the road is not, sadly enough, inhabited; it serves only as a cellar for the wines of the group. Its wine is the least known of the four and not considered to be of the same quality—perhaps for snobbish reasons only, since it receives an indeterminate fate: unlike most of Bordeaux's best, Langoa is not château-bottled but goes to the cellars of its merchant-owners, Barton and Guestier in Bordeaux, for final processing.

West of the village and Route D-2 are châteaux Gruaud-Larose and Talbot, both the property of one of Bordeaux's most respected vintners, M. Jean Cordier. The wines of both these vineyards are made with consummate care and skill; that of Gruaud-Larose in particular is rich and full, with a beautiful deep color. In itself, Gruaud-Larose would suffice to make any commune famous.

The first château one encounters in Pauillac is the aristocratic Latour, one of the four *premiers crus*. Its lonely tower stands amid the vines, once part of an elaborate fortification built by Pauillac in the Middle Ages to defend itself against oceangoing pirates who often penetrated the Gironde. During one of the many wars between France and England, the castle was destroyed by the French themselves, in revenge on an owner who had been an English sympathizer. Few vineyards of the Médoc are as beautifully maintained as those of Latour. The preponderance of egg-sized pebbles speaks for itself; one will notice, also, a large proportion of ancient, gnarled vines. Château Latour exemplifies the vinicultural method called *jardinage*, a practice of allowing the vines to grow to a ripe old age and die a natural death, instead of pulling them and replanting when they pass their peak of production. Traditionally the finest wines are made from old, long-established plants; but the older a vine grows, the less it produces. For those who relish heavy, full-bodied clarets and can afford to wait many years for them to mature, the clarets of Latour have no peers.

Just next to Latour, on either side of the road, are the twin vineyards of Pichon-Longueville; to the name of one is added that of the Baron de Pichon, to the other, the Comtesse de Lalande— former owners. Both vineyards are *deuxièmes crus*, producing wines of high quality, although not as much in demand as many of their neighbors. In any new classification, they would probably lose face.

The town of Pauillac is the largest and most important in this section of the Médoc, at one time a lively port—as evidenced by its broad, shaded quay. Today there are few signs of commercial activity and unfortunately no inns or restaurants one can conscientiously recommend, even for their wine cellars. One must face it: the Médoc is lamentably bereft of good hostelries. Yet one should pause in Pauillac, if only for a glimpse of the river, and perhaps to indulge in a bit of speculation on what the town must have been a century or more ago. Just beyond, off to the left of the Route de Médoc, is Château Pontet-Canet, whose ubiquitous bottles are a familiar sight in almost any wine shop on earth. Pontet-Canet is a *cinquième cru*. Its variable wines—in our own opinion sometimes good, sometimes not quite so good—are bottled in Bordeaux in the cellars of its owners, the large shipping firm of Cruse, a practice that invariably invites suspicion. The château's acreage is one of the largest in the Médoc; yet its production, curiously, is never disclosed.

Adjacent to Pontet-Canet are two giants: Château Lafite-Rothschild and Château Mouton-Rothschild. The château at Lafite, easily seen from the main road, is certainly one of the Médoc's masterpieces: a saffron-colored, handsome country house, commanding the highest land in Pauillac. Bought at auction in the middle of the last century by the Baron James de Rothschild for what would nowadays be the equivalent of $1,500,000, the château and its vineyards consist of about one hundred and fifty acres planted to the two Cabernets, the Merlot, and the Petit Verdot. In great years the wines of Lafite are capable of being the most elegant of all Médocs, and its proud owners, Rothschild descendants, devote much time and effort to keeping them that way. One will notice that Lafite has its own ingenious method of training its vines, calculated to gain a maximum exposure from the rays of the summer sun, and that perhaps, after Château Latour, its vineyards are the most meticulously tended. Only the very best is bottled as Château Lafite—wines from the most mature vines. The balance (from younger vines) is called Carruades de Château Lafite, a less expensive but nonetheless excellent wine, much in demand.

More difficult for the visitor to find is the rival Rothschild château, Mouton, the controversial *deuxième cru* and valued property of a cousin of the present owner of Lafite. Despite the fact that Mouton houses one of the finest wine museums in all France, a fascinating collection tracing back to Roman days, there are few aids to guide an interested tourist. The château and its vineyards border those of Lafite to the south, inland from the main road; thus if one persists in following one's nose and the country lanes, one cannot fail to bump into its fortresslike buildings. Admission to the museum and cellars may be had by telephoning in advance.

The northernmost commune of Haut-Médoc, Saint-Estèphe, contains two important *deuxièmes crus* and one outstanding *troisième*: châteaux Cos d'Estournel and Montrose, and Château Calon-Ségur. Saint-Estèphes are known as the "hardest" wines of Haut-Médoc—in part the result of a larger proportion of clay in the soil, in another part because of the practice of using more juice of the Cabernet sauvignon in the various blends. Saint-Estèphes are anything but "feminine" wines: one would never liken them, for example, to a Château Margaux. Montrose lies off the main road toward the river, an unobstrusive but charming building whose grounds and vineyards, like those of Château

Beychevelle, slope gently toward the river. Some years ago the property was owned by an Alsatian, who capriciously gave Alsatian place names—such as Rue Mulhouse—to all its little lanes and by-ways.

Château Cos d'Estournel, the other *deuxième cru*, produces better-known wines. We suspect you will agree that its principal building—not a residence, but a cellar—is certainly one of the most unusual in the entire Médoc. A medley of Oriental styles and steals, conceived in the first half of the last century by a Bordeaux merchant whose principal trade was with the Far East, the château and vineyards are now owned by the Ginestet family, proprietors of Château Margaux. In contrast to its bizarre château, the wines are among the most distinctive and delicate of the region—exceptionally fruity, and smelling for all the world like the roses that landowners in the Médoc cultivate along the lanes.

The last important vineyard of Saint-Estèphe is Château Calon-Ségur, lying almost on the border of Haut-Médoc and Médoc (Bas-Médoc), a *troisième cru* that most experts would raise to the status of a *deuxième*. Apparently the same sentiments were held by its eighteenth-century owner, the Marquis de Ségur, in that day also proprietor of châteaux Lafite and Latour. "I make wines at Lafite and Latour," the marquis is supposed to have said, "but my heart is at Calon." His words are carved into the mantle of a door at the château, and subsequent proprietors have made further unfortunate commercial use of the quote by printing a symbolic heart on the label. Provided one is able to swallow this dose of sentimentality, one will find that Calon-Ségur produces some of the most virile and hauntingly powerful wine of the region. Even its most ardent admirers rarely allow it its rightful age: some bottles, born in the first decade of our century, are only attaining their zenith today.

Beyond Saint-Estèphe, in that part of the peninsula once known as the Bas-Médoc, one finds the countryside and civilization undergoing a subtle change. One passes acre upon acre of vines, but for the most part the vineyards appear neglected and un-prospering. Wine is made here, but definitely not great wine; nor seemingly with much serious effort. Before too long, one prophesies, the Bas-Médoc will revert to cattle and pines. Which is not to say that the Bas-Médoc is unlovely, or that those who have the time to journey as far as the peninsula's end, the Pointe de Grave, would not do well to go a little farther yet and take the ferry to Royan on the other side of the estuary. The current status of restaurants in the Médoc and the city of Bordeaux being what it is, a short voyage across the Gironde at this point will be well repaid by a visit to one of Royan's two outstanding restaurants—the André and the Chalet. No restaurant in all of Bordeaux can equal the Chalet's roast partridge (*perdrix rôtie salmis*), or its other specialty, a *mouclade* of mussels in a sauce of cream and wine, anointed with shallots, chives, parsley, anise, and Cognac. The cellar is gratifyingly representative of the entire Gironde, including a certain array of pearls.

Except for an unbelievable modernistic church, one may skip the town of Royan—but then, after a meal at the Chalet, one will not be an enthusiastic sightseer anyway. During the last war, a contingent of Germans, sealed off from their own retreating lines, holed up in Royan, necessitating total destruction of the old city by the allies. The town had to be completely rebuilt, with results that are simply not France.

I V : *The Graves*

To the west and south of the city is the red- and white-wine region of Graves, and about twenty miles or so up the Garonne, the sweet-white-wine region of Sauternes and Barsac. Thirty years ago, any account of these two parts of the Gironde would have merited a far larger place in the sun than they deserve today. The Graves region produces both red and white wines, but re-grettably the whites have not maintained the popularity they once had, and the reds, with few exceptions, are no longer as well known on the markets of the world as their equivalents from the Médoc and Saint-Émilion.

Similarly, the sweet, fragrant Sauternes and Barsacs, once so important a factor in Bordeaux's wine trade, have succumbed to a changing world. The taste for dessert wines, and the habit of serving them in their appropriate role, has faded, and with the exception of Château d'Yquem—in some parts of the world a byword for sweet wine—few châteaux in Sauternes and Barsac are free of economic troubles. In fact many of the white-wine vineyards in Sauternes and Barsac, as well as some in Graves, are on the market, and at ridiculously low prices.

Visitors to Bordeaux are always surprised to find that some of the best vineyards of Graves have literally been overrun by the burgeoning city. One such is the most famous of all, the *premier cru* Château Haut-Brion, whose hundred acres of vines are entirely surrounded by busy suburbs. The château has a long and distinguished history. At one time it belonged to Talleyrand, who reputedly took a supply of its wines, along with France's most able chef, to the Congress of Vienna, thereby considerably enhancing his diplomatic negotiations. Haut-Brion's vintages were discovered at an early date in England, when Samuel Pepys sampled them at a London tavern and recorded them as being exceptional quality. Due to the influence of its present owner, Clarence Dillon, one-time U.S. Secretary of the Treasury and Ambassador to France, a good part of the château's production, whose demand always exceeds supply, now goes to the United States.

Graves, in French, means gravel, and parts of the region are in effect a huge gravel bank whose depth sometimes extends several dozen feet below the surface. In the vineyards of Château Haut-Brion, for instance, the roots of the vines penetrate forty feet of pure gravel to obtain moisture and nourishment. The red wines of Haut-Brion and its neighbors have a pronounced richness and fullness—often literally called "earthiness." Château Haut-Brion also makes a small quantity of white wine, Haut-Brion Blanc, considered by many to be the finest of Graves: a wine of extraordinary body and character.

Just down the street, also in the suburbs, are three other excellent vineyards that hyphenate Haut-Brion to their names: La Mission-Haut-Brion, Latour-Haut-Brion, and Laville-Haut-Brion. Laville makes white wines only, Latour red, and La Mission both —though the white, somewhat confusingly, is bottled under the name of Laville. Another of those few vineyards of the Gironde with Church associations, the Mission was at one time the property of an order founded by Saint Vincent de Paul. A statue of the Saint stands in the chapel at the Mission, promoting the legend that concerned his desertion of heaven to drink the wines of Haut-Brion—to be turned to stone by the Almighty for his greediness.

Another nearby red-wine vineyard of Graves, Château Pape-Clément, the source of excellent wines, has a history that is anything but legendary. It was planted in the fourteenth century by one Bertrand de Goth, the archbishop of Bordeaux who skirted conventional channels and succeeded in having himself elected pope. As Pope Clément, he moved the papacy to Avignon, where he undoubtedly had a strong hand in developing the Rhône vineyards at Châteauneuf-du-Pape. After his investiture, Clément deeded his vineyards to the Church in Bordeaux, which owned and controlled them until the French Revolution. It was of the wine of Pape-Clément that Cardinal Richelieu is supposed to have said, "If God did not intend man to drink, why did He make it this good?"

A few miles south of the city is the commune of Léognan, the site of three or four vineyards producing white Graves considered qualitative equals of the reds. This is largely a connoisseur's judgment. As we have implied, white Graves today is not popular on foreign markets. Even though a certain quantity of it is sold to Scandinavian countries and, to a lesser extent, to England, the only real devotees of white Graves are the French themselves, notably the Bordelais. To most others a white Graves is a weak and watery wine, a little too dry, and with a peculiar rusty taste—the combination of white Sémillon and Sauvignon grapes, the two principals prescribed by the *Appellations Contrôlées,* raised on gravelly soil being far more attractive in a sweet wine than in a dry one. Along with the rare Haut-Brion Blanc, the three most deservedly famous are those of the châteaux Carbonnieux and Olivier, and the Domaine de Chevalier.

The countryside of Léognan, in contrast to the Médoc, is hilly, dotted with patches of woodland and crisscrossed by small streams. The châteaux themselves, too, have their distinct charms. Château Olivier is a thirteenth-century building surrounded by a moat—an architectural gem as pristine as its clear, dry white wine. Another is the fourteenth-century Château Carbonnieux, originally a seat of the Benedictines, later a hunting lodge of the Duc d'Epernon, the friend of Henri III, who was also grand admiral of France and owner of Beychevelle in Saint-Julien. The name Carbonnieux involves yet another colorful story—in this case doubtless with a certain vestige of truth. During the regime of the Benedictines, it came to pass that the Sultan of Turkey acquired an unorthodox thirst for white Graves—one version of the story involves a favorite of the harem, an irresistible Bordelaise. Alcohol was, of course, forbidden in Islam; but through the complicity of the Benedictines in Constantinople, the Sultan was enabled to have his wine delivered to the palace innocuously labeled "Eau Minérale de Carbonnieux." Most of the vineyards in Léognan produce both red and white wines. Château Carbonnieux's red, made in small quantity, actually rates higher in the eyes of experts than its white.

Yet another vineyard in the vicinity, the Château de La Brède, is equally worth a visit, even though its wines are today of comparatively little consequence. Its lovely thirteenth-century castle, in an excellent state of preservation, was once the residence of Montesquieu, the great historian and political theorist of the eighteenth century, also an enthusiastic vineyardist. Under his guidance the white wines of La Brède were at one time rated very high among those of the Gironde.

Following up the Garonne, the country again flattens, and we are once more in the midst of vast expanses of vineyards, all of them producing white wine. This somewhat nondescript area is the source of great quantities of *Graves Supérieures*, an appellation requiring a slightly higher alcoholic content than an ordinary Graves. Here is the fount of all those lemon-yellow bottles seen on the shelves of every *épicerie* in France, or on the tables of every French dining car. Luckily there are other uses for this wine in a waning market: at Podensac, one of the towns we pass, great quantities are made into Lillet Vermouth, one of France's nicest *apéritifs*.

V : *Sauternes and Barsac*

The Sauternes region contains five communes, that of Sauternes lending its name to wines of the others. Fargues, Bommes, and Preignac are names more often seen in books than on labels. The fifth commune, Barsac, produces wines that may be legally labeled as themselves—or alternately as Sauternes, an arrangement that in poor years often works to the distinct advantage of Barsac growers. The special charm of Sauternes and Barsac, probably the greatest sweet-wine region in the world, is not easy to pinpoint. Despite an almost imperceptible rolling of the land, one has the impression of a flatness extending infinitely—like a vast desert. In midsummer the heat may be semitropical, and when there is no breeze to ripple the vines, you think you can almost hear the grapes growing. Dotted across this shimmering, verdant desert are little oases: tiny villages or the walled enclaves of the châteaux themselves, their squares and courtyards cool and dark in the shade of thick trees.

Crowning the only hill that one could conceivably flatter with the name are the turreted buildings of Château d'Yquem, a vineyard classified as a *premier grand cru*, along with the *premiers crus* of the Médoc, in 1855. Today the distinction is only technical, of course; yet a terminology indicating a higher rank (*grand*) could hardly have been an oversight on the part of the classifiers, inasmuch as they continued their ratings in Sauternes and Barsac with eleven *premiers crus* and twelve *deuxièmes*. Perhaps it was because they saw eye to eye with Thomas Jefferson who, in the course of his tour of French vineyards, wrote that Château d'Yquem was "the best white wine in all France." More likely, however, the ratings here also had an economic basis. Only a few years before, four casks of d'Yquem had been bought by the czar's brother for the staggering sum of twenty thousand francs ($10,000).

The fame of Château d'Yquem is such nowadays that it may well live long after the names of Sauternes and Barsac have been buried and forgotten. Yet one often wonders why. From a connoisseur's point of view, there are several other *crus classés* of the region with far more individuality—and more realistically priced. Château d'Yquem is oftentimes too luscious, almost too perfect in its purity to hold the interest of the discriminating wine-drinker for long.

The method of making wines in Sauternes and Barsac is, to all intents and purposes, the very same as that used for *liquoreux* wines in Anjou, or for the Beerenauslesen of Germany. The already ripe grapes are allowed to stay on the vine until they have been attacked by the so-called noble mold, the *Botrytis cinerea*, that tiny organism whose roots pierce the skins and sap the water within the fruit. The resulting proportions of sugar, pectin, and glycerine produce a wine that is unusually thick and full-bodied and, because of its high sugar content, attains an extremely high degree of alcohol. And since the juice contains even more sugar than can be naturally fermented into alcohol, the wine is also sweet. As any visitor to the Château d'Yquem or its neighbors may witness, provided he is privileged to be in the vicinity in late October, the shriveled grapes are picked bunch by bunch as they become ready for the press. Sweet wines of this nature are expensive to produce, and in Sauternes the yield is often only three hundred bottles per acre. It is not unusual for the alcoholic content to run as high as 16 percent—two degrees below the theoretical limit.

In the past few decades the diminishing demand for sweet wines has stripped the local growers of Sauternes and Barsac of all but a vestige of their former prosperity. A temporary boom took place during the postwar era in England, where a population too long deprived of sugar eagerly sought sweet wines. But that market soon passed. In desperation many of the growers turned to the production of dry wines—by pressing the grapes before they became affected by the *Botrytis*, but the results have hardly been worth the trouble. Even Château d'Yquem's attempt to make a dry version, labeled Chateau Y, is little better than good white Graves from Léognan. At best one may only be skeptical about the future of all *liquoreux* wines and mention a few outstanding ones while they are still available. Of these, two often seen on shelves or lists are Châteaux Climens and Coutet, both from Barsac, where a more chalky soil endows its wines with a sharper and more pronounced character. Two others are Châteaux Rieussec and La Tour-Blanche, labeled as Sauternes.

Certain gastronomic proponents of Sauternes, led by the late Marquis de Lur-Saluces, owner of d'Yquem, advocate the use of these *liquoreux* wines not only for desserts and as an after-dinner *digestif*, but also as an accompaniment to main courses, especially fish. Such a practice, which instills horror in a modern restaurateur, was considered to be in the best of taste during the eighteenth and nineteenth centuries—George Saintsbury, the late dean of Anglo-Saxon wine snobs, is on record as liking Sauternes with his oysters. Whereas we do not recommend that it perhaps be tried at Maxim's or the Pavillon, there is a handy little restaurant and hotel on the border of Sauternes itself, where eyebrows will not be raised if one commands a Château Coutet with one's *sole au vin blanc*. This is the Hôtel Oliver in the peaceful village of Langon, a few miles up the Garonne from Preignac, one of the Sauternes communes. The Oliver is also one of the very few hostelries on the Graves-Médoc peninsula that merits unqualified recommendation for both cellar and kitchen. And though the coincidence adds nothing to its excellence, it may well be that certain gastronomes may wish to visit it on the sole grounds that it was here that Raymond Oliver, France's famous "television chef" and proprietor of Paris's Restaurant Grand Véfour, underwent his apprenticeship.

V I: *Saint-Émilion and Pomerol*

Twenty miles to the east of the city, beyond the two rivers and the swallow-tailed Entre-Deux-Mers, lie those vineyard lands that have for centuries been known as the *Haut-Pays*, or highlands. In actuality the *Haut-Pays* are anything but high, except by comparison with the flat Graves-Médoc peninsula. Most of the best vineyards are situated on a plateau overlooking the Dordogne valley: an area shared by the little commune of Pomerol and a section of Saint-Émilion called Graves-Saint-Emilion—again indicating a predominantly gravelly soil. With the exception of a handful of great vineyards near the town of Saint-Émilion itself, other parts of the region, including five communes that hyphenate their names with Saint-Émilion, do not produce wines of the same quality. The region as a whole is the second largest wine-producer in Bordeaux, after the Médoc, and legendarily the oldest. Principally the *Haut-Pays* is a red-wine region. White wines are also made, but entitled only to the lowly appellation of Bordeaux.

Vines were certainly grown on the Saint-Émilion plateau long before they appeared in the Médoc; but there remains some question as to whether they preceded vineyards in Graves and Sauternes. To the Romans, in any event, Saint-Émilions were the best. Their praises were bountifully sung by the poet and fourth consul Ausonius (who also appreciated Moselles), and many another. They were also undoubtedly the first wines of this part of France to reach England. King John, who gave Saint-Émilion a charter in 1199, reputedly could never get enough of them; a century later Edward I created what was certainly the first *Appellation Contrôlée* in Europe, with an ordinance requiring that every cask of Saint-Émilion be clearly marked with the town's coat of arms.

In that day wines of the *Haut-Pays* were shipped from Libourne, a port near the mouth of the Dordogne, at the time of equal importance to—if not greater than—Bordeaux itself. This competition was logically resented by the Bordelais, who eventually got their revenge during the reign of Henry III. Among other privileges, Henry allowed Bordeaux (the city) to trade with England with markedly reduced taxes; it was also given its own charter, and the privilege of electing its own mayor and its own government, called the Sénéchaussée. Such was the beginning of the great Bordeaux wine estates, and the monopoly of the wine trade by the antecedents of what are now the great Bordeaux houses. It also meant a long eclipse for Libourne and the *Haut-Pays*. Their wines were perforce channeled through Bordeaux; and their casks waited on the quays of the city until all those of the Bordeaux burghers had been sold and shipped. Obviously, when they finally reached England, *Haut-Pays* wines were in a state of sad deterioration.

It is more than regrettable that the drab town of Libourne bears so little resemblance to what it once must have been, and it is hard to imagine its harbor as once having played host to the great trading fleets of the nations of the north. Nowadays the harbor is hardly more than an overexpanded marina, and its only foreign waterborne visitors are occasional tankers and tramps—barely enough trade to satisfy the corps of quayside streetwalkers, manifestly the only citizens who persist in the assumption that Libourne is still a port. About the only redeeming feature of the town is the Hôtel Loubat, near the station. The Loubat rests on a long tradition of excellence. Its most famous dish is *riz de veau à la crème*, grilled sweetbreads accompanied by a cream sauce filled with chopped truffles, and served on a slice of *pâté de foie gras*. Along with this elegant, caloric dish, there are others of comparable beauty, and a wine cellar that curiously enough lays emphasis on the best of Graves rather than those of the *Haut-Pays*. The Loubat is not necessarily a place to choose to spend the night, but certainly a most recommendable stop for lunch after a late start from Bordeaux.

Just outside Libourne the "wine road" starts to climb gently into the country of Pomerol. Possibly it is only because of the comparison to the flat peninsula one has just left behind, yet one finds the vineyards of the *Haut-Pays* have a refreshing airiness about them, a well-ventilated feeling of being a bit closer to heaven. Soon one is in the thick of the best, for Saint-Émilion and especially Pomerol are small regions with innumerable small estates, all packed closely together. Château Pétrus, the "king of Pomerols," you pass on your right; barely a stone's throw away are l'Évangile and Vieux-Château-Certan. Close by, across an unmarked border, is one of Saint-Émilion's two best, Cheval Blanc, whose undistinguished group of buildings is typical of the rambling farmhouses associated with the names of the famous châteaux of the *Haut-Pays*.

Cheval Blanc was once the site of an ancient inn of the same name. Needless to say, its wines are all red—contrary to the published words of a well-known English writer on the subject, who somehow managed to quit the area with the impression that Cheval Blanc was Saint-Émilion's opposite number to Burgundy's Clos Blanc de Vougeot.

The soil of this part of the *Haut-Pays* is gravelly and stony, alternately mixed with chalk and clay. It produces rich, dark wines with the softness of velvet and lovely fruitlike bouquets, characteristics that have led them to be described as the "Burgundies of Bordeaux." Comparable to Burgundy, too, they mature early: a Château Pétrus of a good vintage is usually at its peak within ten years—at about the same time a very great Pauillac or a Saint-Julien might be tasting like so much warmed-over tea. Saint-Émilions mature less rapidly than Pomerols, but the difference is largely academic.

Although it is not a country for great wines, one should not leave Pomerol without driving higher yet, up the country road through the villages of Saint-Georges, Montagne, and Lussac— this last commune having the highest elevation of any vineyards of the Gironde. All three, along with nearby Puisseguin and

Parsac, hyphenate their appellations with Saint-Émilion. Generally speaking, their wines do not compare with their distinguished neighbors, though those from Saint-Georges often possess much merit.

Taking an alternate road in the direction of the Dordogne, one shortly comes on the charming town of Saint-Émilion itself, on whose outskirts vines even grow amid the ruins of an ancient church. Nearby, also bordering the town, are the Clos Fourtet and Château Canon, two of Saint-Émilion's finest; and just below the town, toward the river, is Château Ausone, thought to be the seat of Ausonius' villa, where he retired in order to be near the source of his favorite wines.

Saint-Émilion, one of France's more fascinating wine towns, is built on dozens of different levels connected by precipitous, narrow streets, many unchanged since the Middle Ages. Its best-known church, the Église Monolithe, is hewn from a cliff of limestone, as was also the maze of wine cellars that underlie the town and extend into the surrounding hills. If one has the stomach for it, one should not miss the Monolithe's catacombs, along with its *oubliettes* designed for mass burials at times when the town was under siege. We warrant that after this tour, one will be eager to climb to the upper level—the equivalent of the roof of the great church—to the shaded terrace of an excellent hostelry known as the Hôtel de Plaisance, an ideal vantage point from which to contemplate the kaleidoscopic rooftops of Saint-Émilion. The cellars of the Plaisance are soundly insulated from the archaeological realities below, and their vinous treasures, however youthful by comparison, will not disappoint any student or lover of the wines of the *Haut-Pays*.

Recent Vintage Years of Germany, Switzerland, and France

RED WINES

	1961	1962	1963	1964	1965	1966	1967	1968	1969	1970
Switzerland	4	3	3	3	4	4	4	3	4	3
Rhône	4	3	2	3	3	4	3	1	4	3
Loire	5	3	2	3	1	4	2	1	4	4
Côte d'Or	5	4	3	3	1	4	2	1	5	5
Southern Burgundy	4	5	3	3	1	4	2	1	5	3
Beaujolais	5	4	1	3	2	4	3	1	5	4
Médoc	4	4	3	3	1	4	3	1	3	5
Saint-Émilion and Pomerol	5	4	2	4	1	4	3	1	3	4
Graves	4	4	3	3	1	4	3	1	3	4

WHITE WINES

	1961	1962	1963	1964	1965	1966	1967	1968	1969	1970
Moselle	3	3	2	4	3	5	3	2	4	4
Rheingau	3	4	3	4	3	4	4	2	4	4
Rheinhessen	3	4	3	4	3	4	4	2	4	4
Rheinpfalz	3	4	3	4	3	4	4	2	4	4
Alsace	5	4	2	3	1	4	4	2	4	4
Switzerland	4	4	3	3	3	4	3	3	4	4
Rhône	5	4	2	4	2	4	3	3	3	4
Pouilly-Fumé and Sancerre	4	4	2	3	1	4	3	2	4	4
Anjou	4	3	2	3	1	4	3	1	3	5
Chablis	4	5	3	3	3	4	3	2	4	4
Côte d'Or	5	4	3	3	1	4	3	1	4	4
Southern Burgundy	4	3	4	3	1	4	3	1	5	4
Graves	4	4	1	4	2	4	2	1	3	3
Sauternes	5	4	1	3	2	3	3	2	3	5

1 = Poor   2 = Mediocre   3 = Good   4 = Very Good   5 = Excellent

APPENDICES

APPENDIX A

Principal Vineyards of Germany

WINES OF THE MOSEL-SAAR-RUWER

Trittenheim

Trittenheimer Apotheke
Trittenheimer Altärchen
Trittenheimer Falkenberg

Trittenheimer Laurentiusberg
Trittenheimer Clemensberg
Trittenheimer Sonnenberg

Neumagen

Neumagener Laudamusberg
Neumagener Engelgrube

Neumagener Rosengärtchen

Dhron

Dhronhofberger

Piesport

Piesporter Goldtröpfchen
Piesporter Lay
Piesporter Schubertslay
Piesporter Falkenberg

Piesporter Güntherslay
Piesporter Taubengarten
Piesporter Treppchen

Wintrich

Wintricher Geyerslay
Wintricher Grosser Herrgott
Wintricher Rosenberg

Wintricher Ohligsberg
Wintricher Neuberg
Wintricher Sonnseite

Brauneberg

Brauneberger Falkenberg

Brauneberger Juffer

Bernkastel

Bernkasteler Doktor
  (und Graben)
Bernkasteler Lay
Bernkasteler Schlossberg
Bernkasteler Badstube

Bernkasteler Doktor
  (und Bratenhöfchen)
Bernkasteler Schwanen
Bernkasteler Pfalzgraben
Bernkasteler Rosenberg

Graach

Josephshöfer
Graacher Abtsberg
Graacher Heiligenhaus

Graacher Himmelreich
Graacher Domprobst

Wehlen

Wehlener Sonnenuhr
Wehlener Klosterlay
Wehlener Rosenberg

Wehlener Nonnenberg
Wehlener Lay

Zeltingen

Zeltinger Schlossberg
Zeltinger Himmelreich
Zeltinger Rotlay

Zeltinger Sonnenuhr
Zeltinger Stephanslay
Zeltinger Kirchenpfad

Erden

Erdener Treppchen
Erdener Pralät

Erdener Busslay

Uerzig

Uerziger Schwarzlay
Uerziger Kranklay
Uerziger Lay

Uerziger Würzgarten
Uerziger Urglück

Kinheim

Kinheimer Hubertuslay

Kinheimer Rosenberg

Cröv (or *Kröv*)

Cröver Niederberg
Cröver Petersberg

Cröver Heislay

Zell

Zeller Burglay
Zeller Dommhen

Zeller Nussberg
* Zeller Schwarze Katz

* Nowadays usually generic, comparable to Moselblümchen.

Traben-Trarbach

Trarbacher Schlossberg
Trarbacher Königsberg

Trarbacher Huhnersberg
Trarbacher Ungsberg

Enkirch

Enkircher Steffensberg
Enkircher Herrenberg

Enkircher Montenubel
Enkircher Battereiberg

Wiltingen

Scharzhofberg
Wiltinger Rosenberg
Wiltinger Braune Kupp

Scharzberg
Wiltinger Gottesfüss

Oberemmel

Oberemmeler Hütte
Oberemmeler Karlsberg

Oberemmeler Scharzberg
Oberemmeler Altenberg

Ayl

Ayler Kupp

Ayler Herrenberg

Ockfen

Ockfener Herrenberg

Ockfener Bockstein

Serrig

Schloss Saarstein
Serriger Heiligenborn

Schloss Saarfels

Maximin Grünhaus

Maximin Grünhauser Herrenberg

Eitelsbach

Eitelsbacher Karthäuserhofberger
  Kronenberg

Eitelsbacher Karthäuserhofberger
  Sang

Kasel (or *Casel*)

Kaseler Niegen

Waldrach

Schloss Marienlay

Mertesdorf

Brutusberger Lorenzberg

Brutusberger Treppchen

WINES OF THE RHINE

Rheingau

Rüdesheim

Rüdesheimer Berg Bronnen
Rüdesheimer Berg Lay
Rüdesheimer Berg Burgweg
Rüdesheimer Berg Roseneck
Rüdesheimer Berg Mühlstein

Rüdesheimer Berg Schlossberg
Rüdesheimer Bischofsberg
Rüdesheimer Berg Rottland
Rüdesheimer Berg Hellpfad

Geisenheim

Geisenheimer Rothenberg
Geisenheimer Decker
Geisenheimer Katzenloch
Geisenheimer Klauserweg

Geisenheimer Lickerstein
Geisenheimer Kosackenberg
Geisenheimer Mäuerchen
Geisenheimer Mönchspfad

Johannisberg

Schloss Johannisberg
Johannisberger Hölle
Johannisberger Mittelhölle
Johannisberger Goldatzel
Johannisberger Hansenberg

Johannisberger Erntebringer
Johannisberger Klaus
Johannisberger Sterzelpfad
Johannisberger Kerzenstück
Johannisberger Nonnhölle

Winkel

Schloss Vollrads
Winkeler Jesuitengarten
Winkeler Dachsberg

Winkeler Hasensprung
Winkeler Honigberg
Winkeler Kläuserweg

Hallgarten

Hallgartener Deutelsberg
Hallgartener Jungfer
Hallgartener Hendelberg
Hallgartener Würzgarten

Hallgartener Schönhell
Hallgartener Mehrhölzchen
Hallgartener Rosengarten

Oestrich

Oestricher Lenchen
Oestricher Eiserberg
Oestricher Klostergarten
Oestricher Hölle
Oestricher Magdalenengarten

Oestricher Doosberg
Oestricher Deez
Oestricher Pfaffenberg
Oestricher Klosterberg

Hattenheim

Steinberg
Hattenheimer Wisselbrunnen

Hattenheimer Nussbrunnen
Hattenheimer Mannberg

Hattenheimer Engelmannsberg
Hattenheimer Hassel
Hattenheimer Willborn
Hattenheimer Rothenberg

Hattenheimer Pfaffenberg
Hattenheimer Hinterhausen
Hattenheimer Bergweg

Erbach
Marcobrunner
Erbacher Steinmorgen
Erbacher Brühl
Erbacher Hinterkirch
Erbacher Herrenberg

Erbacher Siegelsberg
Erbacher Hohenrain
Erbacher Honigberg
Erbacher Rheinhell

Kiedrich
Kiedricher Wasserrose
Kiedricher Turmberg
Kiedricher Heiligenstock

Kiedricher Gräfenberg
Kiedricher Sandgrube

Rauenthal
Rauenthaler Baiken
Rauenthaler Rothenberg
Rauenthaler Herberg
Rauenthaler Wieshell

Rauenthaler Gehrn
Rauenthaler Wülfen
Rauenthaler Pfaffenberg

Eltville
Eltviller Sonnenberg
Eltviller Kalbspflicht
Eltviller Langenstück

Eltviller Klumbchen
Eltviller Taubenberg
Eltviller Mönchhanach

Walluf
Wallufer Walkenberg
Wallufer Unterberg

Wallufer Mittelberg

Hochheim
Hochheimer Kirchenstück
Hochheimer Rauchloch
Hochheimer Raaber
Hochheimer Stielweg
Hochheimer Sommerheil

Hochheimer Domdechaney
Hochheimer Stein
Hochheimer Hölle
Hochheimer Daubhaus

Rheinhessen

Bodenheim
Bodenheimer Kahlenberg
Bodenheimer Rettberg
Bodenheimer Braunloch

Bodenheimer Ebersberg
Bodenheimer Hoch
Bodenheimer Silberberg

Nackenheim
Nackenheimer Rothenberg   Nackenheimer Fenchelberg
Nackheimer Stiel   Nackenheimer Engelsberg
Nackenheimer Rheinhahl

Nierstein
Niersteiner Rehbach   Niersteiner Hipping
Niersteiner Auflangen   Niersteiner Glöck
Niersteiner Flächenhahl

Oppenheim
Oppenheimer Goldberg   Oppenheimer Kreuz
Oppenheimer Kröttenbrunnen   Oppenheimer Herrenberg
Oppenheimer Sackträger

Dienheim
Dienheimer Goldberg   Dienheimer Tafelstein
Dienheimer Guldenmorgen   Dienheimer Kröttenbrunnen

Worms
Wormser Liebfrauenstift

Bingen
Binger-Büdesheimer   Binger Schlossberg
  Scharlachberg   Binger Schwätzerchen
Binger Eiselberg   Binger-Kempter Rheinberg
Binger Rochusberg   Binger Rosengarten
Binger Ohligberg

Rheinpfalz

Kallstadt
Kallstadter Kruez   Kallstadter Kobnert
Kallstadter Nill   Kallstadter Steinacker

Ungstein
Ungsteiner Michelsberg   Ungsteiner Herrenberg
Ungsteiner Spielberg

Bad Dürkheim
Dürkheimer Spielberg   Dürkheimer Michelsberg
Dürkheimer Hochness   Dürkheimer Feuerberg
Dürkheimer Schenkenböhl   Dürkheimer Fuchsmantel

Wachenheim

Wachenheimer Gerümpel   Wachenheimer Böhlig
Wachenheimer Bächel   Wachenheimer Rechbächel
Wachenheimer Goldbächel   Wachenheimer Wolfsdarm

Forst

Forster Jesuitengarten   Forster Kirchenstück
Forster Ziegler   Forster Kranich
Forster Freundstück   Forster Ungeheuer
Forster Langenacker   Forster Langenmorgen

Deidesheim

Deidesheimer Grainhübel   Deidesheimer Kränzler
Deidesheimer Hohenmorgen   Deidesheimer Grain
Deidesheimer Dopp   Deidesheimer Kieselberg
Deidesheimer Geheu   Deidesheimer Rennpfad
Deidesheimer Leinhöhle   Deidesheimer Kalkofen
Deidesheimer Hofstück   Deidesheimer Langenmorgen

Ruppertsberg

Ruppertsberger Nussbien   Ruppertsberger Gaisböhl
Ruppertsberger Hoheberg   Ruppertsberger Hofstück
Ruppertsberger Mandelacker   Ruppertsberger Kieselberg
Ruppertsberger Reiterpfad

WINES OF THE NAHE

Kreuznach

Kreuznacher Kröttenpfuhl   Kreuznacher Hinkelstein
Kreuznacher Kahlenberg   Kreuznacher Forst
Kreuznacher Narrenkappe

Niederhäus

Niederhäuser Hermannsberg   Niederhäuser Hermannshöhle

Norheim

Norheimer Kirschheck   Norheimer Kafels
Norheimer Götzenfels   Norheimer Dellchen

Schloss Böckelheim

Schloss Böckelheimer   Schloss Böckelheimer Königsfels
  Kupfergrube   Schloss Böckelheimer Königsberg
Schloss Böckelheimer Kupferberg

APPENDIX B

Classified Wines of Burgundy

"GRANDS" AND "PREMIERS CRUS"
OF THE CÔTE D'OR

(*Grand Cru* vineyards indicated by CAPITALS)

Red Wines of the Côte de Nuits

Fixin
Clos de la Perrière
Clos des Marcs d'Or

Clos du Chapitre
Les Hervelets

Gevrey-Chambertin
CHAMBERTIN
LATRICIÈRES-CHAMBERTIN
CHARMES-CHAMBERTIN
GRIOTTE-CHAMBERTIN
CHAPELLE-CHAMBERTIN

CHAMBERTIN-CLOS-DE-BÈZE
MAZIS-CHAMBERTIN
MAZOYÈRES-CHAMBERTIN
RUCHOTTES-CHAMBERTIN
Clos Saint-Jacques

Morey-Saint-Denis
BONNES MARES
CLOS DE TART
Clos des Lambrays

CLOS DE LA ROCHE
CLOS SAINT-DENIS

Chambolle-Musigny
MUSIGNY
Les Amoureuses

BONNES MARES
Les Charmes

Vougeot
CLOS DE VOUGEOT

Flagey-Échezeaux
GRANDS ÉCHEZEAUX   ÉCHEZEAUX

Vosne-Romanée
ROMANÉE-CONTI   LA TÂCHE
ROMANÉE-SAINT-VIVANT   RICHEBOURG
LA ROMANÉE   La Grande Rue
Les Malconsorts   Les Suchots
Les Beaux-Monts

Nuits-Saint-Georges
Les Saint-Georges   Les Cailles
Clos des Corvées   Les Vaucrains
Les Pruliers   Les Porrets
Clos de Thorey   Les Baudots
Les Cras   Les Murgers
Les Richemones

Red Wines of the Côte de Beaune

Aloxe-Corton
CORTON   Corton-Bressandes
Corton-Clos du Roi   Corton-Renardes
Corton-Perrières   Corton-Les Maréchaudes

Pernand Vergelesses
Île des Vergelesses

Savigny-les-Beaune
Vergelesses   Lavières
Marconnets

Beaune
Grèves   Fèves
Le Cras   Champimonts
Marconnets   Bressandes
Clos de la Mousse   Clos des Mouches
Les Avaux   Aigrots
Clos du Roi   Les Theurons
Les Cent-Vignes   Les Toussaints

Pommard

Rugiens	Épenots
Pézerolles	Clos Blanc
Platière	Jarolières

Volnay

Clos des Chênes	Clos des Ducs
Caillerets	Champans
Fremiets	Chevret
Santenots	

Auxey
Les Duresses

Chassagne-Montrachet

La Boudriotte	Clos Saint-Jean
La Maltroie (Maltroye)	Morgeot

White Wines of the Côte de Nuits

Fixin

Clos de la Perrière   Clos des Marcs d'Or

Chambolle-Musigny
MUSIGNY BLANC

Vougeot
Clos Blanc de Vourgeot

Nuits-Saint-Georges

Perrière   Clos d'Arlots

White Wines of the Côte de Beaune

Aloxe-Corton
CORTON-CHARLEMAGNE   CORTON

Beaune
Clos des Mouches Blanc

Meursault

Perrières	Genevrières
Charmes	La Pièce-sous-le-Bois
Goutte d'Or	Santenots
	Meursault-Blagny

Puligny-Montrachet

MONTRACHET
BÂTARD-MONTRACHET
Combettes
Folatières
Pucelles
Champ-Canet

BIENVENUE-BÂTARD-
    MONTRACHET
CHEVALIER-MONTRACHET
Chalumeaux
Claivoillon
Cailleret
La Garenne

Chassagne-Montrachet

CRIOTS-BÂTARD-
    MONTRACHET
Cailleret

Ruchottes
Morgeot

BEAUJOLAIS
"Crus" (Sub-regions) of Beaujolais

Brouilly
Chiroubles
Fleurie
Morgon
Saint-Amour

Chénas
Côtes de Brouilly
Juliénas
Moulin-à-Vent

CHABLIS
"Grands Crus"

BLANCHOTS
VALMUR
VAUDÉSIR
BOUGROS

LES CLOS
GRENOUILLES
LES PREUSES
LA MOUTONNE

"Premiers Crus"

Beauroy (Boroy)
Beugnons
Butteaux
Châtains
Séchet
Côte de Fontenay
Côte de Léchet
Les Forêts
Fourchaume
Les Lys
Melinots
Mont-de-Milieu

Montée de Tonnerre
Montmains
Chapelots
Pied d'Aloup
Roncières
Troëme (Troêne)
Vaillons
Vaupulent
Vaucoupin
Vaulorent
Vosgros
Vogiros (Vaugiraud)

APPENDIX C

Classified Growths of Bordeaux

Classified Red Wines of Haut-Médoc (1855)

1.
(Premiers Crus)

Château Lafite-Rothschild | Château Latour
Château Margaux | Château Haut-Brion (Graves)

2.
(Deuxièmes Crus)

*Château Mouton-Rothschild | Château Léoville-Las-Cases
Château Rausan-Ségla | Château Léoville-Poyferré
Château Rauzan-Gassies | Château Léoville-Barton
Château Durfort-Vivens | Château Cos d'Estournel
Château Lascombes | Château Ducru-Beaucaillou
Château Gruaud-Larose | Château Montrose
Château Brane-Cantenac | Château Pichon-Longueville
Château Pichon-Longueville | (Comtesse de LaLande)
(Baron de Pichon) |

3.
(Troisièmes Crus)

Château Cantenac-Brown | Château Giscours
Château Palmer | Château Kirwan
Château Grand La Lagune | Château d'Issan
*Château Calon-Ségur | Château Lagrange

Château Ferrière
Château Marquis
   d'Alesme-Becker

Château Langoa-Barton
Château Boyd-Cantenac
Château Malescot-Saint-Exupéry

4.
(*Quatrièmes Crus*)

Château Gloria
Château Saint-Pierre
*Château Branaire-Ducru
*Château Talbot
Château La Tour-Carnet
Château Duhart-Milon

Château Pouget
Château Rochet
*Château Beychevelle
Château Prieuré-Lichine
Château Marquis de Terme

5.
(*Cinquièmes Crus*)

Château Pontet-Canet
*Château Batailley
*Château Grand-Puy-Lacoste
*Château Grand-Puy-Ducasse
*Château Lynch-Bages
Château Lynch-Moussas
Château Camensac
Château Cos-Labory
Château Clerc-Milon

Château Dauzac
*Château Mouton-Baron Philippe
Château Le (du) Tertre
Château Haut-Bages-Libéral
Château Pédesclaux
Château Belgrave
Château Croizet-Bages
*Château Cantemerle
*Château Haut-Batailley

6.
(*Crus Exceptionnels et Bourgeois*)

Château Villegeorge
*Château Angludet
Château La Couronne
Château Moulin-Riche
*Château Capbern
*Château Dutruch-Lambert
*Château Fourcas-Dupré
*Château Le Boscq
*Château Meyney
*Château Les-Ormes-de-Pez
*Château Paveil-de-Luze

*Château Chasse-Spleen
*Château Poujeaux-Theil
Château Bel-Air-Marquis-d'Aligre
*Château Fourcas-Hostein
*Cru Gressier-Grand-Poujeaux
*Château Lanessan
*Château de Pez
*Château Phélan-Ségur
*Château La Tour-de-Mons
*Château Sénéjac

* Considered by most experts to be deserving of a higher classification

Classified Growths of Graves

RED WINES (CLASSIFIED IN 1953)

Château Bouscaut
Château Carbonnieux
Château Fieuzal
Château Malartic-Lagravière
Château Smith-Haut-Lafite
Château La Mission-Haut-Brion
Château Latour-Haut-Brion

Château Haut-Brion
Château Haut-Bailly
Domaine de Chevalier
Château Olivier
Château La Tour-Martillac
Château Pape-Clément

WHITE WINES (CLASSIFIED IN 1959)

Château Haut-Brion
Château Bouscaut
Domaine de Chevalier
Château Malartic-Lagravière
Château Couhins

Château Carbonnieux
Château Olivier
Château La Tour-Martillac
Château Laville-Haut-Brion

Classified Growths of Sauternes and Barsac (1855)

1.
(Grand Premier Cru)

Château d'Yquem

2.
(Premiers Crus)

Château La Tour-Blanche
Château Lafaurie-Peyraguey
Château Suduiraut
Château Climens
Château Rieussec
Château Rabaud-Sigalas

Clos Haut-Peyraguey
Château Rayne-Vigneau
Château Coutet
Château Guiraud
Château Rabaud-Promis

3.
(Deuxièmes Crus)

Château de Myrat
Château Doisy-Védrines
Château Filhot
Château Nairac
Château Suau
Château Romer

Château Doisy-Daëne
Château d'Arche
Château Broustet
Château Caillou
Château de Malle
Château Lamothe

Classified Growths of Saint-Émilion (1953)

1.

(Premiers Grands Crus Classés)

Château Ausone
Château Beauséjour
Château Canon
Château Figeac
Château Magdelaine
Château Trottevieille

Château Cheval Blanc
Château Belair
Clos Fourtet
Château La Gaffelière
Château Pavie

2.

(Grands Crus Classés)

Château l'Angelus
Château Bellevue
Château Cadet-Bon
Château Canon-la-Gaffelière
Château Chapelle Madeleine
Château Corbin
Château Coutet
Château Curé Bon
Château Fonroque
Château Grand-Barrail-
  Lamarzelle
Château Grand-Corbin-Despagne
Château Grand Pontet
Château Guadet-Saint-Julien
Clos des Jacobins
Château La Clotte
Château La Couspaude
Château Larcis-Ducasse
Château Lamarzelle
Château Laroze
Château La-Tour-du-Pin-Figeac
Château Le Châtelet
Château Le Prieuré
Château Moulin-du-Cadet
Château Pavie-Macquin
Château Petit-Faurie-de-Souchard
Château Ripeau
Château Saint-Georges-
  Côte-Pavie

Château Yon-Figeac
Château Balestard-la-Tonnelle
Château Berget
Château Cadet-Piola
Château Cap-de-Mourlin
Château Chauvin
Château Corbin-Michotte
Château Croque-Michotte
Château Fonplégade
Château Franc Mayne
Château Grand-Corbin-Figeac
Château Grand Mayne
Château Grandes Murailles
Château Jean Faure
Château La Carte
Château La Cluzière
Château La Dominique
Clos La Madeleine
Château Larmande
Château Lasserre
Château La-Tour-Figeac
Château Le Couvent
Château Mauvezin
Château Pavie-Decesse
Château Pavillon-Cadet
Château Petit-Faurie-de-Soutard
Château Sansonnet
Château Soutard
Château Tertre-Daugay

201

Clos Saint-Martin
Château Trimoulet
Château Troplong-Mondot

Château Trois Moulins
Château Villemaurine

Principal Red Wines of Pomerol
(Unofficial classification by the Pomerol Wine Growers Syndicate)

1.
(*Grands Premiers Crus*)

Château Pétrus
Château Certan

Vieux Château Certan

2.
(*Premiers Crus*)

Cru l'Évangile
Château Beauregard
Château Clinet
Château Lafleur
Château La Commanderie
Château Gazin
Château Le-Gay-La-Fleur
Château Guillot

Château Nénin
Château Petit-Village
Le Clos Lacombe
Le Clos de l'Église
Clos du Clocher
(Château) Certan-Sauteloup
Château Trotanov

APPENDIX D

Glossary of Wine Terms

Apéritif (French): Appetizer. Vermouths and aromatic wines used to whet the appetite.

Appellation Contrôlée (French): Officially "controlled" place name; authorized classification for a wine.

Auslese (German): Literally, "selection." German wines made from specially selected ripe grapes.

Beerenauslese (German): Literally, "Berry selection." Sweeter than *Auslese* (q.v.).

Berg (German): Hill or mountain; steep hillside.

Blanc de Blancs (French): Champagne, sparkling or still wine made from white-skinned grapes only.

Bouquet: Wine's fragrance or aroma.

Brut (French): Usually indicates the driest Champagnes or sparkling wines.

Cabinet: See *Kabinett*.

Caves (French): Cellars; wine storehouses.

Château (French): Traditional name for a Bordeaux vineyard; also manor house.

Claret: Red Bordeaux wine.

Côte(s) (French): Hillside; wine-growing area.

Cru (French): Growth, crop; wine from a specific vineyard.

Cru classé: Classified Wine (Bordeaux).

Domaine (French): Estate or holding; control or management of several vineyards.

203

Doux (French): Predominantly a Champagne or sparkling wine term; usually denotes sweet or sweetish.

Dry: Unsweet.

Edelzwicker (Alsatian): Alsatian white wine made from a blend of "noble" (best) grapes. See *Zwicker*.

Eiswein (German): Sweet wine from frost-bitten grapes.

Extra Dry: A fallacious term: actually indicating a sweeter wine than "Brut" (q.v.).

Fass (German): Cask.

Feine (Feinste) (German): Exceptional; fine.

Flasche (German): Typical tall, slim German wine bottle.

Fuder (German): Cask.

Grand Vin (French): Literally, "great" or "big" wine. A meaningless term apt to be slapped on any label. Not to be confused with legitimate classification of "Grand Cru" (principally for best Burgundy vineyards).

Haut (French): Literally, "high." Among French wine terms (Haut-Médoc, Haut-Sauternes, etc.), generally indicates "upriver" or farther away from water. Not necessarily a term meaning superior.

Hochfeinste (German): Finest; most superior.

Hock: British term for Rhine wine.

Hospice (French): Hospital, almshouse; in France frequently supported by income from vineyards.

Kabinett (Cabinet) (German; also Alsatian): Highest quality from a particular vintage.

Lage (German): Vineyard. (pl. *Lagen*).

Liebfraumilch (German): Popular generic Rhine wine.

Light: Light in alcohol content; delicate in flavor.

Liquoreux (French): Sweet, luscious.

Maderizé (French): Oxidized wine, brown and bitter. Literally: like Madeira.

Marc (French): Spirits distilled from the "must" or leavings of pressed grapes.

Marque Déposée (French): Registered brand name.

Mise en bouteilles à la propriété (French): Bottled at the château; estate-bottled.

Monopole (French): Monopoly on a wine, vineyard, or brand name.

Moselblümchen (German): Generic term for a Moselle wine, usually a blend.

Mousseux (French): Sparkling wine.

Natur (Naturrein) (German): Indicates no sugar has been added.

Négociant (French): Shipper.

Oeil de Perdrix (French): Traditional term for a *rosé*.

Original-Abfüllung (*Orig-Abfg.*) (German): Estate-bottled. *Kellerabzug* and *Schlossabzug* are equivalents.

Pétillant (French): Slightly sparkling; fizzy.

Petit (French): Minor; secondary.

Phylloxera: Vine louse of North American origin.

Réserve (French): Special; specially selected. In Alsace, often means *auslese* (q.v.).

Rosé (French): Pink- or rose-colored wine.

Sec (French): Dry.

Sekt (German): Generic term for German sparkling wine.

Spätlese (German): Literally, "late-picked." Wine made from very ripe grapes.

Spritzig (German): Slightly sparkling; *pétillant*.

Supérieur (French): Usually denotes wine of higher alcoholic content.

Tête(s) de Cuvée(s) (French): Traditional Burgundian term for finest vineyard(s).

Trockenbeerenauslese (German): Literally, "dried berry selection." Very sweet dessert wines made from the ripest, sometimes "raisined" grapes.

V.D.Q.S. (*Vins Délimités de Qualité Supérieure*) (French): Official classification of wines, with a status just below *Appellation Contrôlée* (*q.v.*). Recognized superior "country" wines.

Vintage: Year in which wine was made.

Vitis labrusca: Table or "fox" grape.

Vitis vinifera: Wine grape.

Wachstum (German): Indicates unsugared wine. *Gewächs* and *Crescenz* are equivalents.

Weingut (German): Indicates vineyard or estate.

Zwicker (Alsatian): Alsatian common wine or *ordinaire*, as opposed to *Edelzwicker* (*q.v.*), a blend of "noble" grapes.

INDEX

ABBREVIATIONS

Ch. = Chateau(x)
cl. = classification
dist. = wine district; generic growing area
Fr. = French; France
Ger. = German; Germany
gr. = grape; vine
reg. = wine region; officially demarcated area
riv. = river
shp. = wine-grower; merchant; shipper
Switz. = Swiss; Switzerland
vyd. = vineyard
wn. = wine; wine type

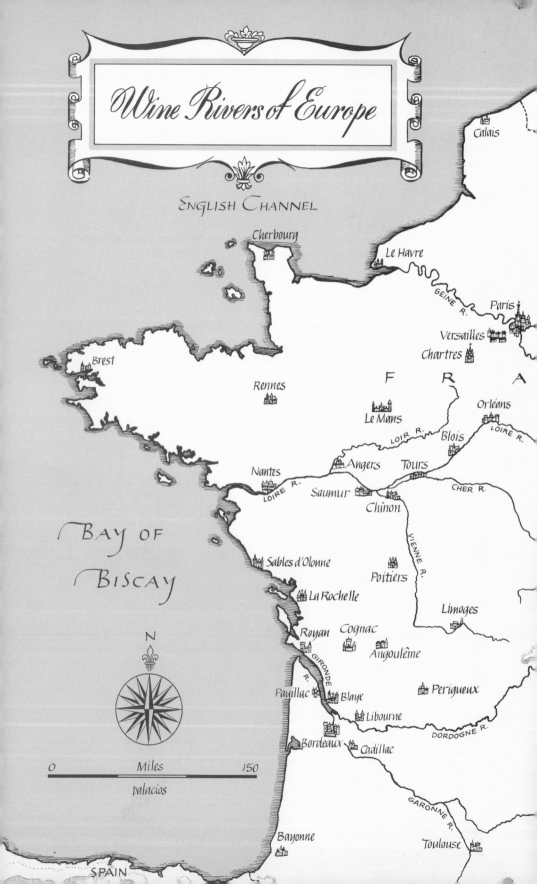

Wine Rivers of Europe

ENGLISH CHANNEL

Calais

Cherbourg

Le Havre

SEINE R.

Paris

Versailles

Chartres

Brest

Rennes

F R A

Le Mans

Orléans

LOIR R.

Blois

LOIRE R.

Angers

Tours

Nantes

LOIRE R.

Saumur

CHER R.

Chinon

BAY OF

BISCAY

VIENNE R.

Sables d'Olonne

Poitiers

La Rochelle

Limoges

N

Royan

Cognac

Angoulême

GIRONDE R.

Périgueux

Pauillac

Blaye

Libourne

DORDOGNE R.

Bordeaux

Cadillac

Miles

0   150

palacios

GARONNE R.

Bayonne

Toulouse

SPAIN